Well
Seasoned

Well Seasoned

Exploring, cooking and eating with the seasons

Russell Brown and Jonathan Haley

An Anima Book

This is an Anima book, first published in the UK in 2018 by Head of Zeus Ltd

9 7 5 3 1 2 4 6 8

A catalogue record for this book is available from the British Library

ISBN (HB): 9781786695055
ISBN (E): 9781786695048

Designed by Matt Inwood
Printed and bound in Spain by Graficas Estella

Head of Zeus Ltd
First Floor East
5–8 Hardwick Street
London EC1R 4RG
www.headofzeus.com

Contents

Introduction

I f you've ever wanted to know exactly when the asparagus season starts, this book is for you. If you like the idea of picking wild garlic but aren't quite sure where to begin, you're in the right place. And if you're looking for fantastic recipes that make the most of Britain's finest seasonal produce every month of the year, we can definitely help you.

We've picked gooseberries in June, foraged cobnuts in October, caught cuttlefish in July and roasted venison in November. Along the way, we've learned how everything we see, eat and experience – from the height of summer to the depths of winter – is inextricably linked to the seasons. To date, other food writers have only told half the story. It's all very well knowing that crayfish are in season in May, but how much better to know how and where to catch them yourself? Spiced squash is the perfect Halloween dish, but so much more satisfying when you've picked your own pumpkin or spiced it with home-grown chillies.

Without learning more about seasonality and the impact it has on the world around us, 'seasonal food' is only an abstract concept. So, this book isn't merely a guide to seasonal eating but to seasonal living.

About the authors

Russell Brown

Russell ran a fly-fishing business in Cornwall before a growing passion for food and cooking led to him taking the plunge and embarking on a new career as a professional chef at the age of twenty-seven. Starting as a commis chef in Truro, various jobs followed before, in 2003, Russell and his wife Eléna opened Sienna in Dorchester. Here Russell was awarded three AA rosettes in 2007 and a Michelin star in 2010. They sold Sienna in 2015 when Russell launched Creative about Cuisine, a business focusing on his food writing, photography and consultancy work. Russell writes for a number of trade and leisure publications, often supplying the accompanying photography. He also continues to cook at guest-chef dinners, demonstrates at various festivals and has a number of wide-ranging food consultancy contracts. Russell's recipes and photography feature throughout the book.

Jonathan Haley

Jon comes from a farming family and loves everything about the great outdoors, particularly when it involves diving, fishing or foraging. He is a strong believer in food ethics and educating the next generation on the importance of food provenance (a cause of unending annoyance to his wife and two children). As the principal author of the *Well Seasoned* blog, Jon was the runner-up in the *Observer* Ethical Awards for Best Blog and his food writing has been widely published. At various times in his life (and with varying degrees of success) he has been an actor, an oceanographer, a diving instructor and a lawyer. Most of the non-recipe writing in the book is his.

How to use this book

We've arranged this book by monthly chapters. We hope that every month (at least) you'll dip into it for ideas of where to go, what to do and, most importantly, what to cook. Each month is divided into four parts:

Out & About

At the start of each chapter, we suggest an outdoor experience – either in your garden or the Great British countryside – that captures the essence of the month. Wherever you live, get out and about to see how the world around us is hard-wired to the seasons.

Food & Foraging

Here you'll find out about some of our superstar seasonal ingredients. These are the real flag-bearers for each month of the year and might only be around for a few weeks, so look out for them in your local shops, markets or hedgerows.

Feasts & Festivals

Dates to note in your diary for the month. Some are long-forgotten, others have evolved into the festivities we know and love today. Each one is a small but important marker in the seasonal cycle.

Recipes

Lastly, Russell's mouth-watering recipes to help you make the most of the month's best produce. Cook, eat and drink as you explore each season.

I n the Appendices you'll find detailed seasonality charts as well as contact information for the various organizations we mention throughout the book. If you like the sound of a particular event or activity then these will usually be a good place to find more information.

Living seasonally means living with some uncertainty. In the modern world, we're not very good at that, but it's important to emphasize that this book is about living with the seasons. We can't dictate exactly when the birds should start nesting, when snowdrops might emerge or when the hedgerows will blossom. Only Mother Nature can do that. All we can do is tell you when she's most likely to.

The same goes for our food and recipes – although the British seasons are actually fairly reliable, we can't know exactly when any particular ingredient will be at its best. You shouldn't feel you have to stick slavishly to the chapter headings or seasonality charts. Whether it's raspberries ripening, sprouts sprouting or crayfish crawling, if something looks and feels good, then feel free to give it a go.

On a practical note, since we spend most of our time in London and Dorset, this book inevitably reflects those places as our seasonal reference points. If you live in the far South West of the country, the micro-climate of Devon and Cornwall means you have a good chance of finding any ingredient or natural phenomenon several weeks earlier than the book suggests, and if you're in Northern Scotland you could be up to a month behind.

Finally, there is an abundance of conflicting views as to exactly when spring, summer, autumn and winter 'officially' start and end. For simplicity, we tend to use the meteorological system, which divides the year into four equal seasons, starting on the first day of March, June, September and December respectively. Obviously, nothing is truly that simple and we'll touch on a few of those differing opinions along our seasonal journey.

Why seasonal?

Our seasonal love affair starts with food: very simply, we believe that ingredients taste best when they're grown in the right place at the right time of year.

It's not that we don't enjoy food and flavours from overseas – you'd be hard-pushed to prize a steamed pork bun out of our hands – but the Great British public has become used to a diet of tasteless tomatoes and bland strawberries, simply because they can be cheaply imported all year round.

In times gone by, our lives would have been intimately intertwined with the seasons. We would have known when to harvest crops for the best yield, which fruits tasted sweetest each month and which animals or fish would provide us with the richest meat. Innovations like fridge-freezers, processing techniques and a globalized food market have changed all of that. Seasonality has largely slipped from our collective consciousness and our eating habits have become almost entirely disconnected from the annual cycle.

Should we care? It is easy to accuse us of being stuck in the past – of failing to embrace change. Many of the advances we have seen have, of course, done wonders for our world. For most people, especially those of us lucky enough to live in the British Isles, food is cheaper and more accessible than it has been at any time in the past. And yet, if you buy food that is artificially grown at the wrong time of year, you are certain to be making at least some compromise – whether that's in terms of taste, cost, nutrition or environmental impact.

There are weighty issues at work here and we certainly don't claim that the answer is always clear-cut. Even with today's technology, comparing things such as carbon footprints, energy consumption or nutritional content can be difficult. Nor do we suggest you need to stick too dogmatically to the principles. There's undoubtedly a place in our cooking for well-sourced, seasonal produce from abroad, particularly those ingredients that don't thrive here. (You'll see we happily feature Seville oranges and clementines in this book, as well as using a plethora of spices and seasonings that can only be imported.)

But it's also undoubtedly the case that food produced in tune with the seasons tastes as nature intended it to (and as our taste buds have evolved over millions of years to appreciate). And if it can also be locally sourced, a short supply chain necessarily means that fewer resources will be required to get it from field to fork. So, adhering to the 'seasonal and local' principle is usually a simple and effective way to buy food with maximum flavour and minimum environmental impact.

Far from being an act of self-denial, seasonal eating is a very positive choice. We choose to forgo green beans in December or peaches in March, looking to the alternatives without any sense of sacrifice; by eating with the seasons we have the excitement of rediscovering perfectly ripe produce and exciting new flavours every month of the year.

The annual cycle brings a cornucopia of new ingredients to our table every few weeks, all bursting with flavour and so often the ideal partners to other in-season produce. We can eagerly await the first squid of summer, be tantalized by the slow ripening of the autumn apple and delight in the earthy sweetness of winter chestnuts.

We can reject the September strawberry in favour of the underrated raspberry. We can refuse to eat insipid plums in June and instead enjoy tart and tangy gooseberries. Does Peruvian asparagus in February actually taste any good? You already know the answer to that one, so why not try freshly picked stems of purple sprouting broccoli instead? Britain produces great-tasting food all year round; our farmers and growers deserve to be championed and their produce deserves to be eaten.

More than that, we live in one of the most seasonally affected countries in the world, and everything we do and experience as a nation, be it wrapping up warm to go to the park on a frosty winter morning or getting unexpectedly soaked to the skin in the middle of an April afternoon, is – and always has been – determined by the seasons.

So, this book is an enthusiastic celebration of British seasonality that goes beyond just food.

You'll find out about the New Forest pannage season, where to spot the first snowdrops of spring and why some rhubarb is forced. We'll tell you the best times of year to spot seals, why St George must have loved asparagus and what makes the ideal Bonfire Night banger. We'll give you a sensational cherry compote recipe for the summer, a wonderful warming soup for winter and a winning wild garlic pesto for the spring.

As you begin to explore, cook and eat with the seasons around you, you'll quickly realize how satisfying and rewarding a seasonal life can be. It is, of course, the natural way to live and before long you'll be wondering why you ever did anything else.

Cooking introduction

Anticipation and excitement, for me, are two of the fundamental reasons for cooking with the seasons. It's Nature's way of providing things to look forward to. As a chef, it gives structure to cooking and menu planning and also means you are cooking with the best, and often cheapest, ingredients around. This in turn means that you, as a cook, have less work to do to create a stunning meal. Some flexibility is needed as the seasons do vary but if the produce tastes amazing and has been carefully sourced, the cooking – and, more importantly, the eating – will be a real pleasure.

Jon and I have tried to choose recipes for the book that are accessible and we really hope there is nothing here that you feel you won't try. Some require specific equipment – such as a food processor – and some are more difficult than others. Making your own hot dog sausages, for example, will require a bit of commitment and won't be for everyone but you could just make the chilli-pickled cabbage and buy some venison sausages. Do feel free to pick and choose, mix it up, take an element from a recipe and use it in one of your own.

If you've bought into the philosophy behind this book, you won't be too worried if your carrots are a little wonky or your apples are different sizes. Accepting that things vary is really important as a cook – ovens vary, the speed at which a pan heats up and how evenly it cooks will vary. Equally, when we cook with natural products – seasonal vegetables, meat, fish and so on – even the taste and size can vary. No two lemons will taste exactly the same, for example, and the thickness of a fish fillet will often differ, which means the cooking times will need to vary too.

I hope you'll use these recipes as a guide, rather than a strict set of rules. Yes, there are exceptions – I wouldn't recommend using plain flour instead of self-raising (we've all done it!) – but what you do need to do is use your senses and develop an understanding of how things differ from day to day.

Learning to trust your senses will make you a better cook, too. Looking, smelling, tasting and listening are all so important. The sound a piece of meat makes when it goes in a pan tells you if the pan is hot enough, and a little taste of that lemon juice will tell you whether it's eye-wateringly sour or actually quite sweet, and you can adjust accordingly. Tasting properly is a mental process, not just a physical one, and you have to engage and concentrate on what you are tasting. Most young chefs I've worked with have had to learn the difference between tasting and eating!

It's also important not to get too hung up on specific ingredients. Buying what is good and then choosing what to cook is often the best way, but even if you do have a particular dish in mind, many elements will be flexible. Fish is a really good example – most recipes for oily fish will work just as well with a different type of oily fish. So, if it's a cod recipe, but the haddock looks better? Buy the haddock. The recipe says sherry vinegar but you only have red wine vinegar? Use it. In many instances it won't be crucial – yes, it will change things, but it shouldn't be a disaster.

I speak to lots of keen cooks who get stressed out in the kitchen, especially when a dish requires several things to be done at the last minute, and my biggest piece of advice here is to adopt a technique from the professional kitchen. Look at a recipe and break it down into what can be done ahead of time. This is called 'mise en place' – literally meaning 'everything in its place', so you're ready to start cooking. If a dish requires fresh herbs to be added just before serving, you don't want to be scrabbling around looking for a clean chopping board and a knife as the fish is overcooking in the pan. The herbs, along with everything else, should be ready before you light the gas.

If you can make one element of the dish a day ahead, or if something, such as pastry, can be taken out of the freezer, that really helps as well. Puréed or mashed potato will be perfectly fine made in the morning and warmed up in the microwave that night. Salad dressings keep for weeks in the fridge and most types of dough freeze really well. It's all about giving the cook more time to concentrate on those last-minute elements. Warm plates will mean you have to worry less about the food going cold, and some things, such as purées, will keep their heat for a fair while in a plastic tub with a lid on. Planning and organization are everything.

Weighing and accuracy

Some recipes in this book do call for a high level of accuracy in the weighing and measuring, particularly for things like bread and cakes. I've given spoon measures for the small quantities based on using a set of measuring spoons, as teaspoons from the kitchen cutlery drawer will vary. All the measures are level and scooped as opposed to packed hard. Where I feel weighing is either easier or more accurate, I've given a gram weight in brackets.

Weighing eggs is also important in some dishes, as a large egg can vary from 63–73 grams. On average, the yolk from a large egg weighs around 18–20 grams. Again, I've given the quantities in numbers followed by a gram weight where it is important.

I always use Maldon sea salt as a personal preference and grind it to the texture of table salt with a pestle and mortar when a fine salt is needed. The weight difference between a teaspoon of finely ground salt (which weighs 5g) and a teaspoon of flakes (3.5g) is quite significant, so if the recipe says, '1 tsp Maldon sea salt, finely ground', it's measured after the salt has been ground.

All gelatine sheets in the recipes are the type readily found in supermarkets that weigh just over 1.5 grams per sheet.

Where it's necessary to preheat the oven, I've mentioned this at the very beginning of the recipe. This is really to flag up the need for a hot oven – when you do this will, of course, depend on whether you are breaking the recipe down into stages or popping out to the shops part way through!

Ingredients

A well-stocked store cupboard and fridge really helps to pull a meal together. My fridge nearly always holds eggs, milk, crème fraîche, cheese, mustard, gherkins, capers, spice pastes, cured meat, bacon, salad leaves, yoghurt, lemons and unsalted butter, plus assorted leftovers, experiments and impulse purchases! The larder will have lots of dried pasta (Rummo is my favourite readily available brand), Maldon sea salt, Arbequina extra virgin olive oil, rapeseed oil, jars of beans and pulses, arborio rice, couscous, basmati rice, various vinegars, dried breadcrumbs, tomato ketchup, Worcestershire sauce, honey, maple syrup, baking powder, saffron, chilli flakes, cumin powder, paprika, smoked paprika, ground coriander, fennel seeds and star anise. The baking cupboard holds a mix of dried fruits, muscovado sugar (both dark and light), caster sugar, golden caster sugar, soft dark brown sugar, plain and self-raising flour, strong bread flour, pasta flour, semolina, granary flour, and wholemeal and rye flours. Chocolate is a usual feature, as is golden syrup, cinnamon, ginger and mixed spice.

As you would expect for someone who has been passionate about food and cooking for the last thirty years, there is much more besides, but if I had to stock a kitchen from scratch that would make a good start. The beauty of the majority of these ingredients is that you will use them time and time again and they won't sit languishing at the back of a cupboard for years.

Equipment

Good equipment does make a difference to your cooking and I'm a great believer in buying something of good quality and only having to buy it once. However, you don't need masses of kit. Yes, I have got a Thermomix, a water bath and a vacuum packer in my kitchen – relics from the restaurant – but how often do I use them? Well, when I'm just cooking for Eléna and myself or for friends, very infrequently. I do use a small food processor and Kitchen Aid mixer a lot and I use good-quality, stainless-steel pans with heavy bases alongside heavy-duty, non-stick pans that will all go in the oven. I also use a griddle pan, baking sheets and tins – all heavy-duty items. I use a number of knives but would happily manage with a serrated paring knife, a serrated pastry knife, a 20cm cook's knife, a filleting knife and a boning knife. Assorted wooden and metal spoons, a couple of palette knives, a strainer and a ladle are all really useful. A sieve, a fine chinois and a colander will cover the straining and draining. Digital scales and a digital temperature probe I rate as essential. An oven thermometer to check how accurate your oven is will be useful, too. That should about do it; although I will freely admit my kitchen is cluttered with a lot more than that!

I've had a great time experimenting, testing and eating as we've worked on *Well Seasoned* over the past year. Many of the dishes I've cooked regularly, and I've become even more enchanted with the incredible seasonal produce available to us. Most of all, though, I really have had fun, and I hope you enjoy reading and cooking from the book as much as I've enjoyed writing it.

Russell Brown

01 | January

Wulfmonath – wolf month, when the wolves came into the villages in search of food

January tends to get a raw deal. It's the cold, dark, hungover month, often now sacrificed to the god of abstinence (or the new false prophet, detox). But as the new year begins, I think we should resolve to think more positively about it.

Cold, crisp mornings, bright blue skies, the days getting longer, snow... January has plenty of positive attributes. Granted, there's still a long way to go until the warmer, brighter weather of spring, but it should be an exciting month. The short days mean we have plenty of time indoors to make plans for the year ahead. So, stock up on outdoor kit in the sales, brush up your nature knowledge and put the year's seasonal adventures in the diary.

On the food front, the game season is still in full swing, with partridge, pheasant and duck all bringing a touch of wild class to our tables. Frost-resistant roots like parsnips, Jerusalem artichokes and carrots are all quite content to sit tight during the coldest part of the year, doing nothing much apart from staying fresh.

Our coastline is still teeming with a great selection of fine fish that thrive in Britain's cool, clear waters. Shellfish such as cockles, mussels and oysters are especially good this month and worth exploring as a tasty, lighter alternative to meat (especially if, like me, your trousers tend to inexplicably shrink over the Christmas period). If you're feeling a bit cold at any point, you might spare a thought for our ever-reliable fishing fleet who are out in (nearly) all weathers so that the worst we have to endure is a slightly nippy stroll to the fishmonger's.

After the gluttony and excess of the festive season, January is a bracing, fresh start to the year and the perfect place to begin our seasonal journey.

Out & About
snowdrops

Food & Foraging
forced rhubarb, Jerusalem
  artichoke, Seville and blood
  oranges

Feasts & Festivals
Twelfth Night
Burns Night

Vegetables
carrots, Jerusalem artichoke,
  January King cabbage

Fruit
forced rhubarb, Seville and blood
  oranges (imported)

Meat & Game
snipe, woodcock

Fish
brown crab, cockles

Recipes

Jerusalem artichoke soup with wild mushrooms
  and artichoke crisps
Seville orange marmalade
Blood orange, chicory and feta salad
Mulled cider with spiced apple jelly
Beer-braised beef cheeks with pickled shallots
Rhubarb and almond tart

Out & About | Snowdrops

The emergence of snowdrops is one of the earliest signs that spring is on the way, and in most years you'll see the very first ones make an appearance in late January. They are also known in some parts as Candlemas because of the time of year they emerge. As the saying goes, 'The snowdrop, in purest white array, first rears her head on Candlemas Day' (see February).

There are several species of snowdrop. Our native wild flowers have drooping white blooms with a small green patch on the inner petal tip and just one flower per stem. If you see any other kind on your winter walk it's likely to originate from a cultivated variety (of which there are many).

So, towards the end of the month, wrap up warm and take a wintery wander through damp woodland near to streams or ponds, keep a close eye on the ground and you should spot them. The delicate flowers you see were actually formed nearly a year ago, but they wait until the following winter before pushing up through the soil. (They contain a natural anti-freeze which helps them survive the icy weather. It's so effective that the wild plants were harvested during the First World War to make de-icing chemicals for tanks.)

I t's usually around January that we really start to miss those mellow fruits of autumn. The bad news is that it'll be some time before any of them return. The good news is that there's a vegetable in season this month that does an excellent impression of one.

Rhubarb was originally a native of Siberia. It's impervious to the cold and, importantly, lack of light – even our coldest winters are positively balmy as far as rhubarb is concerned, so it thrives in Britain. Since the 1800s, growers have been taking advantage of the plant's love of our mild climate by growing it in a rather mysterious way.

'Forcing' rhubarb involves growing the plants outside but then moving them into long, dark sheds in late autumn, just after the first frosts. Astonishingly in this day and age, the sheds are still lit by candlelight so that light levels are as low as possible. Rhubarb sheds are an eerie place. If you stand quietly you can actually hear the rhubarb 'talking' as it creaks while growing.

The dark, warm and moist conditions trick the plants into thinking they are covered by thick Siberian snow. As a result, photosynthesis stops and the plants put all their energy into growing long, slender stems which are a vivid pink (rather than green). The first forced rhubarb harvest takes place in mid-to-late January and it continues through to mid-spring when the field rhubarb season starts. (The two types of rhubarb are actually exactly the same plant, just grown differently.)

West Yorkshire's 'Rhubarb Triangle' once produced more than 90 per cent of the world's forced rhubarb and, at the peak of production, whole trains ran from Yorkshire to London carrying the rhubarb to market. Although sales haven't quite continued at those levels, it's still undoubtedly a success story – Yorkshire forced rhubarb has been given Protected Designation of Origin (PDO) status, putting it in the same league as Champagne, Camembert cheese and Melton Mowbray pork pies.

Try: Rhubarb and almond tart (p. 37)

Food & Foraging | Jerusalem artichokes

As far as names go, the Jerusalem artichoke is about as misleading as it gets. They're not from Jerusalem (they originated in America) and they're not related to globe artichokes (they just taste vaguely similar).

Following their discovery in North America, these little tubers were imported to Europe in the early 1600s, where they were grown extensively for both human and animal fodder. They were particularly popular in France and Italy where they were discovered to be a relative of the sunflower. Thus, the name is most likely a corruption of '*girasole*', the Italian name for the flower and other members of the daisy family. The fashionable food duly made its way to Britain where it has thrived ever since.

Knobbly and gnarly in shape, Jerusalem artichokes range from yellow to pink in colour and are hugely versatile. As with most small tubers, a quick scrub and (if you wish) peel should be sufficient preparation; and in terms of cooking, you can more or less treat them like new potatoes. From a flavour perspective, however, they pack considerably more punch than your average spud, making them a superb feature ingredient in a warm winter salad or the mainstay of a velvety-smooth soup.

In more ways than one, Jerusalem artichokes have an affinity with pheasant. The game birds are so fond of them that some of the large shooting estates still grow artichokes as a fodder crop. In the circumstances (since the pheasants don't have much choice in the matter) it's a bit of a stretch to suggest this is an example of the cook's saying that 'what grows together goes together' but, by happy coincidence, the nutty tang of artichokes complements the gamey notes of pheasant (and other game birds) so you'll frequently find them paired on the plate.

In season from November through to early March, Jerusalem artichokes should feature regularly on your winter and early-spring menu.

Try: Jerusalem artichoke soup (p. 26)

Food & Foraging | Seville and blood oranges

O ne early highlight of our seasonal food calendar is the short season for blood and Seville oranges.

Now, wherever possible our focus in this book is on British seasonal produce but there are some things that just don't grow in the UK, and oranges, unsurprisingly, are one of them.

I excuse myself for this early diversion on two further grounds.

Firstly, despite the continental provenance of the fruit, marmalade (the main use of Sevilles) is quintessentially British; a cup of tea and a thick slice of buttered toast with a generous layer of the stuff are what Sunday mornings were made for.

Secondly, the season for both of these fruits is a matter of weeks. Starting in mid-December at the earliest, it's all but over by the end of January for Sevilles and a few weeks later for blood oranges. It's an early and stark reminder that some seasons really are a blink-and-you'll-miss-it affair – well worth noting as we start the year.

Sevilles – named after the Spanish city they originate from – are often a bit lumpy and bumpy, so don't worry too much what they look like, especially if you're planning to slice them into marmalade. The seeds of the ultra-tart fruit are high in pectin (the natural setting agent), making them ideal for the classic, bitter-sweet preserve.

Blood oranges also come from the Mediterranean and have a similar, though longer season. Aromatic and tart in taste, their distinctive and eye-catching dark red flesh works well in jellies, sauces and winter salads.

Try:
Seville orange marmalade (p. 29)
Blood orange, chicory and feta salad (p. 30)

Feasts & Festivals | Twelfth Night (5th January)

I n the first week of January, Twelfth Night marks the end of the Christmas season and historically culminated in a final party of Christmastide.

There is some ongoing debate as to which day Twelfth Night actually falls on, and this depends whether Christmas Day or Boxing Day is counted as the first night. It's further complicated by the existence of Old Twelfth Night (see below) but in the Christian calendar it's celebrated on the fifth and marks the eve of Epiphany, when the wise men were said to have visited the baby Jesus. It was (and still is) a significant date in the Church year.

As any GCSE English student will tell you, Twelfth Night is immortalized in the famous Shakespeare play, which would have been performed on or around the night itself, and its plot line reflects some of the chaos and calamity that typically surrounded the celebrations. One Twelfth Night custom was to bake a cake that contained a bean or dried pea. The person finding the bean in their slice would be crowned Lord of Misrule for the day. Masters would become servants and vice versa, and the Lord's word was law. Midnight was the end of his rule when the world would return to normal.

Other traditions included creating surprise pies with live fillings to amuse Twelfth Night diners (the origin of the 'four and twenty blackbirds' in the nursery rhyme) and wassailing, a ceremonial blessing of the apple orchards.

Wassailing remains surprisingly common in the cider-producing counties even today. Although usually celebrated on Twelfth Night, some maintain it is most properly observed on 'Old Twelfth (or Twelvey) Night' – 17 January (which would have been the right date before the modern Gregorian calendar was adopted). The word itself is a toast derived from the Middle English greeting 'waes hael', meaning 'may you be healthy'.

The form of the ceremony differs greatly from county to county, but all involve singing, dancing and drinking (lots of drinking) to the health of the apple trees in the hope of a good harvest next year. The largest or oldest tree in the orchard is selected and the cider is liberally sprinkled at its base. Crowds then sing, shout and bang pots and pans to ward off evil spirits and awaken the trees as they come towards the end of their winter slumber.

It has long been thought unlucky to keep Christmas decorations up beyond Twelfth Night, and this probably originated from the belief that spirits inhabited the greenery brought into houses at the beginning of the Christmas period. After twelve nights, the spirits would grow restless and want to be returned to nature.

Try: Mulled cider with spiced apple jelly (p. 33)

Feasts & Festivals | Burns Night (25th January)

I f you've still got any party spirit left in you, Burns Night on 25 January is a great excuse to enjoy some Scottish delicacies.

The great Scottish poet Robbie Burns was born on 25 January 1759. Since his death he has been celebrated at annual Burns Night suppers.

The proceedings open with the 'Selkirk Grace', a thanksgiving poem (not actually written by Burns). The meal then begins, most usually with cock-a-leekie soup, and the main course is, of course, haggis – a sheep stomach stuffed with offal, oatmeal, onions and various herbs and spices.

The haggis is carried into the room by the chef, accompanied by the sound of bagpipes, ending up at the top table. The head of the table pours two large glasses of whisky that are presented to the chef and piper. The haggis is then addressed with Burns's famous poem 'Address to the Haggis', which begins with the lines 'Fair fa' your honest, sonsie face/Great chieftain o' the pudding-race!' A dagger is plunged into it and sliced twice diagonally to represent the cross of St Andrew. The main dish is accompanied with neeps and tatties (swede and mashed potatoes).

The very first Burns Supper was held by the poet's friends on the fifth anniversary of his death (21 July, 1801), but in the late 1800s it was decided that his birthday was a more fitting celebration and it is now a truly global event, celebrated by Scottish communities the world over.

There's no better night of the year for adults to enjoy a wee dram or two, and everyone can finish the evening with some poor-quality Sean Connery impressions. 'Haggish and neepsh? Yesh pleash, Missh Moneypenny.'

Jerusalem artichoke soup with wild mushrooms and artichoke crisps

The silky texture of a Jerusalem artichoke purée or soup has a real sense of luxury to it, and the flavour matches excellently with the earthiness of wild mushrooms or, should the budget allow, a few shavings of truffle.

SERVES 6 AS A STARTER

For the soup

2 sticks of celery, finely sliced
2 large banana shallots, finely sliced
2 tbsp olive oil
1kg Jerusalem artichokes
double cream to taste
Maldon sea salt

For the crisps

4 small artichokes, peeled and thinly sliced
oil for deep-frying
50/50 blend of finely ground Maldon sea salt and cep powder for dusting

For the mushrooms

2 tbsp olive oil
1 clove of garlic, smashed
200g mixed wild mushrooms
20g unsalted butter
1 dsp chopped flat-leaf parsley
Maldon sea salt and freshly ground black pepper

1. For the soup, start to soften the shallots and celery in the olive oil in a heavy, wide-bottomed pan. Peel and finely slice the artichokes, cutting them as thin as you can. Add to the pan and season lightly with salt. Continue to sweat the vegetables until they begin to soften, then just cover with water and bring to a simmer. Cook until the vegetables are completely soft. This time varies but approximately 20–30 minutes.

2. Transfer the contents of the pan to a blender, in batches if necessary, and process until completely smooth. Add a touch of double cream, and season to taste. The seasoning is really key in this recipe. You want to keep adding salt until the maximum flavour is achieved but the soup doesn't taste salty. Pass through a fine sieve and either chill or keep warm if using immediately.

3. To make the crisps, dry the artichoke slices on kitchen paper and then deep-fry in small batches at 160°C until pale golden brown. Drain on kitchen paper and season with the salt mix.

4. For the mushrooms, heat the oil in a heavy, non-stick pan and add the garlic clove. Allow the garlic to brown in the hot oil and then remove, pressing down well on the clove. Add the mushrooms to the garlic pan and sauté over a high heat until they just start to colour and crisp, and finish with the butter and parsley, seasoning to taste.

5. To serve, divide the mushrooms between shallow bowls, pour the soup around and serve the crisps on the side.

Seville orange marmalade

Crisp toast slathered in salty butter with a good dollop of marmalade makes for a pretty special start to the day. As an alternative, try mixing a tablespoon of marmalade into a small pot of fat-free Greek yoghurt along with a spoonful of oats that have been toasted with a little muscovado sugar. Let the mix sit overnight and enjoy in the morning.

MAKES AROUND 6 LARGE JARS

1.1kg Seville oranges, well washed
2 lemons, well washed
2kg preserving sugar
10g unsalted butter

1. Start by halving and juicing all the fruit, retaining all the pips. Use a teaspoon to scrape the membranes out from the juiced fruit.

2. Cut the skins in half again and slice off some of the white pith if it is really thick. Next, slice the skins into strips of your choice of thickness, depending on whether you want a fine shred or a coarser one. The shreds will swell as they cook to an extent. (I add the lemon skins to the mix, although many recipes call for just the juice and I would have to accept that maybe it isn't a true Seville orange marmalade.)

3. Measure the juice from the fruit and make up the quantity to 2l with water. Put the juice and shredded peel into a large saucepan. Tie the pips and around a quarter of the membranes in muslin and add this to the pan. Bring to the boil and then simmer very gently until the peel is tender, around 1–1½ hours.

4. Remove the muslin bag and squeeze all the juice out into the pan – if you have a potato ricer it is brilliant for doing this!

5. Warm the sugar in a roasting tin in the oven set to 100°C for 10 minutes. (This is recommended in many recipes to aid dissolving. I use the oven to sterilize the jars, too.)

6. Add the warm sugar to the pan and stir constantly until it has dissolved, then increase the heat and boil the marmalade rapidly for 5 minutes before starting to check for a set. If using a thermometer it should register 104–105°C. Or pour a spoonful onto a chilled saucer; when the edge of the pool of marmalade is pushed, the skin should wrinkle.

7. Once a set is achieved, pour the marmalade into the sterilized jars and seal.

Blood orange, chicory and feta salad

The arrival of blood oranges is a time of real excitement. I find citrus fruit in general incredibly versatile and the acidity can lift so many dishes, but blood oranges have a complex flavour that moves them to another level. Used in sweet and savoury dishes, blood oranges provide flavour and colour, but most importantly, they can provide balance. This is the key to any really successful dish; that harmony between the tastes – sweet, sour, salty, bitter – and umami, now very much recognized as the fifth taste. Umami is the sense of savouriness and is found in Parmesan cheese, soy sauce, tomatoes, seaweed and cured meats.

In this simple salad, there is no oil other than that clinging to the tomatoes. Extra oil really isn't necessary, as the combination of the blood orange syrup and all the other ingredients makes a balanced dressing.

SERVES 4 AS A SIDE DISH OR LIGHT STARTER

4 blood oranges, segmented and juice
squeezed from the frames
2 heads of chicory, broken into leaves, washed
and dried
40g rocket leaves
8 sun-dried tomatoes, drained of oil and cut into
strips
80g good quality feta
Maldon sea salt and freshly ground black
pepper

1. Place the juice from the oranges in a small pan and reduce until it is slightly syrupy. Allow to cool.

2. Toss all the salad leaves gently with the orange segments and sun-dried tomatoes. Season with Maldon sea salt and fresh black pepper. Arrange in a bowl, crumble the feta over the top and finish by drizzling the reduced orange juice over the leaves.

FOR A SIMPLE PASTA DISH WITH SIMILAR INGREDIENTS:

1. Heat a little oil and sweat off a couple of cloves of crushed garlic.

2. Add the tomatoes, orange juice and half the segments. Reduce until syrupy.

3. Add cooked spaghetti to the sauce.

4. Finely slice the chicory and stir that in along with the remaining orange segments.

5. Add a little of the pasta water and cook until the chicory has wilted. The rocket could also be added for a peppery finish.

6. Season well, divide between bowls and crumble some goat's cheese (instead of the feta) over the pasta.

Mulled cider with spiced apple jelly

Jon has talked about the traditions of wassailing and raising a glass to the orchards; how effective this is for ensuring a successful crop is no doubt up for debate, but a glass of mulled cider will certainly lift the spirits! The spiced apple jelly is non-alcoholic and you could swap the cider and brandy for a really good apple juice. The jelly keeps well in the fridge for several months, so you can easily make a glass or two of mulled cider whenever you fancy. Either way, you will have a drink full of warming spice.

MAKES ENOUGH FOR 8–10 PORTIONS

For the jelly
2l good-quality apple juice
2 star anise, broken into pieces
2 cinnamon sticks, broken into pieces
10 black peppercorns
2cm piece of root ginger, peeled and roughly chopped
2 crisp, sharp apples, roughly chopped
½ orange
100g light muscovado sugar

For one glass of mulled cider
35–40g spiced apple jelly
200ml dry cider
1 tbsp apple brandy (optional)
1–2 drops orange bitters
thin slices of fresh apple
twist of orange peel

1. To make the jelly, combine all the ingredients in a large pan and bring to the boil, stirring frequently. Turn the heat down to a simmer and reduce by half. Turn off the heat, cover the pan and leave to infuse for a couple of hours.

2. Reheat the syrup, then pass the liquid through a fine sieve into a clean pan, pressing down well on the solids to squeeze any liquid out. Continue to reduce the liquid to leave around 300ml. Allow to cool for 10 minutes and then pour into a sterilized jar – it should set to a light gel. The jelly will keep in the fridge for several months.

3. To serve, warm the cider with the jelly in a small pan, but do not boil; you don't want to burn off the alcohol! Place a metal spoon in a glass and pour in the cider, stirring gently to mix. Add the orange twist, apple slices, brandy if using and bitters to finish.

Beer-braised beef cheeks with pickled shallots

This is a great example of a tough cut of meat that becomes yielding and tender with some long, slow cooking. I think the key to good braises and casseroles is cooking in a flavoursome liquid, otherwise all the flavour is in the sauce and the meat can be bland. A combination of beer or wine and a good stock does the trick. The pickled shallot rings balance the richness of the sticky, gelatinous meat and are equally good in a cheese sandwich or on a burger!

SERVES 4 AS A MAIN COURSE

For the beef cheeks
1 small bunch of thyme plus one large sprig
1 star anise
100ml olive oil
1kg sweet white onions, finely sliced
1kg beef cheek, trimmed and cut into 125–150g portions
500ml Doom Bar beer or similar
1 tsp good red wine vinegar

For the pickled shallot rings
2 large banana shallots, peeled and sliced into 4mm-wide rings
125ml red wine
125ml red wine vinegar
125g caster sugar
1 sprig of thyme
1 tsp yellow mustard seeds
1 tsp black peppercorns
½ tsp Maldon sea salt, finely ground

1. Preheat the oven to 150°C.

2. For the beef cheeks, tie the thyme and star anise in muslin. Heat half the olive oil in a pan, add the onions and the muslin bag and slowly caramelize the onions. This will take 45 minutes and the onions should be a dark golden colour.

3. Season the beef cheeks and seal in a hot pan using the remaining oil, colouring well.

4. Once the onions are caramelized completely, add a little water to dissolve any solids. Transfer the onions to a deep roasting tin with the muslin bag, place the sealed cheeks on top, re-season and add the beer. The cheeks should only be one-third covered. Add some beef stock if necessary. Cover with baking parchment and then a double layer of foil. Braise for 2½–4 hours. Check after 2½ hours and then every 20 minutes until the cheeks are completely tender but not breaking up.

5. Remove the cheeks and place in a small roasting tin. Pass the braising liquid through a fine sieve, pressing down well on the solids and the muslin bag. Season to taste and add a sprig of fresh thyme and the red wine vinegar. Bring up to a simmer and then turn off the heat, allowing to infuse for 5 minutes before passing the liquid through a fine sieve over the beef cheeks. At this point you can warm the beef through in the oven, or chill to serve later.

6. For the pickled shallot rings, combine all the ingredients for the pickling liquid in a small stainless-steel pan and bring to the boil. Separate the sliced shallots into individual rings, discarding the small centre pieces. Add the shallots to the pickling liquid, bring back to a simmer and immediately remove from the heat. Allow to cool and chill. The liquid can be reused and the shallots will keep for several weeks in the fridge.

7. To serve, if you have chilled the beef cheeks, warm them in the cooking liquid until hot right through. Baste frequently to create a glaze on the cheeks. Serve with potato purée and some greens. Top the cheeks with pickled shallot rings dressed with a drop of oil and a pinch of salt.

Rhubarb and almond tart

Yorkshire forced rhubarb is the first splash of colour to arrive in the kitchen in the new year and, as such, really is a joy. For me, this is one of my absolute seasonal highs, up there with the first new potatoes, British asparagus and the first partridge of the year.

SERVES 8–10

For the frangipane
150g unsalted butter
150g caster sugar
2½ large free-range eggs, beaten (150g)
50g self-raising flour
150g ground almonds
1 tsp Maldon sea salt, finely ground
bitter almond extract

For the rhubarb
200g Yorkshire forced rhubarb
25g caster sugar
2 tbsp ginger wine

For the tart case
¼ quantity of sweet pastry (see Basics
    pp. 288–9)
1 large free-range egg yolk, beaten with an
    equal quantity of water

1. Preheat the oven to 160°C.

2. To make the frangipane, cream the butter and sugar in a mixer. Gradually add the egg interspersed with the flour, then add the ground almonds and salt. Flavour with a few drops of good-quality bitter almond extract.

3. For the rhubarb, cut the rhubarb into 2cm lengths and place on a baking tray, sprinkling with the sugar and ginger wine. Roast for 2 minutes, until the rhubarb just starts to soften. Drain off any juice from the tray and then chill the rhubarb.

4. Roll out the pastry to line a 26cm flan ring or small flan tins. Use an offcut of pastry to push to the pastry well into the corners. Trim the edges, chill for 20 minutes and then blind-bake until just set, approximately 15-20 minutes. Remove the baking beans and cook until a light golden brown, approximately 4-6 minutes.

5. Brush the pastry case with a yolk-and-water egg wash and return to the oven for 1 minute. Repeat.

6. To assemble, fill a piping bag fitted with a 1cm plain nozzle with the frangipane and, starting in the centre, pipe a thick spiral of frangipane to fill the tart. Push the rhubarb pieces into the frangipane, starting at the centre and working outwards. Leave ½cm gap between the pieces and finish 1cm in from the edge of the pastry case.

7. Bake for 15–20 minutes until golden and firm. Allow to cool but do not refrigerate.

02 | February

Kalemonath – cabbage month, when the first cabbages of the year could be harvested

February is the Rumpelstiltskin of months – short and bad-tempered – and it's hardly surprising if some of that gloom rubs off on us too. It's a bit difficult not to feel grumpy when it's cold, wet and grey outside.

It's in February, above all other months, that you might be forgiven for not sticking to your seasonal principles. There's only so much swede anyone can take, turkey has long since lost its appeal and even the sprouts are running out. But before you fall off the *Well Seasoned* wagon, take a look at what else is on offer this month. It's definitely not all bad news.

If ever there was a month designed for comfort food, this is it. Hearty stews and ragouts, together with the last of the feathered game, will keep us nourished, and although it's true that sweet treats are thin on the ground, forced rhubarb continues to provide plenty of fruity goodness. That superstar of late winter, purple sprouting broccoli, usually hits the shelves this month, while hardy brassicas, onions and carrots are still plentiful, meaning that even if the choice isn't as broad as we might like, there's still plenty of good vegetables to go around.

February is both the shortest month and the last month that we'll feel the full frozen grip of winter. That's definitely worth a celebration or two, and Shrove Tuesday and Valentine's Day fit the bill nicely. If that's not enough, you might be cheered by the fact that we'll see even more of those very early signs of spring this month. The first daffodils will flower, the first garden birds will sing and the first lambs will be born.

No one can stay grumpy after all that... can they?

The dawn chorus of garden birdsong signals the start of the mating season as our feathered friends start looking to attract partners and defend their breeding territories. Beginning with blackbirds and robins in late February, other species will gradually join the chorus through to late May, when it reaches a glorious crescendo.

The sunrise singing provides a fascinating insight into the world of our birds. With a little patience, you'll soon learn to distinguish individual species and the order in which they start to sing each day. They stick to a fairly rigid timetable and you might well prefer simply to soak up the atmosphere as you lie in bed – it begins around 4.30 a.m. this month, and as early as 3 a.m. as we reach the early summer.

The order of the birds song is dictated by the foods they eat and their ability to see in the low morning light. The early birds (blackbirds and robins) literally do catch the worms. These species have comparatively large eyes compared to their bodies and are able to see in the earliest, dim light of dawn. As the sun rises and light levels increase, insect-eaters (wrens) wake from their slumber. Finally, the seed-eaters (finches and sparrows) take their time and wait until just before daybreak.

So, expect to hear, in order:

Blackbird – monotonous *chink, chink, chink* followed by a distinct, low-pitched melody
Robin – high-pitched *tick, tick, tick*, followed by a cascade of warbling notes
Wren – chur, chur, churrrrr (at an impressive volume for such a small bird)
Chaffinch – distinct *pink, pink, pink*, followed by one of several flourishes
House sparrow – chattering and repetitive *chirrup, chirrup*.

The fall in our garden bird numbers over recent years has been well documented, though not fully explained. If you fancy doing your bit to help, take part in the RSPB's Big Garden Birdwatch, which takes place in late January or early February each year. More than half a million people usually participate, helping to provide a valuable snapshot of the bird population.

C auliflower, in its multitude of varieties (and colours, now including green, purple and even orange) is, in one guise or another, available throughout the year. However, in its most familiar, creamy-white winter form (in season from late autumn through to mid-April) it can make a significant contribution to your cold-weather repertoire. The fleshy buds, or florets, are packed full of stored vitamins, making it ideal winter fodder – perfect at a time of year when good root vegetables start to become a little harder to find.

It's another plant (along with forced rhubarb – see January) that you can actually hear growing when conditions are right. In warmer weather, cauliflower heads can grow up to 3 cm (about 1 in) a day, causing a loud squeaking noise. This phenomenon is known by growers as 'cauliflower creak'. (There's a joke there somewhere about cauliflower ears....)

This humble vegetable does suffer a great deal from over-enthusiastic cooking, and if you're not a fan, it's worth pausing to consider whether you've given it a fair chance. Its subtle, savoury flavours are easily spoiled by too much time in the pan. All too often you're left with grey mush and the sulphurous odour of over-cooked brassica. Cooked properly (which usually means briefly), cauliflower should be firm and flavoursome with a slight nutty taste.

For a vegetable, the cauliflower is relatively high in protein, which together with its firm, filling texture, makes it a favourite in vegetarian cultures, not least on the Indian subcontinent where it is frequently paired with bold flavours like cumin and turmeric. More traditionally, blitzed and sieved until smooth, it makes a hearty winter soup as well as a sublime bed for a starter of seared scallops.

To select a good-quality cauliflower, look for firm, bright florets, surrounded by fresh, green leaves. (Although usually discarded, the leaves are similarly flavourful and can be cooked in a similar way to a cabbage.)

Try:
Whole roasted spiced cauliflower with almonds and sultanas (p. 48)
Winter piccalilli (p. 51)

A medieval beast stalks our countryside, but is so elusive that many people aren't even aware of its existence. You might be surprised to learn that there are wild boar alive and well in British woodlands.

In the past, large numbers of boar inhabited our woods and fields. The Tudors loved to hunt them, and a spit-roasted wild boar was the centrepiece of many a medieval banquet. Sadly, sometime in the seventeenth century, British boar were hunted to extinction and nothing was seen of them for many years. But then, in the 1980s, boar farms breeding imported animals were established in Britain. In several incidents, most notably the great storm of 1987, some of the animals escaped, and in a few rare cases they were able to establish themselves as free-living populations.

Although there is some debate as to exactly how widespread they are, breeding populations have existed since at least 1990 and are now certainly established in Kent, Sussex, Dorset and the Forest of Dean.

Wild boar are extremely wary, generally venturing out only at night. They cause problems for a number of groups, including farmers who have to deal with the damage they do to land (boar feed in the same way as pigs, quickly reducing the ground to a hummocky quagmire) and ramblers who on several occasions have startled boar with their dogs, unexpectedly finding themselves in the middle of a canine/porcine rumpus.

They are also hardy beasts, with no natural predators in this country, so most land managers agree that they need to be culled in the same way as deer. This ensures a healthy population and limits the damage they do to crops, land and fencing. The upside is that if your butcher can get hold of it, wild boar meat is a seriously tasty treat.

Wild boar breed during the warmer months and so, while there isn't an official season for them, reputable dealers will only sell truly wild meat from late autumn through to the spring. That shouldn't, however, stop you from buying farmed meat, which is invariably free range and of high quality all year round.

Try: Pappardelle with wild boar ragout (p. 53)

I f you're brave enough to go to the beach in February, try hunting for razor clams (or, as they're known in Scotland, 'spoots'.) These elongated molluscs resemble the shape of a cut-throat razor, hence the name, and they make for excellent eating. Despite the risk of some pretty inclement weather, February is a good time to collect and eat shellfish because most will spawn during the warmer summer months.

For some reason (as with many of our shellfish) we don't eat many razor clams in the UK, but they are gobbled up by our continental cousins, and for good reason. Their flesh is firm and meaty, and although it has a fairly subtle taste, it partners very well with some big, bold flavours. In Portugal and Spain they are frequently cooked up with chorizo and other spicy meats.

If you want to try catching your own, first you need to locate a likely razor clam bed. There's nothing like a bit of local knowledge, so do some research and ask around first, but sandy, flat beaches are their preferred habitat. You'll need to check tide tables and aim to be on the beach at the beginning of the slack, low, spring tide (the very lowest tide) in order to have an hour at the lowest water line. Then look for little keyhole-shaped holes in the sand.

Using a large spouted bottle, pour several tablespoons of fine table salt into the hole and wash it down with water from a squeezy washing-up-liquid bottle or similar. The high salt levels irritate the clam and after a few moments you should see the surface being pushed upwards before the top erupts out of the sand. Grip the shell between two fingers, then firmly but slowly pull the clam out from its burrow. Make sure you grab the shell quickly and hold on; if you let go or wait too long they will bury themselves back in almost as quickly as they came out.

Your razor clam should be at least 10 centimetres (4-inches) in length. If it is, put it in your bucket. If not, put him back for another day.

Try: Razor clams with herb crumb, lemon and parsley butter (pp. 54–5).

I n the pagan calendar, 1 February (which falls halfway between the winter solstice and spring equinox) was known as Imbolc. It marked the beginning of spring and the festival of Brigid, Celtic goddess of fire, fertility and early spring.

Imbolc was seen as a time of great significance, when the worst of winter was over and the days were noticeably longer. Celebrations would start at sunset on the last day of January and continue until the same time on the following day. Whilst there are few reliable records of exactly what the original Imbolc celebrations would have entailed, fires and candlelight undoubtedly played an important role, representing the return of new light and warmth to the world around. It was a time for decluttering, cleaning and ritual bathing to create space and allow newly planted seeds (actual and spiritual) to take root.

As with so many of the old pagan festivals, a Christian feast cropped up to ensure that the converted could still have a good party, and so it is also now celebrated as the Feast of St Brigid.

There's another event that follows immediately after Imbolc. The second of February (Candlemas in the Christian calendar) is Groundhog Day. Most of us know the day from the 1993 Bill Murray film but it's a real event that actually started in Europe... with a badger.

Tradition has it that if the badger/groundhog sees his shadow when he emerges from his burrow in February, winter will last for six more weeks. If it's a cloudy day, spring will come early.

There is an interesting seasonal theory about the tradition's origins. The suggestion is that the day originally developed to allow for a compromise between the two conflicting views of when spring actually begins. More modern Western societies held that spring started on the vernal equinox (in mid-March), whereas the older cultures favoured Imbolc. By allowing the badger to choose between the two possibilities, the date could vary from year to year.

If Candlemas be fair and bright,
Winter will have another flight.
If Candlemas brings clouds and rain,
Winter will not come again.
(Traditional)

Feasts & Festivals | Shrove Tuesday (3rd February–9th March) and Easter

Shrove Tuesday is the last day before the start of Lent, the forty-day period leading up to Easter. The word 'Shrove' comes from 'shrive', meaning confession and absolution, as Lent was a time for fasting, penance and the confession of sins.

Because meat and fatty foods (originally including dairy products) were forbidden during Lent, it was common to use up stocks of foods, including eggs, butter and milk, on Shrove Tuesday, hence why the day became so closely connected with pancakes.

Shrove Tuesday is followed by Ash Wednesday, the first day of Lent, which can fall any time from 4 February to 10 March, as Easter can fall on any date from 22 March to 25 April.

How so? Well, unlike most religious celebrations, Easter is a 'moveable feast', meaning that it doesn't have a fixed date. The reason is that, in the past, some religions (including Judaism and Islam) used a lunar calendar with 354 days in the year, whereas others (Egyptians and Christians) used a solar one (with the now-standard 365 days). The complex rules around Easter are a result of trying to harmonize the two.

As a general rule, Easter falls on the first Sunday after the full moon on or after 20 March (in many years, but not all, the spring equinox – see March).

Unfortunately, it's not actually that simple, because occasionally different definitions of a full moon, including an 'ecclesiastical' moon, are used, and the more accurately we understand the astronomical cycles, the harder it becomes to reconcile the two calendars.

Various attempts have been made to fix Easter and there is, in fact, already a 'legal' Easter which was set out in the Easter Act (passed in 1928) that defines it as 'the first Sunday after the second Saturday in April'. But the Act was never brought fully into force so the exact date of Easter continues to vary from year to year.

Because of its association with pancakes, Shrove Tuesday has become widely known simply as Pancake Day. And for almost as long as people have been cooking pancakes, they've been dressing up in silly clothes and running with them.

Olney in Buckinghamshire hosts the original and most famous pancake race. Since at least 1948, competitors have lined up in the market square and raced the official 415 yards (380m) originally through but now past, the churchyard, flipping pancakes as they go. According to the pancake authorities, the event may date back as far as 1445, possibly to when a local housewife who was late for church on Shrove Tuesday dashed to the service, still holding her frying pan. It seems pretty unlikely and is unsupported by anything other than local legend, but it's an engaging tale nonetheless.

Try: Pancakes with blood orange marmalade (p. 57)
Pancakes with leek, Parmesan and prosciutto (p. 57)

Whole roasted spiced cauliflower with almonds and sultanas

This is a good example of the food I love to cook at home and uses some of my favourite spices. Cumin is, for me at least, one of the truly wonderful spices, rich and aromatic with a deep savouriness. I use it often.

Make this dish when the cauliflowers are abundant and serve as the main event with couscous and charred spring onions, or alternatively use it to accompany a slow-roasted shoulder of lamb.

SERVES 4 AS A SIDE DISH

1 whole cauliflower
50ml olive oil
1 tsp yellow mustard seeds
1 tsp ground cumin
1 pinch chilli flakes
60g unsalted butter
30g flaked almonds
1 lemon
50g sultanas, soaked in boiling water for 20
   minutes
Maldon sea salt and freshly ground black
   pepper

1. Preheat the oven to 200°C.

2. Remove the leaves from the cauliflower and cut out the core. Wash under a running tap and then steam or blanch in simmering water for around 6 minutes. Drain and dry off.

3. Heat the oil in a deep sauté pan, toast the mustard seeds then add the cumin and chilli flakes. Add the butter and, when it starts to foam, place the cauliflower in the pan, then season and baste with the butter. Transfer to the oven and cook, basting frequently, for approximately 15 minutes.

4. Remove the cauliflower, put the pan over a medium heat and add the almonds to the pan, allowing to toast. Remove from the heat and add a good squeeze of lemon juice. Grate some lemon zest into the pan, drain the sultanas and add them to the mix. Check the seasoning and adjust as required.

5. Pour the sultana mix over the cauliflower to serve.

Winter piccalilli

Our traditions of preserving, pickling and jam-making are strong in the UK. The origins of these traditions lie in the days long before the deep freeze, when salt, acid, smoke and vinegar were all employed to make food last longer. Today, the necessity may have gone but the delicious flavours continue to live on.

Recipes for piccalilli are numerous and each has its own nuance. I first made this only a couple of years ago in the depths of winter and I used what came to hand. A summer version could contain courgettes or red peppers, roasted and peeled of course, but the stalwart is undoubtedly the cauliflower; as we have seen, having three growing seasons in the UK, it is available nearly all year round.

MAKES 4 LARGE JARS

For the vegetables

1 small cauliflower, cut into florets
100g baby onions, peeled
150g celeriac, cut into 1cm cubes
1 bunch winter radishes, halved or quartered
100g salt
2l water
1 Bramley apple, peeled, cored and diced
1 bunch spring onions, cut into 2cm lengths

For the sauce

1 tbsp olive oil
2 tsp yellow mustard seeds
1 tsp cumin seeds
¼ tsp cayenne pepper
1 tsp turmeric
500ml cider vinegar
75g runny honey
50g caster sugar
25g cornflour and 15g English mustard powder
    mixed to a smooth paste with 200ml cold
    water
Maldon sea salt and freshly ground black
    pepper

1. First prepare all the vegetables and fruit, reserving the baby onion and the apples. Make a brine with the salt and water and use to cover the vegetables. Brine overnight, drain and wash off thoroughly.

2. For the sauce, heat the oil in a large pan and toast the mustard and cumin seeds, then stir in the cayenne and turmeric. Add the vinegar and bring to a simmer. Stir in the honey and sugar.

3. Add all the brined vegetables. Cook for around 6 minutes until the vegetables just start to soften. Take a ladleful of the hot vinegar mixture and combine with the cornflour mix and then gradually stir this back into the pan. Allow to thicken. Remove from the heat and adjust the seasoning. Stir in the spring onion pieces and the diced apple, then transfer to sterile jars.

Pappardelle with wild boar ragout

People often ask me about the merits of fresh versus dried pasta, but I think you have to look at them as two different products. The more robust texture of dried pasta made with just durum wheat semolina is not really comparable with fresh egg pasta. I like both in equal measures and have no qualms about using good-quality dried pasta. I feel it works better for something like a carbonara, as the texture stands up to the pancetta or guanciale and it gives the whole dish body. With a meltingly tender ragout or encasing soft ricotta, however, fresh egg pasta is the way to go.

The most important thing for me with a pasta dish is that the pasta shouldn't be overshadowed by the sauce or filling. It has an equal role in many dishes but can also be the star, with the sauce just providing moisture and seasoning.

SERVES 6 AS A MAIN COURSE

For the wild boar ragout

650g wild boar or good-quality pork, diced
100 ml olive oil
125g coarse pork mince that is fairly fatty
1 carrot, peeled, quartered lengthwise and cut
    into ½cm pieces
1 stick celery, halved lengthwise and cut into
    ½cm pieces
1 large onion, finely diced
2 cloves of garlic, sliced
1 tsp ground fennel seeds
1 tsp chilli flakes
150ml white wine
6 sage leaves and 1 bay leaf, tied in muslin
1 tsp dried oregano
½ a 400g tin of good-quality chopped tomatoes
100ml semi-skimmed milk
Maldon sea salt and freshly ground black
    pepper

To serve

420–480g dried pappardelle, or 600–750g fresh
    egg pappardelle (see Basics pp. 287–8)
aged Parmesan (24 months is a good choice)
olive oil

1. Preheat the oven to 140°C.

2. To make the ragout, season the boar, heat the olive oil in a large casserole or heavy pan, and fry the boar in small batches to colour well. Drain and set to one side.

3. In the same pan, fry the pork mince, breaking it up into small chunks as you go. You are looking to colour the meat so use a fairly high heat and don't overcrowd the pan. Remove from the pan and set aside with the boar. Tip off excess oil to leave around 2 tbsp.

4. Add the carrot, celery, onion and garlic to the pan and cook until starting to soften – around 10 minutes. Add the fennel seeds and chilli flakes and cook until aromatic. Add the wine and reduce by two-thirds. Add all the remaining ingredients, including the meat, and bring to a simmer. Season well, cover and place in the oven for at least 3 hours, stirring occasionally and topping up with water if the meat is getting too dry. The boar should be breaking up into flakes when it is cooked. It may need a little encouragement with a fork. Adjust the seasoning and leave the sauce to rest while you cook the pasta.

5. To serve, bring a large pan of salted water to the boil – around a litre for every 100g of pasta, with 1 tsp of salt per litre. Cook the pasta according to the packet instructions for al dente if dried, or 1–3 minutes if fresh.

6. Heat the ragout and, using tongs, transfer the pasta to the ragout. Don't drain the pasta too carefully, as the starchy water that comes with it will emulsify the sauce and allow you to cook the pasta and sauce together for a minute or two.

7. Finish with a good glug of your favourite olive oil and some freshly grated Parmesan.

Razor clams with herb crumb, lemon and parsley butter

These are a little fiddly to prepare but for this particular recipe all the prep can be done in advance so it will take the pressure off! Once the clams are steamed open, the meat will pull easily from the shell and the inedible parts can be cut away.

Lay the clam flat on the board with the rounder end to the left, cut this off close to the dark sac. Lift the frilly wing up and slice off the cylindrical piece of meat with the pointed end. Now trim the wing away from the dark sac. Scrape off any odd bits of sand as you go. Now the meat can be sliced into half-centimetre pieces ready to use. If you're unsure at any point, the internet has plenty of useful videos on fish and shellfish preparation.

SERVES 4 AS A STARTER

For the clams
1kg live razor clams, thoroughly washed (Razor claims should be alive when cooked; open shells should close when tapped – discard any that don't. Any shells that don't open once cooked should be discarded also.)
75ml white wine

For the butter
50g unsalted butter
½ lemon, grated zest only
2 tsp lemon juice
freshly ground black pepper
reduced clam cooking liquid
1 dsp chopped flat-leaf parsley

For the crumb
1 tbsp olive oil
1 clove of garlic, smashed
40g day-old bread, preferably a rustic loaf, torn into pieces.
1 tbsp chopped flat-leaf parsley

To serve
lemon wedges and crusty bread (optional)

1. Before you start cooking the clams, have a roasting tin of ice ready to chill them as soon as they are cooked.

2. To cook the clams, heat a large casserole or sauté pan that has a tight-fitting lid. When really hot, drop in the clams and pour in the wine. Put

the lid on immediately and steam over a high heat for 1 minute until the clams are open. Use tongs to drop the clams onto the ice.

3. Pass the cooking liquid through a fine sieve into a small, clean pan and reduce until syrupy. Allow to cool.

4. Prepare the clams as described above and then chill the sliced meat for a few minutes.

5. Beat the butter together with the lemon zest, juice and a few grinds of pepper. Gradually beat in the clam cooking liquid, checking the seasoning as you go. The liquid will be salty so stop when the butter is well seasoned. Add the parsley and mix in the clam flesh.

6. Select eight of the largest and best-looking shells, give them a scrub and then place in a pan of water and bring to the boil to sterilize. Drain and dry off. Allow to cool.

7. For the crumb, heat the olive oil in a small pan and add the garlic. Cook, turning frequently, to make a garlicky oil. Don't let the garlic go beyond golden or it will start to take on some bitter notes. Blitz the bread with the parsley, garlic and oil to make coarse breadcrumbs.

8. To serve, fill the clam shells with the buttery clam meat and top with the breadcrumbs, grill under a hot grill for 2 minutes until bubbling and golden. Serve immediately with lemon wedges, and bread for mopping up the juices.

Pancakes

Pancakes are something we should have more often than just on Shrove Tuesday, but for many of us this is the only time we will make them. This is a shame as they make a versatile carrier for all sorts of sweet and savoury dishes. They certainly have a place alongside the pitta and tortilla.

At this time of year, the fresh fruit and vegetable selection can be a little limiting, but preserves and store-cupboard ingredients can certainly elevate the pancake. One fresh fruit that crosses over from January into February is the blood orange, and these, along with some marmalade and sweetened whipped cream, make a sticky, sweet-and-sour filling. If a savoury pancake is your preference, I would reach for leeks, Parmesan and prosciutto.

MAKES APPROXIMATELY 16 PANCAKES

For the pancakes

270g plain flour
1 tsp Maldon sea salt, finely ground
2 tbsp caster sugar
3 large free-range eggs
200ml water
400ml semi-skimmed milk
35g unsalted butter, melted

1. Preheat the oven to 230°C.

2. Sift the flour, salt and sugar into a bowl. Combine the eggs, water and milk in a jug. Gradually whisk the liquid into the flour mix to achieve a smooth batter. Whisk in the melted butter and then let the batter rest in the fridge for at least an hour before using.

3. Heat a little oil and butter in a good non-stick frying pan and swirl in a thin layer of the pancake batter. Cook over a medium heat until the pancake is set and lightly coloured on the underside. Turn or flip and brown the other side. Pile them up and keep them warm while making the remaining pancakes.

BLOOD ORANGE AND MARMALADE FILLING (FOR 8 PANCAKES)

125ml double cream
2 tsp semi-skimmed milk
2 tsp caster sugar
seeds from ½ vanilla pod
120g Seville orange marmalade
3 blood oranges, segmented and juice
   squeezed from the frames

1. Whip the cream and milk with the sugar and vanilla to soft peaks, and set to one side.

2. Place the marmalade and juice from the oranges in a small pan and bring to the boil. Cook for 1 minute. Allow to cool slightly then add the orange segments. Spoon the orange mix onto warm pancakes and top with the vanilla cream.

LEEK, PARMESAN AND PROSCIUTTO FILLING (FOR 8 PANCAKES)

3 large leeks, halved lengthwise and sliced into
   1cm pieces
3 tbsp crème fraîche
2 tsp Dijon mustard
50g grated Parmesan plus 10g for grilling
lemon juice to taste
8 slices of prosciutto
Maldon sea salt and freshly ground black
   pepper

1. Place the leeks in a pan with a couple of tablespoons of water and season. Cover with a tight lid, place over a medium heat and steam for approximately 5–6 minutes or until tender. Remove the lid and continue to cook over a high heat to dry out. Add the crème fraîche and mustard and mix well. Remove from the heat, add 50g of the Parmesan and adjust the seasoning with the salt, pepper and lemon.

2. Place a slice of prosciutto on each pancake and top with one-eighth of the leek mix. Roll up to encase the filling and place in an oven proof dish. Sprinkle with the remaining Parmesan and warm through in the oven for 5 minutes.

Sticky ginger cake

This is a variation on the method for making a sticky toffee pudding and straddles the line between cake and pudding very nicely. It would work well with roasted rhubarb and clotted cream for a dessert, is excellent with honey-roasted pears and sits quite happily alongside a flat white.

SERVES 8

125g Californian raisins
4 pieces of stem ginger in syrup
100ml Muscat wine
100g unsalted butter
80g dark muscovado sugar plus 1 tsp for sprinkling on top
1½ tbsp syrup from the stem ginger, plus 2 tbsp for finishing
2 large free-range eggs, beaten
½ tsp bicarbonate of soda
150g self-raising flour
1 tsp Maldon sea salt, finely ground
1 tbsp ground ginger
1 lemon, grated zest only

1. Preheat the oven to 170°C.

2. Place the raisins, ginger and wine in a pan, bring to the boil and simmer for 5 minutes. Transfer to a food processor and blitz to a rough purée.

3. In the meantime, cream the butter, muscovado sugar and ginger syrup together and gradually beat in the eggs. Use a little of the flour to stop the mix splitting.

4. Add the bicarbonate of soda to the raisin mix and blend in.

5. Sift the remaining flour together with the salt and ground ginger. Fold the flour mix into the egg mix and then fold in the raisin purée and the lemon zest. Pour the batter into a greased 20cm loose-bottomed cake tin and sprinkle 1 tsp of muscovado over the surface. Bake for 20 minutes and then reduce the heat to 150°C and cook for a further 15 minutes. The cake should spring back when gently pushed and be a dark brown colour.

6. Remove from the tin and transfer to a cooling wire. Using a pastry brush, coat the top of the warm cake with the 2 tbsp of ginger syrup.

03 | March

Lenctenmonath – lengthening month, when the days start getting noticeably longer

It's practically impossible not to feel positive in March. The first month of spring brings with it longer days, warmer sun and the beginnings of new growth all around us.

As if to hammer the point home, we've artificially created one of the most abrupt seasonal changes with British Summer Time, when, at the end of the month, the clocks suddenly reward our patience through the dark winter months with an extra hour of evening sunlight. It almost, but not quite, coincides with the vernal equinox, which for many of us represents the natural start of spring and reignites a sense of optimism that has been absent for the past few months.

Unfortunately, all that positivity is bound to suffer a set-back at some point. The one thing you can guarantee about March weather is that there are no guarantees; one day it'll be bright sunshine and the next we could have torrential rain or even a blanket of fresh snow. No, there's simply nothing predictable about March.

Nevertheless, whatever twists and turns we experience along the way, we know we're heading in roughly the right direction. The first spring lambs will be out in the fields by now, daffodils will definitely have flowered and we'll see the early green shoots of the summer crops. It's no coincidence that every religion that's ever been prevalent in the UK has some form of celebration of birth and new life around this time.

And so it is in the kitchen – optimism and a sense of expectation abound. February and March are comparatively lean months, but by the time the clocks go forward, things start to look up a little as the first crops of broccoli, spinach and early lettuces all arrive. It's a pretty good month for seafood, too and although the feathered game season closes at the end of January, there's still good meat in the wild larder, with rabbit and venison both on the menu.

It's also the time when we can start to think about going outside without looking like we're planning an assault on Everest, and with the new growth all around us, it's usually a good month to start foraging for some wild ingredients, including nettles, dandelions and that pungent perennial, wild garlic.

Out & About
chillies

Food & Foraging
wild garlic, kale, gurnard

Feasts & Festivals
Spring Equinox
Mothering Sunday

Vegetables
kale, purple sprouting brocoli

Fish
gurnard, shrimp, lemon sole

Hedgerow Harvest
wild garlic

Recipes

Potato gnocchi with wild garlic pesto
Chicken, leek and wild garlic pie
Fillet of gurnard with a warm potato and caper
   salad
Roast pork belly with sage and onion
Warm salad of kale, roasted onion, chickpea and
   soft goat's cheese
Lemon and white chocolate roulade

Out & About | Chillies

Anyone interested in seasonal eating should grow an annual crop of chillies. Whether you're green-fingered or all thumbs, you'll find it a rewarding experience and, unless you're a real heat freak, you don't need much space – a small number of plants will satisfy most of your culinary needs. March is the month to plant most seeds for a crop in September (although for some slower-growing varieties you might even think about planting them as early as January).

Chillies originate from South America and Asia and so need hot, humid conditions to thrive. This does mean that in the UK they need to be planted indoors and should be transferred outside only once the summer weather really takes off.

First, choose your chillies. Your selection will depend on the amount of space you have, whether you want to keep them indoors and how much heat you can handle. (If you're a novice, you might start with something like a Super Chilli – not actually that 'super' in terms of heat but an excellent all-round cooking chilli and very simple to grow in a confined space.)

Plant into seed trays (follow the instructions on your seed packet for depth and quantity) and keep them warm and moist. Within a week or two you should see the first green shoots, and by the time any risk of a frost has passed in early May they should be ready to plant outside (if you want to – many smaller varieties will thrive potted, indoors). You can expect them to flower in mid-summer, after which they will develop small green fruits which will grow and ripen until early autumn, when they'll be ready for picking.

Although it's always best to use fresh chillies in your cooking when you can, if you have a good crop you'll definitely want to keep some for future use and you should pick them all before the first frosts of autumn.

My preferred method of preserving chillies is to dry them. Once properly dried, they can last for years and will retain much of their flavour and heat. It's vital to remove all of the moisture so they are crisp and brittle; otherwise they will rot over time.

You can buy purpose-made food dehydrators but unless you're intending to work on an industrial scale, you can achieve much the same effect with your oven. Turn it to a very low temperature (about 100°C or 200°F), then spread the chillies in a single layer on a baking tray lined with baking paper and place in the oven. It's critical to keep an eye on them. If you burn the chillies they will be bitter and unusable. Start by baking for ten minutes and then check every few minutes until they are crisp and dry. Once completely dry, remove and allow to cool before storing in an air-tight container.

If you have a bit more time on your hands, you can dry chillies in a classic string or *ristra*. Simply take a needle and a few feet of fishing line or strong thread, tie a large knot at

the end of the line and thread your chillies on (piercing at the top of the chilli, just below the stalk). Hang in your airing or boiler cupboard for at least two weeks until dry and crisp. Once dried, either store in an airtight container or hang in a warm, dry place to avoid them reabsorbing moisture. Next to a bright kitchen window is ideal.

One other alternative, which gets you slightly nearer to a fresh chilli taste when cooking, is to freeze your fruits. Spread on a baking tray so they aren't touching, and place in the freezer overnight. Once separately frozen, they can be bagged up and stored until needed for cooking. They will keep for six months or longer this way.

Before cooking with any chilli you should taste a small piece to test the strength; even those from the same plant can vary considerably. The heat is caused by the chemical capsaicin and, if you want to get scientific about it, is measured on the Scoville scale. Mild chillies such as jalapeños have a rating of around 1,000 Scoville heat units (SHUs) and the hottest chillies in the world, including the Dorset Naga and the Carolina Reaper, measure well over 1,000,000 SHUs.

W ild garlic (also known as ramsons or bear's garlic) comes into season this month and you'll find it easily thanks to its unmistakable smell.

In early spring the woodland air in many places is thick with the pungent, garlicky aroma of ramsons crops for several hundred yards around. Once you locate a likely crop you can confirm its identity by looking for small, star-shaped white flowers and waxy green leaves. It's unlikely you'll go wrong (although be aware that Lily of the Valley, which is toxic, does bear some resemblance). In fact, so familiar and identifiable are wild garlic colonies that 'garlic woods' feature as landmarks on many old maps of the countryside. It's one of the first reliable wild crops of the year and its arrival causes great excitement for foragers across the country.

Despite its strong smell, the flavour of wild garlic is usually subtle and you can use the leaves in place of spring onions in most dishes. Gather what you need (taking no more than a couple of leaves from each plant), then get your foraged crop into the kitchen as soon as you can, especially if it's destined for the salad bowl. If necessary, you can revive any slightly wilted leaves by standing them in a glass of fresh water for twenty minutes or so.

If you can't find any in the woods then you should have better luck at the larger farmers' markets and can also now buy online from a few good suppliers.

Try:
Potato gnocchi with wild garlic pesto (p. 70)
Chicken, leek and wild garlic pie (p. 73)

Food & Foraging | Kale

Kale grows all year round but is most plentiful from mid-autumn to early spring. Like parsnips it's said to be at its best after the first frost, which it happily resists, making it a real cold-weather stalwart and perfect in March, when other leafy greens are still getting their act together.

This butch, bold brassica is packed full of flavour but, despite all its generosity, it seems to divide the nation – in recent years demand from in-the-know foodies has gone through the roof, with some touting it as a 'superfood' (a nonsense word that I would cheerfully ban), but just as many choose to reject its culinary charms.

It's possible that, along with other cheap and nutritious ingredients such as rabbit, it has suffered from its connections with wartime rationing. The Dig for Victory campaign of the Second World War extolled its easy-growing and nutritious virtues, but perhaps that's exactly why it subsequently fell out of favour at the end of the war when other more exciting foods returned to the menu. Another possibility is that people aren't cooking it properly – we have a habit of keeping cabbage in the fridge for too long (kale becomes increasingly bitter the longer it is kept) and then boiling the bejesus out of it (a quick flash in the pan is all kale needs. In fact, you can even eat it raw).

There is no such uneasiness elsewhere. In Northern Germany where kale is universally celebrated as a star ingredient, clubs and societies will regularly host an (unfortunate-sounding) *Kohlfahrt*, meaning 'cabbage walk', during the winter months when kale stews (together with lots of sausage and schnapps) are enjoyed in huge quantities.

Kale really is a seasonal hero as it's one of the few green vegetables that is available throughout the coldest months. There's even a variety called 'Hungry Gap' because it plugs the unproductive early-spring period (see April).

Try: Warm salad of kale, roasted onion and soft goat's cheese (p. 79)

I f there were underwater beauty pageants, the poor gurnard probably wouldn't come last (that dubious honour would go to the monkfish) but it certainly wouldn't win any prizes.

Also known as Robin of the Sea, thanks to its wing-like pectoral fins, this little fish with a big head has been the victim of discrimination for centuries.

Historically in the British Isles, it was completely ignored as an eating fish, used only to bait lobster pots and often simply discarded as unwanted by-catch. Our more enlightened European neighbours would at least bulk out the occasional fish stew or bouillabaisse with it, but it was only ever a filler and never the star attraction.

Thankfully, recent years have seen a turn around in the gurnard's culinary fortunes. All of the species – red, grey and yellow – are now seen as affordable, sustainable and plentiful. Most importantly it's a flavoursome fish that makes an excellent alternative to more common white fish (including its ugly and over-exploited chum the monkfish).

Although the red gurnard is more common and striking in appearance, there is little to choose between the three species in terms of flavour. Their chunky, firm flesh holds together well and so is particularly suited to curries and stews. Roasting gurnard whole is also popular, not least because it avoids having to tackle their unorthodox bone structure, which can be tricky to master.

A small footnote of caution – the Marine Conservation Society has noted that gurnard stocks are stable but, because they are not subject to any fishing quotas, their sustainable status is uncertain. As with any wild stocks, we need to be prudent, so avoid eating gurnard during the summer spawning season and avoid any immature fish under 25 centimetres (9in) – as there is no minimum landing size, you will occasionally find these legitimately for sale.

Try: Fillet of gurnard with a warm potato and caper salad (p. 74)

| # Spring Equinox (20th or 21st March)

Every year on either 20 or 21 March the vernal equinox reputedly (but, as it happens, wrongly) marks the point after which the days become longer than the nights.

The March equinox (meaning literally 'equal night') is the point that the sun sits directly over the equator, marking the start of astronomical spring in the northern hemisphere. For most cultures it is a symbolic day and one which has long been viewed by many as the 'official' start of the new season.

As we've already seen (Shrove Tuesday), the equinox is an important date in determining when Easter falls.

The vernal equinox's counterpart falls on 22 or 23 September, and the Sunday of the full moon closest to the autumn equinox was usually celebrated as part of harvest festivities. Together with the two solstices, the equinoxes make up the four great solar festivals of the calendar year.

If you're a real stickler for detail, the equinox is not actually the day on which the day and night are of equal length in Britain. Due to the refraction of the sun's light over the horizon before it rises, this equality happens a few days before the equinox on a day known as the spring equilux. The converse is true in autumn, when the equilux falls slightly later, around 25 September.

| # Mothering Sunday (middle Sunday of Lent)

Mothering Sunday is the middle (fourth) Sunday of Lent, when mothers across the country are treated to an enthusiastically made breakfast and cold tea in bed – usually around 6 a.m. Historically, the middle Sunday of Lent was a day when the rules of fasting were relaxed in celebration and commemoration of the biblical miracle of the Feeding of the Five Thousand (when five loaves and two fish were said to have fed a multitude). Due to the welcome relief, it was also known as Refreshment Sunday.

There is some evidence to suggest that the name Mothering Sunday existed before Christian times because of the Roman festival of Cybele (the mother goddess), who was also feted in the springtime. But, in any event, it became a date when servants, especially young girls, would be released for the day to visit their family and attend their 'mother church', where they would have been baptized (as opposed to their 'daughter church', nearest to where they lived). Special services were held for the occasion.

On the journey home, the children picked spring flowers to take to the church or to present to their mother, and over time the celebration became widely known simply as 'Mother's Day'.

Simnel cake is traditionally associated with Mothering Sunday and the Easter period generally. It's a rich, marzipan-covered fruit cake with eleven balls of marzipan on top (representing the eleven Christian disciples other than Judas). It's not clear where the name 'simnel' came from but it may simply be from simila, a very fine wheat flour.

Potato gnocchi with wild garlic pesto

This is classed as one of my signature dishes and shows how simple my cooking has become over the years. All the components can be made in advance and the pesto is a great way of extending the wild garlic season. You won't need all the pesto for this recipe so just store any surplus in the fridge for another day. Mixed with equal quantities of crème fraîche and mayonnaise, it's great in a chicken sandwich or as a dip.

SERVES 4 AS A STARTER

For the gnocchi
600g Maris Piper potatoes
100g pasta flour
50g fine semolina
2 tsp Maldon sea salt, finely ground
1 large free-range egg yolk (20g)

For the pesto
150g wild garlic leaves, washed and de-stalked
85g Parmesan, coarsely grated
100g pine nuts, toasted
light olive oil
lemon juice to taste
Maldon sea salt and freshly ground black
  pepper

To serve
150ml vegetable stock (see Basics p. 284)
Parmesan for shaving

1. To make the gnocchi, steam the potatoes or boil in their skins until completely tender. While still warm, peel and rice the potatoes, or push them through a coarse sieve. Don't mash or overwork the potato as this tends to make the gnocchi heavy. Weigh out 400g of the riced potato and place on the work surface. Sift the flour, semolina and salt together and sprinkle half over the potato. Drizzle with the egg yolk and then sprinkle on the remaining flour mix.

2. Use a metal dough-scraper or a large kitchen knife to chop the mix together, repeatedly turning it over and then chopping again until the egg is reasonably well distributed, taking care not to overwork the mix. Once the mix is evenly blended, bring together by hand and knead very briefly. Divide the dough into four pieces and cover with cling film.

3. Working with one piece of dough at time, roll out into a sausage 1.5cm thick and cut into sections 1cm long. Roll each piece into a ball and then form on a gnocchi paddle or the back of a large fork. Alternatively, use the back of a dinner knife to cut the dough sausage into pillows.

4. Repeat with the remaining dough, placing the finished gnocchi on a tray dusted with semolina.

5. Bring a large pan of salted water to the boil, turn down to a simmer and add the gnocchi a quarter of the batch at a time. Stir the pan, and when the gnocchi float to the surface, cook for 1 minute. Remove into iced water. Once all the gnocchi are blanched, drain and toss in a little olive oil. The gnocchi can be refrigerated or loose-frozen.

6. For the pesto, place the wild garlic, Parmesan and pine nuts in a blender and pulse until roughly blended. Pulse in enough olive oil to make a paste that can be quenelled. Season with salt, pepper and lemon juice.

7. To serve, bring a large pan of water to the simmer and add a generous amount of salt. Drop in the gnocchi and heat until they just start to float. Remove with a slotted spoon and drain on a clean cloth. Heat some olive oil in a large non-stick pan and fry the gnocchi in batches until they are golden brown. Heat the vegetable stock and add 1 heaped tablespoon of pesto per portion. Add the fried gnocchi, toss together and adjust the seasoning. Divide between shallow bowls, shave some Parmesan over the top and drizzle with your favourite olive oil.

NOTE: At the start of the wild garlic season, the leaves are often stronger so you may only need a reduced quantity.

Chicken, leek and wild garlic pie

Crisp, buttery pastry, tender chicken and a wonderfully pungent, garlicky sauce mean this is a dish of bold flavours. Simple greens as an accompaniment make a good foil and both cavolo nero and purple sprouting broccoli should be plentiful at this time of year.

It is hard to decide whether the chicken, the pastry or the wild garlic is the star of the show but the garlic is such a seasonal treat. The same quantity in a fish pie is really good too.

SERVES 4 AS MAIN COURSE

For the flaky pastry
200g plain flour
1 tsp Maldon sea salt, finely ground
150g salted butter, chilled
1 large free-range egg yolk
100ml cold water

For the filling
2 tbsp olive oil
2 skinless, boneless chicken breasts, cut into
    large dice
4 rashers of smoked, streaky bacon, cut into
    1cm pieces
500g leek, trimmed, sliced and washed
100ml dry white wine
300ml chicken stock (see Basics p. 285)
1 tsp Dijon mustard
75g crème fraîche
cornflour to thicken
50g wild garlic, stalks removed
1 large free-range egg yolk mixed with 1 tbsp of
    water to glaze the pastry
Maldon sea salt and freshly ground black
    pepper

1. Preheat the oven to 170°C.

2. For the pastry, sift the flour and salt onto the bench, grate the butter over the flour using a coarse grater. Stop every now and again to toss the butter through the flour with your fingertips and to dust the grater with flour.

3. Make a well in the centre, then beat the yolk into the water and pour into the well. Gradually bring in the flour with your fingertips to create a dough. Knead briefly and then wrap in cling film and rest in the fridge for 30 minutes before using.

4. To make the filling, season the chicken breast and fry in the olive oil in a very hot pan. This is just to colour the chicken, not to cook it through. Remove the chicken to a plate and add the bacon to the pan. When the fat is starting to render, add the leeks and cook until just beginning to soften. Add the leek mix to the chicken.

5. Pour the wine into the pan. Reduce the wine to a syrup and add the chicken stock. Reduce this by around two-thirds then whisk in the Dijon mustard and crème fraîche. Mix 1 tsp of cornflour with a little cold water and use this to thicken the sauce – a thick double cream consistency is what you are looking for.

6. Add the chicken mix to the sauce and adjust the seasoning. Finely chop the wild garlic and stir it in.

7. Divide the pastry into two pieces; one-third and two-thirds. Roll out the larger piece to line the base of a 22cm x 16cm pie tin. Add the filling to the tin and then roll out the remaining pastry for the lid. Egg-wash around the rim of the pie base and lay the lid over. Crimp the lid onto the base, sealing well, and trim off excess pastry. Egg wash the lid.

8. Bake the pie for around 40 minutes until the pastry is a dark golden colour and there are signs of the filling bubbling.

9. Serve immediately with your chosen veg. Any leftover pie is delicious cold!

Fillet of gurnard with a warm potato and caper salad

As we've seen, gurnard is one of those fish that is less commonly eaten but does deliver some great flavour. It feeds mainly on crabs and shrimps, which I think gives the flesh some shellfish notes. It has a firm, creamy, white meat and is often used in fish stews or baked whole. It is not the easiest fish to fillet, given its shape, but my personal preference is for fish off the bone so, to me, it is worth the effort. Of course, a good fishmonger will happily fillet the fish for you.

As with many fish dishes, you can change the fish according to what is best at the time from your supplier. The potato and caper salad is hugely versatile and you could easily swap the gurnard for pollock or John Dory.

SERVES 4 AS A STARTER

For the dressing

6 sun-dried tomatoes
1 tbsp small capers, drained and rinsed
1½ tbsp lemon juice
50g crème fraîche
75ml light olive oil
1 tbsp chopped flat-leaf parsley
Maldon sea salt and freshly ground black
  pepper

For the potato salad

50ml olive oil
350g small unpeeled new potatoes, boiled and
  cut into 1cm-thick rings
1 banana shallot, diced
1 tbsp small capers, drained and rinsed
½ lemon, zest only
1 tbsp chopped flat-leaf parsley
Maldon sea salt and freshly ground black
  pepper

For the fish

50ml olive oil
2 large gurnard, filleted, pin-boned and trimmed
1 tbsp plain flour mixed with 2 tsp semolina,
  seasoned well
25g unsalted butter
Maldon sea salt and freshly ground black
  pepper

1. To make the dressing, combine all the ingredients except the parsley in a small food processor. Blitz until smooth. Adjust the seasoning and add the parsley.

2. For the potato salad, heat the oil in a medium, non-stick frying pan and add the potatoes, followed by the diced shallot. Cook over a medium heat, turning frequently, until lightly coloured. Add the capers to the pan and remove from the heat. Grate the zest from the lemon on top and season. Set to one side while you cook the fish, and finish by stirring in the parsley just before serving.

3. To cook the fish, heat the oil in a large, non-stick pan, dust the skin side of the fillets with the seasoned flour mix and lay gently into the hot oil. Cook over a medium-high heat until the fish begins to crisp – around 2 minutes. Season the flesh side of the fish and add the butter to the pan. When the butter is foaming, baste the fish and then flip over. Cook on the flesh side until you can pierce the fish with a cocktail stick without feeling the fibres tearing. This will only take around 1 more minute. Remove the fish and drain on paper towel.

4. To serve, divide the potato salad between the plates, lay a fillet of gurnard across the top and dot some dressing around. If you wanted to serve this as a light lunch, a chicory salad would go well with the dish.

Roast pork belly with sage and onion

As with all meat, it is best to source the highest quality you can get, and with pork, the effort and extra cost really pay dividends. The key for me is a reasonable quantity of fat; if I have had problems getting good crackling on a piece of pork it has always been when the meat is lean. When I look at a piece of pork belly I want to see a ratio of around 60:40 lean to fat, and a nice dry skin.

Roasting the pork on the bed of onions provides one of the accompaniments for the dish, and the combination of high heat and slow cooking will give succulent meat and that all-important crackling.

SERVES 4 AS A MAIN COURSE WITH LEFTOVERS

NOTE: Start this recipe 24 hours in advance.

For the marinade
1 small bunch of sage
3 cloves of garlic, peeled
1½ tbsp Maldon sea salt
1½ tbsp fennel seeds, toasted in a dry pan until fragrant
olive oil to make a spreadable paste

For the pork
2–2.5kg piece of pork belly – bone in, skin on
6 medium onions, peeled and cut into eighths
4 sprigs of sage
olive oil
Maldon sea salt
500ml water
250ml dry cider
1 tsp of cornflour, slaked in 1 tbsp of cold water

For the sage and onion purée
50g crème fraîche
1 tbsp chopped sage
Maldon sea salt and freshly ground black pepper

1. Preheat the oven to 250˚C.

2. Place all the dry marinade ingredients in a small blender and blitz to a paste using just enough olive oil to make a spreadable consistency.

3. Score the skin of the pork belly with the tip of a sharp knife in a diamond pattern with around 1cm between the score lines. Lay out a couple of sheets of cling film, overlapping them slightly, then lay two more sheets on top at right angles, again overlapping slightly. Place the pork belly skin side down on the cling film and pierce the flesh side all over with the tip of a knife. Spread on the marinade, rub in well and wrap up tightly. Transfer to a tray, skin side up, and refrigerate overnight.

4. The next day, place the onions and sage in a roasting tin, unwrap the belly and place skin side up on top of the onions. Drizzle with olive oil and season liberally with Maldon sea salt, rubbing it in well. Add 500ml water to the roasting tin and cook for 20 minutes, when the skin should start to crackle.

5. Reduce the oven temperature to 150˚C. Add the cider to the roasting tin and carefully place a piece of baking parchment over the meat, followed by a double layer of foil. Seal tightly and cook for 1 hour. Unwrap the pork, adding a little more water if the tin is getting dry. Cook for a further 40 minutes. Pierce the meat with a carving fork; it should push through with little resistance if the meat is cooked. Cook for longer if not, checking again at 10-minute intervals.

6. When the meat is cooked, carefully remove to a tray. Turn the oven back up to 250˚C. Place a sieve over a small pan and tip in the onions and liquid from the roasting tin. When the oven reaches temperature, return the pork to the oven to finish the crackling. This should only take 5–10 minutes. Keep a close eye on the crackling's progress as it can burn easily. Remove the pork to rest in a warm place but do not cover.

7. While the pork is resting, purée the onions with the crème fraîche. Pass through a fine sieve to remove any bits of fennel seed, add the chopped sage and adjust the seasoning.

8. Skim the fat from the pan juices, reheat and thicken with the cornflour to make a gravy.

9. Place the pork on a chopping board, crackling side down, and remove the bones. Slice into thick slices, cutting through the meat and then pushing down through the crackling.

Serve with the onion purée and your favourite seasonal veg – purple sprouting broccoli, buttered leeks and the last of the parsnips, perhaps?

Warm salad of kale, roasted onion, chickpea and soft goat's cheese

This is a dish that is about subtle flavours and a really good combination of textures and temperature. The minerality of kale, the richness of thyme-roasted sweet onion and the cool creaminess of tangy goat's cheese work so well together. Good-quality balsamic vinegar ties everything together and is something that is worth spending a few pounds on. Much of my cooking is Italian-influenced even though British ingredients are to the fore. Things like really good-quality oils and vinegars do make a big difference and can transform something very ordinary into something sublime. Chickpeas bought in jars are generally much more tender and creamy than those from tins, so are worth looking out for.

SERVES 4 AS A MAIN COURSE

For the onions

50ml olive oil

4 sweet white onions, cut into eight wedges

20g unsalted butter

6 sprigs of thyme

1½ tbsp good balsamic vinegar

Maldon sea salt and freshly ground black
   pepper

For the kale

350g kale, large stems removed

2 tbsp good olive oil

2 tbsp good balsamic vinegar

Maldon sea salt and freshly ground black
   pepper

For the chickpeas

2 tbsp olive oil

1 large banana shallot, sliced

1 clove of garlic, sliced

75ml white wine

200ml vegetable stock (see Basics p. 284)

2 sprigs of thyme

250g cooked chickpeas

Maldon sea salt and freshly ground black
   pepper

To serve

150g soft goat's cheese

good balsamic vinegar

extra virgin olive oil

1. Preheat the oven to 170°C.

2. For the onions, heat the oil in a roasting tin and add the onions, turning them through the oil. Add the butter, season well and scatter the thyme over the onions. Roast at 170°C for 30 minutes, turning every 10 minutes. If the onions are catching, add a little water to the tin. You are looking for the onions to be well caramelized. Once cooked, remove from the oven and drizzle with the balsamic. Keep in a warm place until you are ready to assemble the dish.

3. While the onions are cooking, blanch the kale in boiling, heavily salted water until just tender. Immediately refresh the kale in a bowl of iced water. Drain and pat dry with a clean cloth.

4. For the chickpeas, sweat the shallot and garlic in a little oil until tender, add the wine and reduce to a syrup, add the stock and thyme and reduce by half. Add the chickpeas, season well and cook until the liquid is just coating the pulses. Check and adjust the seasoning.

5. To serve, warm 2 tbsp of olive oil in a large pan, add the kale. Season and dress with the vinegar. Cook for a further minute, stirring frequently. Transfer the kale to a large serving platter and scatter the warm onion and the chickpeas over it. Crumble the goat's cheese on top and serve with more oil and vinegar.

Lemon and white chocolate roulade

This roulade is light and zingy with fresh lemon flavours. If you have the time, making your own lemon curd will make it even more delicious. It works both as an afternoon-tea cake or as a dessert. You will probably have a little mousse left over which could be served with the roulade or just treated as the cook's perks!

SERVES 8

For the mousse
220g good-quality white chocolate
1½ leaves of gelatine, soaked in cold water
130ml double cream
210ml double cream mixed with 1½ tbsp semi-skimmed milk, whipped to very soft peaks

For the sponge
3 large free-range eggs, separated
85g icing sugar, sifted
1 lemon, zest only
25g cornflour
25g soft pastry flour
2 tsp caster sugar

To serve
120g lemon curd
6 green pistachios
white chocolate shavings

1. Preheat the oven to 160°C.

2. To make the mousse, melt the chocolate in a heatproof bowl either on a low setting in the microwave or over a pan of gently simmering water. Soak the gelatine in cold water.

3. Bring the 130ml of cream to a simmer, remove from the heat and add the soaked gelatine, stirring well to thoroughly dissolve. Gently whisk this into the white chocolate to form a ganache.

4. Check that the temperature of the ganache is around 35–40°C and then fold in the whipped cream/milk mix. Pour into a plastic container and allow to set in the fridge for at least 2 hours.

5. For the sponge, whisk the yolks with two-thirds of the sugar until thick and pale. In a separate bowl, whisk the whites to soft peaks and then whisk in the remaining sugar. Continue to whisk until a thick, glossy meringue is formed.

6. Stir one-third of the meringue into the yolk mix and then gently fold in the remainder using the whisk. When three-quarters mixed, grate the lemon zest over the top, then sift in the flours and continue to fold together until just incorporated.

7. Line a Swiss roll tin with baking parchment and then lightly butter and flour. Pour the sponge mix into the tin and level with a palette knife. Bake for 8–10 minutes until risen, firm and golden. Sprinkle with caster sugar and immediately invert onto a sheet of baking parchment. Remove the lining paper, trim the edges of the sponge and roll up with the paper into the classic roulade shape. Allow to cool.

8. To assemble, unroll the cooled sponge and, with a palette knife, spread the lemon curd over the inside surface, keeping a 2cm margin around the edges. Top the lemon curd with three-quarters of the white chocolate mousse, working from the centre to the outside edges. Roll the roulade up and position with the seam at the bottom. Use the remaining mousse to spread a thin layer over the roulade. Shave curls off the back of the chocolate bar by pulling a heavy cook's knife towards you at an angle of about 30 degrees. Scatter the chocolate shavings over the soft mousse on the roulade and then, with a fine grater, grate some pistachio over the top. Chill the roulade for 4-5 hours to set firmly, removing from the fridge 1 hour before serving.

o4 | April

Eostremonath – Eostre's month, after the goddess of spring

A pril marks something of a turning point in the calendar. The countryside will change colour this month – we'll see fields of new green shoots, the first delicate white flowers of the blackthorn will blossom in the hedgerows, and by the end of the month, entire landscapes will be painted with the vivid yellow of rapeseed flowers.

The weather is still far from perfect and we will almost certainly have a mixture of warm sunshine and cold showers (or, if we're really unlucky, a 'blackthorn winter' when the pure white petals disappear against a backdrop of frost or even snow).

Despite the spectacular and colourful growth all around us, April isn't a particularly abundant time of year. It's seen as the start of the 'Hungry Gap' – the period which starts when stores of winter root crops finally run out and ends with the first harvests of June. In the past, our ancestors would have managed their larders very carefully around this time and they would certainly have been looking forward to the more generous months of summer. These days, thanks to advances in farming, we're unlikely to starve, but the slightly thinner pickings are perhaps a gentle reminder that you can't rush nature.

All that said, there are some real seasonal treats to look forward to in April. We'll see the first new potatoes arrive this month and foragers will eagerly await the arrival of morels and St George's mushrooms.

When you're out and about in April, keep an ear out for cuckoos. Their unmistakable call traditionally heralds the true start of springtime (and, if you're a cider fan, confirmation that the first barrels from the previous autumn are ready for drinking).

Out & About bluebells	*Fruit* field rhubarb
Food & Foraging spring lamb, asparagus	*Fish* plaice
Feasts & Festivals Swallows Day St George's Day	*Meat* spring lamb
Vegetables asparagus, spring greens	*Hedgerow Harvest* morels, St George's mushrooms

Recipes

Asparagus and Old Winchester tarts
Asparagus with duck egg and romesco sauce
St George's mushrooms on toast
Salad of spring lamb, watercress, caper and lemon
Roast rib of beef
Chocolate, mascarpone and raisin cake

The British Isles are home to nearly half of the world population of bluebells. So, we're truly fortunate to be able to witness the stunning sight of forest floors turning from green to violet every spring, as hundreds of thousands of these delicate flowers bloom for a few short weeks.

The timing is no coincidence; at this time of year, early warmth reaches the woodland floor together with, importantly, plenty of light. As the canopy of trees grows over in early summer, the light levels will fall and the bluebells die away for another year.

Both the National Trust and the Wildlife Trusts have excellent directories of publicly accessible bluebell woods so you can search for one near you (it's worth calling ahead to check that they are in full bloom before you travel any distance). Make sure you take a camera to capture this fleeting natural spectacle.

Because of their association with spring, the appearance of bluebells is also linked with Beltane (see May) but they were rarely picked as part of those celebrations – the flowers were thought to be protected by fairies. Far from the dainty creatures we think of today, the fairies of old were malevolent and powerful, so great care was taken not to anger them.

O f our reared meats, lamb is the only one that really retains a marked seasonal element (although see pannage pork in September). Customarily first eaten in the spring and particularly at Easter, it's a pale, extremely tender meat. It also has a very subtle flavour, so don't be tempted to do anything too adventurous with it this early in the year.

A lamb is usually defined as any sheep up to a year old, but most spring lamb is between four and six months old and the very earliest will usually become available in February or March. Those that avoid the chop in spring will graze throughout the summer, taking on a layer of fat and increasing depth of flavour. So, bring it back to the menu in the autumn when it will take well to a range of spices and bolder accompaniments.

There is, however, an obvious ethical footnote to this timing. Most British-born 'spring lambs' are not reared in the warming sun of April but the cold nights of the preceding winter, their ewes having been scientifically induced to early breeding. If it happens to be a late spring, the earliest lambs don't have any opportunity to live or feed outdoors and are reared entirely on indoor bedding and artificial feeds.

Personally, I don't forgo spring lamb altogether but I do like to wait until a little later in the season when the animals will undoubtedly have lived a more natural life, giving both better flavour to the meat and some salve to my conscience.

If your sense of culinary decency leads you to shun lamb, either in whole or in part, try asking your butcher for hogget (a sheep between one and two years old) or mutton (perhaps surprisingly, anything over two years old). Both will have lived at least one season outdoors, resulting in a darker-coloured meat and even more flavour, with the added advantage of a non-premium price.

Traditionally mutton came from a wether (a castrated ram) but more recently it has come to mean ewes that have reached the end of their breeding life. Either way, it makes good use of surplus animals, and whilst it's true that it can be slightly tougher than lamb, slower cooking can turn it into an exquisite dish.

In 2004, in the aftermath of the foot-and-mouth crisis, the Prince of Wales launched the Mutton Renaissance campaign, with a view to providing vital extra income for sheep farmers. Although we are still a long way off the historic high point for mutton sales, the campaign has undoubtedly been a success, leading to a renewal of interest in this once-common meat.

Try: Warm salad of new season's spring lamb (p. 99)

The British asparagus season is tragically short, 'officially' running for just eight weeks from St George's Day to the summer solstice. It's hard not to get excited about this rock star of the vegetable world.

In common with most sweet vegetables, as soon as asparagus spears are picked, the sugars in them start to turn to starch, so it really is important to eat them fresh (and good reason not to buy cheaper imports flown in from abroad). It's hard to find a good British restaurant that doesn't feature asparagus during the season, and this need for a plentiful supply with maximum freshness means the harvest has to be a well-timed military operation. Picking asparagus is back-breaking work and, since a stem can grow by as much as 10 centimetres (4 in) in a day, new spears pop up overnight and the same fields will be reworked several times before the end of the harvest. Once picked, they will be washed, trimmed and graded before making their way to market.

When buying asparagus look for bright green, fresh stalks. If they are floppy, brown or at all shrivelled, give them a miss. The woody ends should snap when you bend the stem, leaving the tender, edible part ready to cook. Fresh spears need no more than a quick rinse and few minutes' cooking time, and once cooked they should still be firm to the bite.

Simple preparation is certainly the best way to highlight the intense savoury flavour of asparagus. The traditional way is to steam it and serve with either melted butter or hollandaise. But asparagus is hugely versatile and the flavour is quite robust so it will also partner well with strong, hard cheeses like Parmesan, as well as eggs and cured meats.

In addition to the familiar green asparagus, there are two relative newcomers to the stalky scene – purple and white asparagus. The former is a different strain, grown for its dark purple hue and lighter flavour. The latter is grown using a similar technique to forced rhubarb. By covering the asparagus (first with mounded earth and then, as the tips begin to protrude, black plastic cloches), chlorophyll production is halted, leaving a ghostly white spear. France and Germany are the main growers of white asparagus (where it is often sold brined or pickled) but in recent years a few British producers have been getting in on the act. The additional work involved makes it a premium-priced treat.

The Vale of Evesham in Worcestershire is arguably Britain's asparagus capital and every year hosts a festival devoted entirely to the spring spears. Lasting a month, the whole area dedicates itself to the delicacy with pubs, restaurants and pop-ups celebrating the harvest.

Try:
Asparagus and Old Winchester Tart (p. 92)
Asparagus with duck egg and romesco sauce (p. 95)

Food & Foraging | St George's mushrooms and morels

S t George's mushrooms are one of two particularly tasty species that you'll find in April, debunking the commonly held belief that the fungi season is purely autumnal.

You'll find the small (usually about 10 centimetres/4 in tall) entirely creamy-white mushrooms in grass fields and on verges, particularly on limestone soils. They sometimes form 'fairy rings' as the spores propagate in all directions around a mushroom from the previous season. Naturally, they get their name from the fact that they first appear in the UK in mid-to-late April, near to the saint's day.

St George's are a real forager's favourite. Their flesh is firm with a distinct smell, often described as 'wet flour'. Once cooked, the mealy odour largely disappears and they taste terrific, matching the flavour of any shop-bought competitor. The season usually ends in June when the first truly hot weather arrives.

Also this month, keep an eye out for morels. They are a strange-looking mushroom, quite different to most of the edible species – a bit like a small honeycombed sponge on a stick. As they can't be cultivated (at least, all efforts to date have failed), they are a wild and rare treat. You'll find them in sandy soils in woodland, under trees and hedgerows. Morels often grow where the land has been burned. In fact, in the eighteenth century a notorious spate of forest fires in Germany was caused by mushroom-mad locals trying to create perfect morel-growing conditions.

Both morels and St George's tend to appear in the same place each year, so once you find them, note the spot and check back regularly every year at around the same time.

The fact that these spring fungi species are edible and wild means, naturally, that other things like eating them, too. Both need to be given a good shake before cooking to ensure there's no extra protein on board.

More importantly, you also need to be 100 per cent sure of your identification. Both fungi have common but toxic look-alikes. (Take a look at October's chapter for general tips on collecting fungi.)

Try: St George's mushrooms on toast (p. 96)

Swallows Day (15th April)

The fifteenth of April is 'Swallows Day' when, traditionally, the first swallows are expected to return from their migration.

British swallows mostly spend their winter in South Africa, travelling through France, Spain and Morocco on the way there and following the same route back in the spring or early summer. They can fly up to 200 miles in a single day on the migration route.

Naturally, they don't all stick exactly to the schedule ('One swallow does not a summer make. . .') but once the warm weather returns in mid-spring, we'll invariably see the return of these beautiful birds.

Swallows are easily identified by their quick, darting flight and glossy blue feathers with red throat and white underside. They feed on insects and enjoy open pastureland with water sources nearby.

In September and October the birds will gather in huge flocks to prepare to migrate south again for the wintering season. (Until the 1800s this habit of gathering in reed beds before suddenly vanishing en masse led to the widely held belief that they hibernated in mud banks.) It's another great time to watch them.

Feasts & Festivals | St George's Day (23rd April)

The twenty-third of April is St George's Day. George was a soldier, martyr, and slayer of a mighty dragon. . . or possibly a grumpy crocodile.

It's not entirely clear what the basis of the legend is. George, an officer in the Roman army, is typically depicted on horseback, clad in armour, battling a mighty tongued beast. It's most likely that the dragon was only ever an allegory (either for the devil or a pagan cult) but some ancient texts refer to the slaying of a large crocodile that was nesting near an important water source in the Holy Land. He was executed on 23 April AD 303, having refused to convert from his Christian faith in favour of the Roman gods. His martyrdom and dragon-slaying skills were enough to install him as one of our most venerated saints.

Hagiographic (good word, isn't it?) uncertainties aside, George was adopted as a patron saint of England in the fourteenth century. His permanent place in English culture was secured at the Battle of Agincourt (where Henry V's outnumbered army beat the French thanks to their new-fangled longbows), when English troops reported having seen him fighting alongside them.

St George's Day became a national day of feasting and celebration on a par with Christmas. Sadly, during the 1700s the day's popularity waned, possibly after the Act of Union was signed between England and Scotland (although the same fate didn't befall St Andrew north of the border). The hymn 'Jerusalem' is still sung in English churches on the Sunday closest to the twenty-third but that really is as far as it goes in terms of official recognition these days.

Although there are some festivals and pageants scattered across the country, it's a shame that England doesn't celebrate St George's Day in a bit more style. It's probably down to the famous English reserve (and possibly a slight embarrassment of the connections between the flag of St George and some of the less savoury elements of its history). More recently, however, some efforts have been made to reclaim the day as one of national celebration and there are continued appeals to declare the day a bank holiday.

Asparagus and Old Winchester tart

Traditionally, the British asparagus harvesting season has a clearly defined timescale, beginning on St George's Day (23 April) and finishing on the summer solstice (20th–22 June). These days there is a little latitude on this, what with modern farming methods and the vagaries of the British weather, but there are still growers who follow these strict dates for the first and last cuts.

For me, this limited window of opportunity makes it all the more special. I enjoy looking at new ways of using asparagus each year as it is a truly versatile vegetable, and one that I make a concerted effort to use as much as possible during the short season. This recipe is essentially a classic quiche. The secret is making sure that the filling for the tart is fairly dry, using the egg custard just to bind together.

Old Winchester is a British cheese from Lyburn Farm in Hampshire and has characteristics similar to a Parmigiano Reggiano, i.e. slightly crystalline and packed with flavour. Old Winchester is made with vegetarian rennet.

SERVES 6-8 AS A STARTER OR LIGHT LUNCH

400g rough puff pastry (see Basics p. 288)
2 tbsp olive oil
1 small onion, finely diced
white of 1 small leek, halved lengthwise and finely sliced
4 large free-range egg yolks, plus 2 whole eggs
80ml double cream
2 tsp Dijon mustard
140g Old Winchester, grated
2 bunches medium British asparagus, prepared and blanched
Maldon sea salt and freshly ground black pepper

1. Preheat oven to 160°C.

2. Start by making the pastry case. Roll out the puff pastry into a rectangle around 3mm thick. Brush with water and roll up like a Swiss roll. Press in from the ends to compress a little then stand upright and press down into a disc. Chill for 10 minutes. Roll out the pastry into a circle just big enough to line a 25cm flan dish or tin. Prick the base of the pastry case with a fork and chill again. Blind-bake for 25–30 minutes, then remove the baking beans and cook for another 10–15 minutes until the pastry is just golden. If you are using a quiche tin (as opposed to a ceramic quiche dish) the pastry may well cook more quickly.

3. Sweat off the onion and leek in the olive oil with a pinch of salt. Cook until completely tender and then allow to cool.

4. To make the filling, mix the egg yolks, eggs and double cream together, whisk in the mustard and then season. Stir in the cheese and the onion/leek mix. Retain 12 asparagus tips and chop the stalks and any remaining spears. Add the chopped asparagus to the custard mix. Fill the tart with the custard and lay 12 asparagus tips onto the top of the tart.

5. Bake for 25–30 minutes until golden and just set. Serve warm with a green salad, as a starter or light lunch.

Asparagus with duck egg and romesco sauce

It would have been easy to fill the whole of April's chapter with asparagus recipes, but one thing is for sure: asparagus has an amazing affinity with eggs. Quails' eggs, scrambled hens' eggs and poached duck eggs all work, and here the romesco sauce links the two elements together – the smoky acidity lifting the asparagus and cutting the richness of the egg, with the crumb providing some crunch.

Poach the duck eggs ahead of time and refresh in iced water to make the dish easier to put together at the last minute.

SERVES 4 AS A STARTER

For the romesco sauce
100g rehydrated nora peppers or piquillo
  peppers
1 clove of garlic, peeled, smashed and covered
  in boiling water for 5 minutes
1 tbsp tomato purée, fried in 1 tbsp olive oil
50g Marcona almonds, ground
25g stale breadcrumbs
75ml Arbequina olive oil
lemon juice to taste
50ml vegetable stock (see Basics p. 284)
Maldon sea salt and freshly ground black
  pepper

For the garlic crumb
1 clove of garlic, peeled and smashed
50g sourdough or ciabatta, torn into small
  pieces
olive oil for frying
Maldon sea salt

For the asparagus
20 medium asparagus spears
20g unsalted butter

For the eggs
4 duck eggs, poached and then refreshed in
  iced water

1. To make the sauce, peel and deseed the peppers as required. Place in a blender with the smashed garlic. Add the fried tomato purée to the peppers and blitz to a rough paste. Add the almonds and the breadcrumbs and blitz together, then drizzle with the oil and season to taste with lemon juice, salt and pepper. Thin with the vegetable stock.

2. For the garlic crumb, warm 2 tbsp of oil in a small, non-stick pan, add the garlic and cook gently until it is golden brown. Discard the garlic and fry the bread crumbs until golden. Drain on paper towel and season.

3. Next, trim the bases of the asparagus spears if necessary and wash well. Blanch in boiling salted water until just tender, drain and then transfer to a small roasting tin. Toss in the butter and season to taste. Keep warm.

4. To serve, reheat the eggs in a pan of gently simmering water, then drain on paper towel. Make sure the asparagus is still warm and arrange on the plates. Place a duck egg on each pile of asparagus and season. Dress the asparagus with romesco sauce and sprinkle with some garlic crumb.

St George's mushrooms on toast

Buttery mushrooms and crisp toast have a real affinity; the toast lends heft and texture and the juices from the mushrooms make the toast yield, especially if it is a good slice of sourdough. Garlic adds its savoury kick and some spinach brings freshness and balance. This is a long way from a slice of Mother's Pride with some button mushrooms but the essence is the same. A poached egg and a salad of bitter leaves turns this into a more substantial lunch but I think this really is snack food of the finest order.

Any of the more robust, fleshy mushrooms are a good substitute for the St George's; girolles, blewits, field mushrooms and chestnut mushrooms would all work in this dish; classic button mushrooms, too, but those I like best raw. Mushrooms contain huge amounts of water so a fairly high heat and long enough in the pan to evaporate some of that liquid will help to intensify their flavour and give them some colour. This is certainly a dish to adapt to your own tastes; a little grated Parmesan to finish, some thin slices of lardo laid across the top, a few shavings of truffle, maybe?

SERVES 4 AS A SNACK OR STARTER

40ml olive oil
500g St George's mushrooms or an alternative, sliced or torn into pieces if large
2 cloves of garlic
60ml medium sherry or Madeira
40g unsalted butter
150g spinach
60g crème fraîche
4 thick slices of sourdough or rustic bread
Maldon sea salt and freshly ground black pepper

1. Start by cleaning your mushrooms. There is much debate about whether to wash mushrooms or not. For me personally, I would rather wash them and let them dry rather than run the risk of a gritty dish. Of course, some mushrooms will only need a wipe or a brush but if you do wash them, dip them into a bowl of lukewarm water and brush with a pastry brush to remove dirt from the gills. Place in a single layer on a tray covered with a tea towel and allow to dry at room temperature.

2. Heat the oil in a large, non-stick pan and add the mushrooms, seasoning with a little salt, and fry over a high heat. The mushrooms will start to release their water, so continue to cook until the water has evaporated and then add the garlic. Allow the mushrooms to take on a little colour. Add the alcohol and reduce completely. Add the butter and, once foaming, stir in the spinach and crème fraîche. Once the spinach has wilted, adjust the seasoning and cook until the creamy, buttery liquid just coats the mushrooms. Toast the bread, or chargrill if you prefer. Pile the mushrooms onto the bread and serve immediately.

Warm salad of new season's spring lamb

It is only later in April that spring lamb becomes more widely available. There may have been some for Easter but, as Jon has mentioned, leaving it until a bit later in the season is a sensible option. From the cook's point of view, it is the delicacy of spring lamb that we want to enjoy; the meat is paler and has a sweeter flavour than when it is more mature, and this really shines through in this light warm salad.

The prime cuts of lamb – the loin, fillet, rack and rump – all work well cooked to medium rare or medium, while the harder-working muscles, such as the legs or shoulders, benefit from slower roasting or braising. The one problem with small portions of lamb is that the membrane between the fat and the meat very rarely breaks down before the meat is cooked. A rump will usually work, given its larger size, but a piece of loin is often better cooked as a lean eye of meat.

SERVES 4 AS A LIGHT MAIN COURSE

1 x 300g piece lamb loin, trimmed of all fat and sinew. (Reserve the fat.)
oil for frying the lamb
25g unsalted butter
100g rustic bread, cut into croutons
1 head of chicory
100g ricotta
2 tbsp light olive oil
15g Parmesan, finely grated
1 lemon
100g watercress, large stalks removed
2 tsp capers
Maldon sea salt and freshly ground black pepper

1. Start by rendering the lamb fat for frying the croutons. Cut the fat into small pieces and colour in a heavy pan. Add enough water to cover by 1cm and then simmer gently until all the water has evaporated. You should be left with liquid fat and the solids. Strain and reserve the rendered fat.

2. Season the lamb loin well with salt and pepper. Heat a tablespoon of oil in a heavy non-stick pan. Seal the lamb all over to create a rich, dark colour. Add a second tablespoon of oil to cool the pan slightly and then add the butter, turning the lamb in the foaming butter over a low to medium heat for 3–4 minutes – aim for medium rare. Remove the lamb to rest on a plate in a warm place, retaining a dessertspoonful of the fat from the pan.

3. Fry the croutons in the rendered lamb fat until crisp and golden.

4. Break the chicory into individual leaves and cut any really large leaves in half at an angle. Wash and dry.

5. In a small food processor, blend the ricotta with the olive oil, Parmesan, a good grating of lemon zest and 2 tsp of lemon juice. Season to taste.

6. Toss the leaves together and scatter the croutons on top. Slice the lamb thinly and arrange on the leaves. Mix any lamb juices with a little of the fat from the frying pan and drizzle over the meat. Spoon the dressing and scatter the capers over the top. Sprinkle with a little sea salt and a little more grated lemon zest.

Roast rib of beef

As a chef, I worked mainly in small restaurants and hotels where the cooking was generally to order and was centred on portions for one or two people. My only real experience of big volumes was in my first job as a commis chef in a busy hotel. Even then, Sunday was usually one of my days off, so roasting large joints of meat is something that I have limited experience of. Spending a considerable amount of money on a big piece of beef to roast at home can seem daunting, but a four-bone rib is a real celebration joint.

Over the years I have tried several different approaches to a large joint and find a short burst at a really high temperature followed by a low temperature and some liquid in the tin works a treat. Keeping the meat out of direct contact with the tin is also important, either by positioning the joint on its bone or by using a trivet of vegetables. A digital temperature probe removes any uncertainty.

SERVES 8–10, PROBABLY WITH SOME LEFTOVERS

1 four-bone rib of beef, approximately 5kg
   (remove from the fridge 1 hour before
   cooking)
2–3 onions (if the joint isn't tied to the spinal
   bone), roughly chopped
500ml water
1 bunch of thyme
Maldon sea salt and freshly ground black
   pepper

1. Preheat the oven to 270°C.

2. Season the meat all over with a generous amount of salt and pepper. Heat a large roasting tin on the hob and seal the meat, starting on the fat side. Turn the joint carefully to seal all over. Turn the joint back again so it is fat side up and resting on the bone.

3. A good butcher will have trimmed the beef, cut it away from the spinal bone and then tied it back onto that piece of bone. This acts as a trivet to protect the meat and makes carving much easier. Prepared like this, the meat goes straight into the oven for 20 minutes.

4. If the rib does not have the spinal bone, roast for 20 minutes, then remove the meat from the tin, place the onions in the tin and put the meat on top.

5. Either way, after that initial 20 minutes turn the oven down to 150°C and add about 500ml water and the thyme. The water shouldn't touch the meat, just be coming part way up the bone or the onions.

6. The cooking time will vary but the joint will take another 1½–2 hours for medium rare. Use a probe to check the core temperature; you are aiming for 45°C. Check after 1 hour and then every 15 minutes. Top up the water if the tin is getting dry. A core temperature of 50°C will give you medium and 55°C will give medium well. The suggested core temperature may seem low but the meat will continue to cook after it comes out of the oven.

7. Once cooked, remove the meat from the oven and transfer to a large tray. Cover the meat very loosely with foil or preferably with a sheet of baking parchment and a couple of clean tea towels. Foil can allow a lot of condensation to form which softens the crisp fat and can keep the meat too hot. Place the meat on the edge of the stove, out of any draughts. If you have a second oven that is off and cool, this is a perfect place to rest the meat. A resting time of around an hour really is necessary with a joint this size, to allow the juices to flow back through the meat.

8. Strain any juices and fat from the roasting tin, allow to settle and pour off the fat. You can use this along with any juice from the resting meat as a base for your gravy.

Chocolate, mascarpone and raisin cake

There is very little around in the way of fruit at this time of year; some rhubarb, yes, and maybe the late blood oranges, but it is a tough time if you enjoy something sweet. This cake relies on the store-cupboard staples of chocolate, dried fruit and spice, which also brings in some of the flavours we associate with Easter. The mascarpone filling is not at all sickly, and good-quality dark chocolate brings its own bittersweet notes.

SERVES 10–12

For the cake
100g dark chocolate
150g unsalted butter
50ml vegetable oil
60g golden syrup
3 large free-range eggs
50g plain yoghurt
80ml semi-skimmed milk
250g self-raising flour plus ½ tsp baking powder
25g cocoa powder
1 tsp Maldon sea salt, finely ground
150g light muscovado sugar

For the filling
125g raisins
1 cinnamon stick
½ vanilla pod, split and seeds scraped out
1cm piece of root ginger, peeled
water to cover
50g light muscovado sugar
150g mascarpone

For the ganache topping
100g good-quality milk chocolate, broken into small pieces
80ml double cream

1. Preheat the oven to 160°C.

2. For the cake, melt the chocolate, butter, oil and syrup together in a large bowl, either on a low setting in the microwave or over a pan of simmering water. Combine the eggs, yoghurt and milk, beating together well. Sift the flour, baking powder, cocoa and salt together and rub through the sugar, making sure to remove any lumps. Mix the egg mix into the chocolate mix, then make a well in the flour mix and add the egg/chocolate mix, using a whisk to make sure everything is completely combined.

3. Pour into a greased and lined 20cm loose-bottomed cake tin and bake for 60–70 minutes (check after 30 minutes and cover with foil if it is starting to get too dark). The cake should be well risen, may have some cracking and a skewer will come out virtually clean.

4. Allow to cool for 10 minutes in the tin, then remove and wrap in cling film while still hot. This helps to keep the cake moist. Place on a wire rack to cool completely.

5. To make the filling, place the raisins, cinnamon, vanilla and ginger in a small pan and just cover with water. Bring to the boil and then simmer until the liquid has completely evaporated. Tip onto a plate, discard the vanilla and cinnamon and chill. Beat the muscovado into the mascarpone and allow to stand for 15 minutes. Beat again and check the sugar has dissolved. Fold in the cold raisins and grate in the piece of ginger from the pan using a fine grater. Mix well.

6. For the topping, heat the cream to simmering point in a pan, pour the chocolate over it and let it sit for 5 minutes. Use a small whisk to emulsify the cream and chocolate together. Press cling film directly onto the surface and allow to cool.

7. To assemble, split the cake in half and trim the top if it is really uneven. Fill with the mascarpone and raisin mix and then coat the top with the ganache. Shave some chocolate curls over the top using a potato peeler if desired.

05 | May

Thrimilce – month of three milkings, when lush grass meant cows could be milked three times a day

I t's hardly a surprise that our ancestors celebrated the arrival of May with particular enthusiasm. Across the countryside, crops planted back in March now cover the fields, elderflowers and hawthorn blossom (mayflower) abound in the hedgerow and the dawn chorus reaches a deafening peak, all hinting at the summer bounties to come.

This month on the rivers, the first mayfly will hatch (signalling the start of 'Duffers' Fortnight', when the inexperienced angler supposedly has the best chance of catching a trout) and in our gardens the honey bees will start their work in earnest.

With two bank holidays we should have plenty of time on our hands and although we may still get the occasional heavy shower, May is usually dry and warm (though rarely too hot).

Talking of showers, this month you'll first notice that distinctive smell that accompanies early-summer rainfall. It's known as 'petrichor' and it's the result of scent-laden plant oils being sprayed into the air by the first heavy rain drops. The word come from the Greek *petra* (meaning rock) and *ichor* – the blood of the gods.

The gods certainly have their hands full this month – the whole landscape is bursting into new life and we're on the home straight to summer.

In the kitchen, it's a reliably good time for one particular group of ingredients – herbs. As if to make up for the lack of big, bold fruits and vegetables, the herb garden provides everything we need to make the very best of those ingredients we do have. Chervil, chives, lovage, parsley, rosemary, sage, sorrel and thyme all come into their own this month and lend themselves to fragrant, fresh dishes that just shout spring at you (in a nice way). There's every reason to be stuffing them into chickens, crusting them onto new-season lamb and smearing them over fresh fish all month long.

Out & About
wildflower meadows

Food & Foraging
elderflowers, crayfish, pigeon

Feasts & Festivals
Beltane and May Day
Oak Apple Day

Vegetables
courgette flowers, lettuce,
    watercress

Fish
crayfish, brown trout

Meat
pigeon, spring lamb

Hedgerow Harvest
elderflowers

Recipes

Crayfish cocktail
Warm salad of pigeon breast, charred spring onion
    and bacon
Roast lamb rump shepherd's pie and spring greens
Fillet of brill with crushed jersey royals, asparagus
    and herb butter sauce
Harry Mckew's elderflower cordial
Beltane cake

B ritain's wild flowers tend to thrive on poor, chalky soils where grass grows thinly (which means they are competing less for light and nutrients). Unfortunately, much of our natural flower meadow land has been lost due to intensive farming (it's estimated that we have lost up to 99 per cent of this valuable 'unimproved grassland' since the Industrial Revolution), but our remaining meadows are found in some of the most picturesque areas of the countryside and are unquestionably worth a visit in late spring or early summer when they are in full bloom.

The flowers themselves are just one important element of a complex and sensitive ecosystem. They support a host of pollinating insects, including bees and butterflies, that provide food for small mammals and birds, which in turn are prey for apex predators like owls and foxes. For ground-nesting species including the lapwing and skylark, the long, uncut grass provides both nesting material in the spring and protection for their newly hatched young in the summer months.

So, pack a picnic and an identification guide and go wandering among the wildflowers in May. You'll find buttercups, daisies and primroses all thriving alongside rarer orchids and cowslips in these stunning, spacious and diverse habitats.

A note of caution – the flora and fauna of our ancient meadows exist in a fine equilibrium. This balance can be easily upset by unintentional trampling of plants or nests, so stick to marked footpaths and picnic sites wherever possible.

You can also grow your own wildflower meadow relatively easily – not only does it create a very attractive, low-maintenance area of your garden, those bees and butterflies will love you for it. You'll need a patch of lawn in a sunny spot, and garden centres now sell mixed bags of wildflower seed for all types of soil. The best time of year to sow is in the autumn but, if you're in a hurry, you can also buy established plug plants and even ready-sown wildflower turf.

I t's sometimes said that the elder defines summer – the season starting when the tree blossoms and ending when its berries ripen. Certainly, the emergence of the creamy-white, unmistakably fragrant flowers in late May is a sure sign that the warmer weather has arrived.

At once both instantly recognisable yet shrouded in mystery, the elder is one of our most culturally significant wild species. For centuries it has been the subject of stories and folklore, connected with fairies and magic (it's no coincidence that J. K. Rowling chose an elder wand to feature in Harry Potter's adventures).

Elders were once thought to be inhabited by a witch-like spirit known as the Elder Mother. Her potent powers, it was said, meant that elders were never hit by lightning. There's perhaps some semi-scientific truth behind that myth – elders are usually found on the edge of woodland, close to taller trees that are more likely to be struck.

Elderflowers (and the cordial made from them) lend themselves to a variety of light, sweet and summery recipes. It's important to harvest them on a dry day. If you collect them wet you'll lose much of the pollen which accounts for their unique, delicate flavour.

Using a pair of scissors, take heads from a couple of trees if you can – there is usually more than one around. (And return in early autumn when the summer sunshine will have transformed the remaining flowers into an abundance of little purple elderberries. They make a tasty and colourful addition to any autumnal pie or crumble.)

Try: Harry McKew's elderflower cordial (p. 122)

The American signal crayfish was introduced to the UK in the 1970s. Many escaped from poorly managed farms and entered our ponds and river systems where they have wreaked havoc. Not only do the signals compete for food with our native white-clawed crayfish, they also carry a virus which, whilst harmless to the signal, is deadly to our indigenous species. Worse still, the signals have a significant impact on our fish stocks because they feed on, among other things, fish eggs.

Thankfully, crayfish also happen to make excellent eating. As a wild pest, there is no legally enforced season for them but they are easiest to catch from mid-April through to October, as the water warms up and they become more mobile.

I've experimented with various ways to collect crayfish, but the simplest way is to trap them. It's easy enough to get hold of traps online; they come in a variety of shapes and sizes but all are designed on the same principles as lobster pots. Unfortunately, a sea (or perhaps more of a freshwater pond) of red tape awaits you if you want to trap your own crayfish legally. You'll need written consent from the Environment Agency (EA) and your trap should be marked with official EA identity tags.

The EA has strict rules about the type of trap you can use because of the risk to water voles or otters, so check out their website before you invest in any equipment. Once you've got hold of your trap and tags, bait them up and leave them (tethered discreetly to the riverbank or pond edge) overnight. A punctured tin of tuna in oil as bait will produce a small, steady slick of oil that the crayfish can follow from some distance away.

Another straightforward but slightly more labour-intensive alternative is to use a baited drop net – in heavily infested areas these can be very productive when left for an hour or so, baited with a bit of chicken carcass or an oily fish head.

It's technically illegal to release any signals back into the water, so any you do manage to round up should be taken home in a sealed container. Before you eat any, purge them in fresh water for twenty-four hours to ensure they are free from muddy lake or river water.

You can also now buy crayfish live from some farmers' markets and fishmongers. To prepare your crayfish: put them into the freezer for half an hour (which will put them into a state similar to hibernation) before plunging them into a large pan of boiling water (which kills them instantly), then bring it back to the boil and cook for five minutes. They will turn bright orange and look just like mini lobsters. Once cooked, allow them to cool and peel in the same way as big prawns. You can substitute crayfish meat for lobster or prawns in most dishes.

Try: Crayfish cocktail (p. 114)

I f you want a low-fat, iron-rich, tasty meat that's quick to cook, cheap and plentiful, May has the answer. The wily wood pigeon is abundant for much of the year, but it's when the fresh shoots of spring arrive that the pigeon party really starts, and this is the ideal time to eat them.

Fields drilled with rapeseed and wheat back in March become a magnet for vast flocks of these birds, who first plunder the newly planted seeds and then strip new green growth from the young plants. With more than ten million pigeons in the UK, farmers can expect regular visits from their feathery friends right through to the harvest season, when grain crops provide even richer pickings (or peckings). Growers always expect to lose a proportion of their crops to pigeons but a heavy infestation can be devastating, so you really will be doing some good by enjoying this rich, red meat.

It's because they are such proficient food-finders that pigeons can be eaten most of the year round. But it's in late spring and early summer that young birds (squabs) hatched earlier in the year will be particularly plump and tender.

Incidentally, you should never make the mistake of confusing a wild pigeon with the feral variety found in city centres. They're literally breeds apart, and a fresh wood pigeon is a very attractive, clean-living bird with bright, iridescent plumage. A pigeon breast, properly cooked, can be as good as a rare steak, with a very slightly gamey note, but at a fraction of the cost.

You'll find them in most butchers and markets throughout the spring and for much of the rest of the year.

Try: Warm salad of pigeon breast, charred spring onion and bacon (p. 117)

Feasts & Festivals | Beltane and May Day (1st May)

S omething stirs in May. It's the time of year when spring turns to summer. For centuries our ancestors have known it and the result was a massive knees-up. Our Celtic forbears knew the first day of May as Beltane. The Romans honoured Flora, goddess of flowers, and to Victorians it was known simply as May Day.

The original Celtic rite was a serious affair. Animal sacrifices were commonplace and there is some evidence of darker practices; Beltane was said to be the day on which a king could be sacrificed.

More recent May Day celebrations were much lighter in theme and popular across the entire country. It's difficult to overstate the importance of those past festivities. At their peak, they rivalled Christmas and Easter in scale.

Customs varied considerably from town to town, combining elements of different faiths and local folklore. But communities everywhere rejoiced as the warmer months arrived, crops began to thrive and people could live in comfort for many months to come. At a time without central heating or reliable hot water, that was certainly worthy of a good party. Despite the regional variations, there were plenty of common themes, including:

Greenery and flowers – Fresh mayflowers and green leaves embodied everything that was being celebrated, and 'bringing in the May' to adorn houses and churches was essential. Girls and young women would wake early to gather the decorations and to wash their faces in the May Day dew to maintain their youthful complexions.

Bonfires – Fires were lit on hilltops in celebration of the longer days and as a way of creating a sense of shared celebration between neighbouring towns.

Food – With the cold dark days behind them and summer in sight, people were keen to enjoy their remaining store foods, and a spring lamb was usually roasted.

Beltane cake – It's difficult to find any reliable historical text which might give us an authentic recipe, but there are plenty of references to cakes being enjoyed by the revellers made from simple, abundant ingredients including eggs, oatmeal and honey. (Russell's version is admittedly more fancy homage than authentic original!)

Maypoles – The maypole was, at its most basic, a stick adorned with flowers to dance around. Over time they became the elaborate, ribbon-festooned poles we know today. Some maypoles were huge. In the City of London, in the shadow of the Gherkin, you will find a church called St Andrew Undershaft, so named because it was dwarfed by the huge maypole set up opposite it each May. The shaft was destroyed in 1547 when it was denounced by a puritanical mob as a 'pagan idol', though it's possible they just really hated morris dancing.

Try: Beltane cake (p. 125)

Oak Apple Day (29th May)

After his defeat to Oliver Cromwell at the Battle of Worcester, Charles II was exiled to Europe. To avoid capture as he fled, he hid in an oak tree, and its leaf was adopted as a symbol of the king and his supporters.

On 29 May (his birthday) in 1660, Charles returned to London and restored the monarchy to England. His return was cheered by the masses and declared as a day of national celebration. Songs were sung, bonfires were lit and church bells were rung. Royal Oak Day, also known as Oak Apple Day, marked a welcome return to the rather less puritanical ways of country life.

'Parliament had ordered the 29th of May, the King's birthday, to be for ever kept as a day of thanksgiving for our redemption from tyranny, and the King's return to his Government, he entering London that day.'
The Diary of Samuel Pepys, 1 June 1660

On Oak Apple Day, children and adults alike would wear oak leaves on their lapels, and horses and carts would be adorned with sprays of leaves and branches. It then became particularly a celebration for children and developed the rather cruel custom of beating people who didn't participate with bunches of nettle leaves, leading to the day also becoming known less appealingly as 'nettling day'!

As fresh new oak leaves will be out during the month of May, a long walk through an oak woodland at a beautiful time of year is an ideal way to celebrate the day.

Crayfish cocktail

OK, I know it's a Seventies classic, revived many times and perhaps still regarded in a slightly derogatory manner, but you like a cocktail sauce as much as I do, don't you? It's all about that sauce, really. Even the worst examples of frozen, watery and utterly tasteless prawns are kind of OK drenched in Marie Rose sauce. So, imagine if you have some good shellfish and we make that sauce from scratch with a couple of twists. How good is that going to be?

In essence, a prawn cocktail is a great dish, having many elements that add up to something satisfying. The crunch of crisp lettuce, the delicate chew of good shellfish, and a sauce that not only manages to be rich and creamy but has a touch of heat and some gentle acidity. I'm using freshwater crayfish for this recipe but good-quality prawns, lobster or langoustines all work well, too. Of course, if you can get hold of some live crayfish as Jon describes (see p. 110), that will give you the perfect ingredient!

SERVES 4 AS A STARTER

For the sauce

1 large free-range egg yolk
½ tsp Dijon mustard
1 tsp chipotle chilli paste
1 tsp tomato purée
1 tsp Worcestershire sauce
1½ tbsp cider vinegar
1 tsp caster sugar
100ml rapeseed oil
40g crème fraîche
Maldon sea salt and freshly ground black
   pepper

For the salad

1 Little Gem lettuce
1 ripe avocado
1 handful of pea shoots
200g cooked shellfish of your choice
freshly ground black pepper

1. The sauce can be made ahead of time and kept in the fridge until required. Be sure to source 'lion marked' eggs, store them in the refrigerator and use before the best-by date as the egg is going to be served raw. Use the sauce within 24 hours.

2. In a small blender, or using a stick blender, combine the yolk, mustard, chipotle paste, tomato purée, Worcestershire sauce, cider vinegar and sugar, and gradually drizzle in the oil with the motor running. Blend in the crème fraîche and season to taste.

3. For the salad, discard any damaged outer leaves from the lettuce and then break into individual leaves. Halve the avocado and remove the stone. Peel off the skin and slice thinly. On four plates, build up a salad of the lettuce and avocado. Top with the shellfish and then dress generously with the sauce. Grind a little black pepper on top and finish with a tangle of pea shoots. This is one of those dishes that you can make as refined or as rustic as you please. A big platter to share or built up in elegant martini glasses, it is all down to personal choice and the occasion.

Warm salad of pigeon breast, charred spring onion and bacon

The dark red meat of a rare-roasted pigeon breast is tender and full of flavour, as well as being quick to cook and relatively cheap. The flavour is delicate with a slight irony note. The quickest way to put someone off pigeon is to serve it well done; as with most game there is little fat and the meat needs to be rare to give it succulence. Well cooked and rested, pigeon makes for really good eating. Cooking on the crown also helps to keep it moist. Your butcher or game dealer should be able to prepare them like this for you. Ask for the wishbone to be removed to make carving easier. The legs and back are best used for stock.

SERVES 4 AS A STARTER

For the pigeon

2 pigeon crowns (remove from the fridge 30
    minutes before cooking.)
2 tbsp olive oil
1 clove of garlic, smashed
4 sprigs of thyme
25g unsalted butter
50ml water
Maldon sea salt and freshly ground black
    pepper

For the dressing

4 rashers of smoked, streaky bacon, cut into
    1cm pieces
50ml stock; pigeon, chicken or vegetable
1 tbsp olive oil
2 tbsp good balsamic vinegar
Maldon sea salt and freshly ground black
    pepper

For the salad

1 bunch spring onions, trimmed and washed
2 tsp olive oil
60g watercress, large stalks removed
Maldon sea salt and freshly ground black
    pepper

To serve

a handful of freshly made croutons

1. Preheat the oven to 180˚C.

2. Season the pigeon crowns well and heat half the oil in a heavy-based frying pan. Place the pigeons in, laying them on one breast. Cook for 1–2 minutes until the skin is golden and then turn onto the other breast and repeat. Add the remaining oil then the garlic, thyme and butter. Baste the pigeons and then turn to sit breast up.

3. Add the water to the pan and transfer to the hot oven for 2–3 minutes. Press the pigeon at the fattest part of the breast to check for doneness; the meat should feel firm not flabby but have lots of give still. Remove to rest on a wire rack, breast down. Tip the butter and herbs over the top.

4. To make the dressing, cook the bacon in a small, non-stick pan until crisp and golden. Add the stock and reduce by half, then stir in the oil and vinegar. Adjust the seasoning.

5. For the salad, toss the spring onions with the oil and a little seasoning, and cook in a hot chargrill pan, turning frequently. Covering with a lid to create a little steam helps to cook the onions through. Total cooking time will be 3-4 minutes. Slice into three pieces and toss with the watercress.

6. To serve, add a little of the dressing to the watercress and spring onions, and then divide between the bowls or plates. Carve the breast from the pigeons and slice each into five or six slices. The skin will vary; sometimes it has enough fat to crisp nicely but on other occasions it can be chewy, so make a call and peel it off before slicing if necessary. Scatter the croutons over the salad, arrange the pigeon slices and then spoon the warm dressing on top.

Roast rump of lamb, shepherd's pie and spring greens

This dish is based on a late-spring/early-summer dish I used to serve at the restaurant, which in turn was probably based on my mum's shepherd's pie! We served a trio of lamb at the restaurant: a piece of roast loin, a brochette of lamb's kidney and button onions, and the shepherd's pie. The one that always drew the best comments was, of course, the pie.

The principle behind the dish was to use every last bit of a lamb saddle. The lean eye for a rare-roasted prime cut, the kidneys for the brochette, the fat for cooking the loin, all the trim for mince in the shepherd's pie and the bones for a stock. I love cooking like this, pairing the cheaper cuts with the prime, and a slightly simplified version is great to do at home. Buying trimmed lamb rumps and minced lamb for the pie reduces the workload.

SERVES 6 AS A MAIN COURSE

For the lamb ragout
500g lamb mince
1 medium onion, cut into ½cm dice
1 stick celery, cut into ½cm dice
1 carrot, peeled and cut into ½cm dice
150ml red wine
½l lamb stock or beef stock (see Basics pp. 284–5)
½ x 400g tin good-quality chopped tomatoes
thyme and rosemary bouquet garni in muslin
cornflour to thicken
Maldon sea salt and freshly ground black pepper

For the mashed potato topping
1kg Maris Piper potatoes (peeled weight), boiled and mashed with a little milk and butter

For the rumps
3 lamb rumps, trimmed and fat scored
50ml olive oil
25g unsalted butter
1 clove of garlic, smashed
4 sprigs of thyme
Maldon sea salt and freshly ground black pepper

For the greens
2 heads of spring greens
25g unsalted butter
100ml water
Maldon sea salt and freshly ground black pepper

1. Preheat the oven to 180°C.

2. To make the shepherd's pie, first brown the mince and then add the vegetables. Cook for 5 minutes and then drain off any excess fat. Deglaze with the red wine and reduce completely. Add the stock, tomatoes and bouquet garni. Season and simmer for 2–3 hours, topping up with water as necessary. It really is worth taking the time to slowly cook the ragout for those 2–3 hours. Before making the final adjustments to seasoning, give the muslin bag a hard squeeze to get all those herby juices out.

3. Thicken the sauce with a little cornflour slaked in some cold water. Pour the ragout into an ovenproof dish or individual dishes and top with the mashed potato. I like to push the mash through a sieve to make it silky smooth and then pipe it onto the meat mixture, but spooning it on and finishing with a fork works well, too. Grated cheddar cheese is always an option to finish. Bake in the oven for 20–30 minutes until piping hot and golden brown on top.

4. Heat a heavy-based frying pan and season the fat on the lamb rumps, placing them fat side down in the pan. Cook over a medium heat to render the fat. Season the flesh and colour well all over. Add the oil, butter, garlic and thyme. Turn the meat so it is fat side down, baste and transfer to the hot oven. Cook for 4–8 minutes, basting occasionally, until the required doneness is reached. I am a big fan of using a temperature probe for cooking meat; medium rare will be around 48˚C when the meat comes out of the oven. Remove to rest on a wire rack, fat side up.

5. While the lamb is resting, cook the greens. Remove any tough or damaged outer leaves and cut the heads into quarters. Remove the core and then cut the cabbage roughly into 2cm squares. Rinse in a colander and then tip into a large shallow pan that has a tight-fitting lid. Add the butter, water, a good pinch of salt and a generous grind of pepper. Place over a high heat and, when the water starts to boil, put the lid on. Cook for 3–4 minutes until the leaves are nearly tender, remove the lid to evaporate all the water.

6. Slice the lamb rumps into thick slices and either plate if using individual dishes for the pie or pile onto a board for all to help themselves.

Fillet of brill with crushed Jersey Royals, asparagus and herb butter sauce

Brill is perhaps considered inferior to turbot but it cooks in a very similar way and has a lovely delicate texture. Price-wise it is usually a cheaper option than turbot, too. Bigger fish will fetch a premium but it is worth a few extra pounds to get a fish that yields thicker fillets. I always choose a bigger fish and freeze any that I don't need for another day. One trick you can use on the smaller fillets is to fold the thinner, tail end under to create a portion that is a more even thickness. As the proteins set during cooking, the folded piece will stick to the top piece.

New potatoes, a delicate sauce and the freshness of British asparagus make this a truly special dish. Make sure that the sauce is well seasoned and has enough acidity to cut through the buttery potatoes. The herbs are really a matter of personal choice but I like the onion note of chives and the fresh punch of flat-leaf parsley.

SERVES 4 AS MAIN COURSE

20–30 spears of British asparagus, peeled and
washed

For the sauce
½kg new potatoes, washed/scraped (Jersey,
Royals, Cornish News or other regional
variations)
70–80g unsalted butter
2 tbsp dry vermouth
50ml white wine
200ml vegetable stock (see Basics p. 284)
lemon juice to taste
Maldon sea salt
1 dsp finely chopped chives
1 dsp roughly chopped flat-leaf parsley

For the fish
2 tbsp olive oil
4 x 150g brill fillets, skinned and trimmed
flour for dusting the fish
Maldon sea salt and freshly ground black
pepper

1. Cook the potatoes in boiling salted water
until tender. Drain and add 25g unsalted butter.
Crush the potatoes with a fork, trying not to
work to a mash. Adjust the seasoning and add
more butter if a little dry. Keep warm.

2. In a small pan, reduce the vermouth and
white wine to a syrup. Add the stock and reduce
to approximately 50ml. Remove from the heat
and gradually whisk in enough cold unsalted
butter to thicken slightly. You want to keep
moving the pan off and on the heat, enough to
allow the butter to melt into the sauce but not
enough to boil it. Adjust the seasoning with salt
and lemon juice. Rich and tangy is the result you
are looking for.

3. Cook the asparagus in boiling salted water
until just tender, drain and add a knob of butter.
Keep warm.

4. In one large – or two medium – heavy, non-
stick frying pans, heat a couple of tablespoons of
olive oil. Season the flesh side of the brill fillets,
dust lightly with flour and shake off any excess.
Lay the fillets gently into the pan, flour side
down. Cook until golden brown on the flesh side,
then season the skin side and add approximately
20g unsalted butter to the pan(s). Baste the fish
with the foaming butter, then turn over and cook
through. Test by pushing a cocktail stick into the
fillet; when it is undercooked you will feel the
fibres tearing as you push the stick in, once done
it will slide in smoothly. Remove from the pan
immediately and drain on some kitchen paper.

5. Warm the sauce and add the herbs.

6. To serve, mound the potato into the centre of
four shallow bowls, place the fish on top of the
potato and strew the asparagus spears around.
Spoon the sauce around the fish.

Harry McKew's elderflower cordial

Recipe by Jon

Harry McKew was my grandfather and a master maker of cordials, jams and pickles. He taught me a great deal of what I know about preserving. While I was researching this book, his original recipe, written on a tatty scrap of paper, fell out of the pages of an old paperback. It's as if he wanted me to share it with you.

The citric acid is essential if you want your cordial to last (it will help it keep for months rather than days) but not if you plan to drink it straight away.

MAKES APPROXIMATELY 1.5L OF CORDIAL

25 elderflower heads
1.7l water
1.5kg sugar
4 oranges and 2 lemons, chopped
50g citric acid (available from chemists)

1. Cut off any leaves and inspect each elderflower head for any insect passengers. Pour the water into a large pan and bring to the boil. Take off the heat and add the sugar, stirring until dissolved. Add the heads, fruit and citric acid to the pan. Stir well then cover and leave to infuse for 24–48 hours.

2. Strain the liquid though a clean tea towel or muslin, then pour into sterilized bottles and seal.

3. To serve, dilute the cordial about 10:1 with still or sparkling water. (You can also add it to sparkling wine for a classy dinner-party aperitif.)

Beltane cake

The impression I get from the little information available on Beltane cake is that it would have been a heavy affair, so I hope we have lightened things up in this recipe while staying true to the spirit of the original.

The Victoria sponge and the carrot cake have both influenced my recipe, with part of the sugar being replaced with honey, and toasted ground oats replacing some of the flour. Elderflower and lemon zest in the cream cheese frosting give a real summery flavour. I don't think a cup of tea or something sparkling would go amiss served with this cake fit to celebrate the coming of summer.

SERVES 8–10

For the cake
100g oats
100g self-raising flour
1¼ tsp baking powder
½ tsp Maldon sea salt, finely ground
1 tsp ground ginger
200g unsalted butter
100g light muscovado sugar
100g honey
4 large free-range eggs

For the frosting
60g unsalted butter
85g icing sugar
300g cream cheese
50ml elderflower cordial
1 lemon, zest only

To assemble
50g lemon curd
30g oats
15g honey
1 tsp vegetable oil

1. Preheat the oven to 170°C.

2. To make the cake toast the oats in an ovenproof dish until golden brown – this will take about 20–25 minutes. Allow the oats to cool before blitzing to a powder in a food processor. Turn the oven down to 160°C.

3. Mix the oats together with the flour, baking powder, salt and ginger, using a whisk to combine thoroughly. In a separate bowl, beat the butter until light and fluffy and then beat in the sugar and honey. Add the eggs one at time, interspersing with a spoonful of the flour mix to prevent splitting. Fold in the rest of the flour mix.

4. Divide the mix between two greased and floured 20cm sponge tins and bake for approximately 20 minutes, until risen and firm to the touch. Transfer the cakes to a rack and allow to cool for 5 minutes before tipping out to cool completely.

5. For the frosting, beat the butter until soft and fluffy, then gradually add the icing sugar and then the cream cheese. Finish by whisking in the elderflower cordial and lemon zest.

6. To assemble, spread the curd over the top surface of one cake and half the frosting over the other. Sandwich the two halves together and use the remaining frosting to cover the top of the cake. The frosting can be spread on with a palette knife or piped on as desired. Mix the oats, honey and oil in a small ovenproof dish. Turn the oven up to 170°C and toast for 15 minutes, turning frequently until golden and crisp. Allow to cool and sprinkle over the top of the cake.

o6 | June

Midsomermonath – the month of midsummer

June marks the start of the summer season. It's when we first really get to reap the rewards of our spring labours on the vegetable patch. The first significant salad crops can be picked and plump potatoes can be dug, both making ideal accompaniments to some fantastic, light, early-summer dishes.

The soft fruits are catching up, too. Gooseberries are first out of the starting blocks, and it won't be long before the raspberries and strawberries are putting their juicy little hands up, just begging to be made into summer tarts, smoothies and jams (or maybe to add 'the healthy bit' to a glass of Pimm's).

For seafood fans, if they haven't already the ever-obliging mackerel will almost certainly arrive on our shores this month, to be found on the fishmonger's slab alongside more exotic specimens like squid and spider crab.

If you didn't manage it last month, you'll definitely be able to have your first barbecue at some point in June, and fishing trips, picnics in the park and long days on the beach should all feature on a list of outdoor activities that's longer than a prize cucumber.

Now, in Spain they say, '*No vendas la piel del oso antes de cazarlo*' (Don't sell the bear's fur before you hunt it) and our equivalent is, obviously, 'Don't count your chickens before they hatch.' Both are worth bearing in mind this month, as June weather can occasionally be a bit of a let-down.

However, there should probably be another saying along the lines of 'What's bad for the garden party is good for the allotment' (I've no idea what that is in Spanish). If we do get a lot of rain and warmth at this time of year, take heart – it will make for a bumper, fruit-filled autumn.

The Pick Your Own (PYO) food concept has been around for many years. In fact, the first PYO strawberry farm was established in the 1960s. During the 1970s and 1980s it was extremely popular, but then took a dramatic nose-dive thanks to the year-round imported fruit and veg offerings of the supermarkets.

Thankfully PYO is making a comeback and with good reason. It's the ultimate field-to-fork experience and a much more enjoyable day out than trundling round the supermarket aisles. Farmers still get a good price for their produce and you'll know exactly where your food came from. In fact, the only people who lose out are the supermarkets, who would otherwise be happy to pay a pittance to the farmer and charge us a hefty mark-up once they've packaged the spotless produce in plastic (and discarded up to 40 per cent of the crop that is perfectly edible but not deemed aesthetically up to scratch).

In the early years, PYO farms only offered fruit, and opportunities to pick your own vegetables were very limited. Fast-forward to today and all that has changed. The largest farms have several hundred acres open from late spring to autumn, where you can pick anything from plums to pumpkins and strawberries to squash.

Most PYO farms will open in April or May but with only one or two early crops (usually asparagus and rhubarb) on offer. From June through to September things really get going and you'll be able to check off your weekly fresh-produce shopping list with ease. You won't have to park in a multistorey, either.

In recent years the PYO principle has been taken even further. Some farms and cooperatives now offer 'Pick your Own Pig' and similar meat schemes, allowing you to choose livestock, take an interest in its rearing and then collect the meat once it has been slaughtered. It won't be to everyone's taste, but if you are interested in animal welfare and food ethics, it's a logical step and one which takes traceability of your meat to the next level.

There's something marvellously British about the tart and tangy gooseberry. They're a little quirky, a bit hairy and, like bold, pasty-fleshed holidaymakers on Clacton beach, they're ready to go earlier in the summer than any of their softer relatives. The season is fairly short – usually beginning in late May and stretching to early August at the latest.

Gooseberries have rather fallen out of favour in recent years. But they have been grown in Britain since Elizabethan times, and in the 1800s they were all the rage. Stripy green (or white or red) goosegogs had fan clubs up and down the country, particularly in the north where regular annual fairs were held for competitors to show their prized fruits.

Only two fairs of any size still exist – one at Egton Bridge in Yorkshire (worth a visit if you're in the area on the first Tuesday in August) and another in Cheshire (hosted by the very factually named Mid-Cheshire Gooseberry Shows Association).

Not content with being our earliest summer fruit, gooseberries are also very versatile, lending themselves to a wide range of dishes, both sweet and savoury (including, incidentally, as an accompaniment to that other June favourite, mackerel).

Try: Gooseberry and elderflower cheesecake (p. 149)

Food & Foraging | Strawberries

Strawberries are synonymous with the British summer. The arrival of these fragrant, juicy red fruits (usually towards the end of the month) is a sure sign that the new season has begun and now runs well into the autumn.

Sadly, good strawberries were one of the early victims of food globalization. It's not unusual to find 'early season' British strawberries on the shelves from February onwards and industrially produced, water-hungry imports are now available all year round.

The quality of these crops varies considerably and it's fair to say that significant technological improvements have been made in recent years, leading to some high-quality fruits being available out of season. But you'll certainly do well to find an outdoor-grown British strawberry on the shelves before mid-June and, in my view, it's well worth waiting for these slow-grown, locally produced varieties to arrive before diving in.

A good strawberry should be bright red, slightly soft to the touch and with a floral, obviously ripe aroma. Anything else is likely to disappoint (and it's worth remembering that some berries, particularly the ubiquitous Elsanta, colour well before they are ripe).

The origin of the strawberry's name isn't clear. It may be from the fact that straw was (and still is) used to keep the berries fresh and free from rot when they were grown outside. But it's also possible that its root is in the word 'strewn', because native wild strawberries appear 'scattered' on the ground.

If you're very lucky, you'll occasionally find the wild berries growing from mid-June through to the autumn in areas of thin woodland or semi-wild grassland where plenty of light can reach the ground. They are rarely abundant and the berries are small, so you'll need to look very carefully. The wild fruits are more delicate than their cultivated (distant) cousins, so always handle them with care.

As we all know, the strawberry's traditional bedfellows are cream and sugar, but do experiment with savoury pairings, too. They work surprisingly well with both black pepper and balsamic (or cider) vinegar.

Try: Iced strawberry parfait (p. 146)

I should start this page by acknowledging that Russell and I feel quite differently about mackerel. To me, it's a strikingly beautiful fish, full of rich, distinct flavours, and a particularly tasty highlight of the summer. He, on the other hand, would rather eat his own socks. I won the argument, so it has a place in this book, but Russ wants you to know that he hasn't changed his mind. So when you read this section and cook the accompanying recipe, feel free to imagine him with his arms folded in the corner of your kitchen, tutting occasionally.

Mackerel are present in our waters all year round, but they come close inshore in late spring, peaking in number around June and July as the water temperature increases. During the summer months, they can be easily caught from small inshore boats or the beach with a simple fishing rig and hooked 'feathers'. For many anglers, including me, mackerel will be their first sea-fishing success and the start of a lifelong passion.

If you want to catch your own, your local tackle shop will be more than happy to kit you out with a basic set-up to match your budget. Once on the beach, signs to look for that will confirm the mackerel's presence include a thin slick of oil on the surface and seabirds diving into the water. The birds are actually eating the smaller bait fish – usually sand eels – that the mackerel are chasing, and you'll occasionally see the surface of the water bubbling, sometimes just yards from the beach, as the eels try to escape. Mackerel are voracious predators (the reason they are so easy to catch) and have even been known to beach themselves in their frenzied hunt for food.

The best times to fish for mackerel are at high tide and in the hours either side of sunrise and sunset. I have enjoyed many long summer evenings on either Chesil Beach or Brighton Pier 'fluff chucking' (as more experienced anglers disparagingly refer to it), and there are few finer dinners than a freshly caught fish cooked on a beach barbecue, finished with nothing more than a squeeze of lemon. But this rich, firm and oily fish also works well with strong, spicy flavours or smoked, particularly as a paté.

Freshness is key and mackerel spoils quickly, so if you're buying rather than catching, look for iridescent blue stripes, clear eyes and bright red gills. Greying, wrinkled skin and soft flesh are definitely to be avoided at all costs.

The shoals move offshore again in September or October as the coastal waters start to cool, so make the most of this versatile fishy treat from now until the early autumn.

Try: Harissa mackerel flatbreads with quick pickled cucumber (p. 136)

St Barnabas' Day (11th June)

St Barnabas' Day on 11 June traditionally marked the first day of the hay-cutting season.

In some parts of the country, flowers, especially white roses, are still worn to mark St Barnabas' Day. The mowing season was an important time in the seasonal calendar, as a good supply of dry hay throughout the colder months ensured animals would be well fed. Heavy rain, which flattened the grass and made it impossible to scythe, could spell disaster.

Before the adoption of the Gregorian calendar, St Barnabas' Day used to coincide with the solstice, hence the saying 'Barnaby bright, Barnaby bright, the longest day and the shortest night.'

Try: Hay-baked leg of kid goat (pp. 139–40)

Feasts & Festivals | Summer Solstice (20th-22nd June)

The summer solstice – the longest day – falls between 20 and 22 June each year. Although some people view the solstice as the start of summer, technically it's the beginning of the end, as the days now start getting shorter. Despite the fact that there is (hopefully) much warm weather still to come, it's a little reminder that the seasons keep on turning and that the long hot days won't be here forever. Enjoy them while you can.

The word 'solstice' comes from the Latin, meaning 'the sun stands still'. Many cultures around the world mark the summer solstice with rites and rituals that celebrate renewal and fertility, as well as the abundance of autumn and the harvest season ahead. Druidic cultures celebrated it as a day when the heavens and earth were wed, and the belief that to be married in June is lucky has endured to this day. As one traditional poem puts it, 'Married in month of roses, June, life will be one long honeymoon.' From a practical perspective, guests were also free to attend the nuptials because June was a relatively quiet time in the farming calendar, being midway between the main sowing and harvest periods.

Stonehenge in Wiltshire is perhaps the most famous of our ancient monuments, with its large, arched entrance designed to frame the rising midsummer sun. Although years of academic debate have yet to establish conclusively what its purpose was, there's no doubt that it was an important site of worship and it has long been a place of mystery as well as midsummer gatherings. After many years of unrestricted access to the stones, damage caused by revellers led to them being fenced off. However, more recently, English Heritage has agreed to 'managed open access' to the site, and seeing the sun set on the solstice (at around 9.20 p.m.) is a moving, if rather chaotic, experience. White-robed druids gather among the standing stones to perform a unique ritual. A central candle is lit and that flame is spread to a circle of surrounding candles. If you can make it through the night, the first rays of the new sun are celebrated with song and dance at around 4.40 a.m.

Historically, the solstice marked the time when important herbs planted at the spring equinox could be picked for healing rituals and medicines.

Try: Basil pesto (p. 142)

Harissa mackerel flatbreads with quick pickled cucumber

Recipe by Jon

These spicy flatbreads are perfect for an informal summer lunch. The cooling cucumber and light yoghurt dressing are a great match for punchy North African spices and rich fish.

To remove the pin bones (the line of small bones that runs down the centre of each fillet), use a small, very sharp knife and cut at an angle either side of the line, creating a V-shaped channel. Lift one end of the strip with the tip of the knife and pull away gently in one piece. As an alternative, the bones can be pulled out with a pair of needle-nosed pliers or tweezers while pressing down gently on the fillet behind the bone. It's not difficult but your fishmonger will also happily do it for you.

SERVES 4 AS A GENEROUS STARTER OR LIGHT LUNCH

For the dressing
150g natural yoghurt
40g harissa paste
½ lemon, juice only

For the pickled cucumber
½ large cucumber
Maldon sea salt
50ml cider (or white wine) vinegar
50g caster sugar

For the fish
4 large, fresh mackerel, filleted and pin bones removed
4 tsp harissa paste
1 tbsp oil for frying
8 large, soft flatbreads (see Basics p. 287)

1. Preheat the oven to 150°C.

2. Make the dressing by spooning the yoghurt into a small bowl. Stir in the harissa, add the lemon juice and stir well.

3. Peel the cucumber and slice in half lengthwise. Remove the seeds using a teaspoon and slice into ½cm crescents. Season the cucumber with a generous pinch of salt.

4. Prepare the pickling liquid by stirring the sugar and vinegar together until dissolved. Pour the liquid over the cucumber pieces and put to one side, turning occasionally while you prepare the fish.

5. Spread ½ tsp of harissa paste onto the flesh side of each mackerel fillet. Add the oil to a large, non-stick frying pan on a high heat and fry the fish, skin side down, for about 3 minutes. The fillets will curl up as they hit the heat but gentle, firm pressure from a palette knife will flatten them out again. Don't be tempted to move them around the pan. When the skin is browned and crispy, turn and fry for 30 seconds more, flesh side down.

6. Meanwhile, warm the flatbreads for 2 minutes in the oven (if they are ready before the fish, take them out and wrap in a clean tea towel to keep warm). Remove the fish from the pan and place a fillet onto each flatbread. Drain the cucumber, pat dry with some kitchen towel, then scatter evenly over the fish. Spoon a couple of teaspoons of the yoghurt dressing over each flatbread, roll and serve immediately. You can also serve all the components on a large board or platter for people to help themselves.

Hay-baked leg of kid goat

In many ways, goat is responsible for this book's existence. Some years ago, former River Cottage Canteen chef James Whetlor wrote a piece for Jon's blog, including a goat recipe. When Jon began to look into collaborating with someone on a book, he approached James to see if he would be interested in writing the recipes. James passed but introduced Jon and me to each other. This was nearly four years ago now, but it started us on the journey to *Well Seasoned*. We owe you one, James!

A by-product of the goat dairy industry, kid falls into the same category as veal; the male young are generally of no use in the dairy industry and many are slaughtered soon after birth. Both kid and rose veal produced in Britain are superb products, and the more widely they are used the better.

James's company, Cabrito, began by selling kid goat meat sourced from British dairy farms to London restaurants. Since then, they have grown to supply restaurants, butchers and catering suppliers nationwide. They now have a network of farms producing high-quality meat from a previously wasted resource.

James is a great chef and I have been lucky to eat some different and tasty kid recipes that he has cooked. A raw kid dish, similar to a tartare, called 'kibbeh' was a real revelation. The raw hand-chopped meat is combined with bulgar wheat, herbs, lemon juice, chilli and spices to give a clean, punchy dish. A whole kid cooked on an asado grill over an open fire was just perfect. I have baked the kidneys in pastry made with their own suet and barbecued butterflied shoulders, and the meat has always lived up to its promise. The flavour is distinctive but delicate, slightly sweet and nutty.

Here, we are baking a leg of kid in hay, an ancient technique that keeps the meat particularly moist and imparts a lovely perfume to the joint. Braised green lentils and a salsa verde or chimichurri sauce are my favourite accompaniments for the meat.

If you fancy trying out some more kid recipes, look out for James's book, *Goat*, which has recently been published.

Continued on page 140

Continued from p. 139

SERVES 6 AS A MAIN COURSE

3–4 tbsp olive oil
2–2.5kg leg of kid goat
Maldon sea salt, finely ground
freshly ground Tellicherry black pepper
80g unsalted butter, softened

NOTE: You will also need a 60cm square of muslin and a small bag of fresh sweet hay. The choice in a pet shop is quite staggering: meadow hay, herb hay, hay with camomile, hay with carrots, organic hay. . . and the list goes on! I settled for some local meadow hay.

1. Preheat the oven to 180°C.

2. Choose a large roasting tin which will hold the leg with about 5cm of space all around. Half-fill the kitchen sink with cold water and add several large handfuls of hay. You need enough to completely encase the leg. Leave to soak for 20 minutes.

3. Meanwhile, heat the olive oil in the roasting tin, season the meat generously and seal. Lay the muslin on a board and place the sealed leg on top. Spread the butter all over the top surface of the leg and season again. Wrap the muslin over to encase the leg. The muslin isn't strictly necessary but it makes the leg much easier to clean up after cooking.

4. Drain the hay and squeeze out any excess water. Line the roasting tin with a layer of the hay and then place the leg into the tin. Add more hay, filling the gaps around the edges and laying a thick layer over the top. Cover the tin with foil and bake the kid for 75 minutes. Remove from the oven, take off the foil and allow to rest for 30–40 minutes before carving.

Basil pesto

As a taste of summer goes, basil has to be high in the charts; an association with Mediterranean holidays, maybe? On a warm summer's day, is there anything much better than a plate of perfectly ripe tomatoes drenched in good olive oil, strewn with freshly torn basil leaves and finished with crunchy sea salt, perhaps with a chilled glass of good rosé to hand?

There are various types of basil used in many different national cuisines but I guess the strongest association is with Italy and genovese pesto. In Dino Joannides's excellent book on Italian cuisine, *Semplice*, he talks about the unique terroir where Ligurian basil is grown, the sweetness of its aroma and how the leaves are harvested young before being combined with pine nuts, pecorino cheese and the best sweet olive oil. As with other green sauces such as salsa verde, the actual recipe isn't vitally important, as everyone has their own preference. The key is the best possible ingredients you can lay your hands on.

I have a love of Spanish Arbequina olive oil, a brand called Mestral, but you will have your own favourite. I like a little lemon juice in my pesto to give some acidity, but using a sharp pecorino cheese will help in this direction. Most recipes evolve over the years; when I was first taught to make pesto it was in large quantities in a food processor and we always toasted the pine nuts, but I have come to prefer using untoasted ones for a sweeter, creamier flavour. Old Winchester cheese is a good alternative to the Parmesan often used in pesto, but feel free to blend and experiment.

Making pesto is a great way of extending the season or using up a glut and isn't the exclusive domain of basil. I find wild garlic pesto (see recipe on p. 70) keeps well in the fridge for several weeks, but basil pesto has more delicately nuanced flavours and is best served as fresh as possible. Equally important if you are using pesto in a hot dish is to add it at the last minute to preserve the colour and flavour.

SERVES 4 FOR A PASTA MAIN COURSE

1 clove of garlic
1 tsp Maldon sea salt
30g pine nuts
50g basil leaves, roughly chopped
20g pecorino, coarsely grated
30g Old Winchester, coarsely grated
50–60ml light, fruity olive oil
1–2 tsp lemon juice

1. Using a pestle and mortar, pound the garlic, salt and pine nuts to a paste. Gradually work in the basil leaves, pounding and rotating with the mortar.

2. Once all the basil has been incorporated, mix in the cheese and then the olive oil. Check the seasoning and add a little lemon juice to taste. You can, of course, use a food processor for this – just check that the blades are sharp and use the pulse button.

Sea salt and olive oil focaccia

Freshly baked bread is a real joy. The focaccia is a distinct contrast to the Viennese loaf that features later in the year and, for me, it is a summer bread. It makes a great accompaniment to the squid with chorizo in July, it could have this month's basil pesto spooned into the holes you push in the dough, and is really good chargrilled either in a griddle pan or on the barbecue. I like it as the base for a brunch dish, with crushed avocado, crispy bacon, fried eggs and a chipotle chilli sauce. Leftover bread is ideal in a panzanella-style salad.

The process of making a starter dough extends the fermentation time, leading to deeper, more complex flavours. Fresh yeast is, to my mind, preferable if you can find it, but if not then use half the quantity of dried active yeast hydrated in the same way as described for fresh.

NOTE: Start this recipe 24 hours ahead

For the starter dough
7g fresh yeast
100ml bottled water (100g)
100g strong bread flour
35ml olive oil (35g)

For the dough
7g fresh yeast
275ml bottled water (275g)
400g strong bread flour
75g semolina
2½ tsp Maldon sea salt, finely ground (12g)

To shape and finish
extra virgin olive oil
Maldon sea salt

1. Preheat the oven to 220°C.

2. To make the starter dough, mix the yeast with half the water and leave for 15 minutes until beginning to froth. Add the remaining ingredients (including the remaining water) and mix well. Wrap the bowl in cling film and place in the fridge to ferment for 24 hours or at least overnight.

3. The following day, make the dough. In the bowl of a stand mixer, mix the yeast with a little water and leave for 15 minutes until beginning to froth. Scrape in the starter dough and then add the remaining water, the flour, semolina and, lastly, the salt. Mix on a low speed for 12 minutes.

4. Scrape the dough onto a floured flat tray, forming a rough ball. Cover with oiled cling film and a tea towel and leave for 30 minutes.

5. With your fingertips, press and stretch the dough into a rectangle approximately. 35cm x 25cm. With the short edge towards you, fold the top edge down two-thirds of the way and then the bottom up to the top. Turn the tray through 90 degrees and repeat the folds. This should put the dough back into a rough ball shape. Lift the ball and flour the tray before replacing. Cover and prove for 30 minutes.

6. Repeat this process twice more. After the third prove, transfer the dough to a 30cm x 20cm bakewell tin. Press and stretch the dough to fill the tin. Cover and prove for 30 minutes. While the dough is on its final prove, place a metal tin in the bottom of the preheated oven.

7. Drizzle oil over the surface of the loaf and spread gently with your fingers. With your fingertips, gently push holes into the loaf all over its surface. The best way is to push right to the bottom of the tin. Scatter Maldon sea salt crystals over the top of the loaf.

8. Place the loaf in the oven on the middle shelf, and pour a cup of cold water into the metal tin to create some steam. Bake for 15 minutes, then reduce the temperature to 170°C and cook for a further 20–30 minutes until the loaf is golden and sounds hollow when the base is tapped.

9. Once cooked, remove to a wire cooling rack and drizzle with more olive oil. Allow to cool for 15 minutes before cutting.

Iced strawberry parfait

I dug up a wild strawberry plant some years ago from a hedge in my mum's garden. Remarkably, given the neglect and various house moves, it is still alive and producing fruit. The harvest of a small handful of fragrant berries indicates that the strawberry season has properly started. There aren't enough for a dish so instead they get muddled in the bottom of a flute and topped up with some sparkling wine. Pure essence of summer!

We need to look for a more abundant supply for this iced parfait, a classic combination of ripe fruit and something creamy. The essential part is a really flavoursome fruit purée, so choose your berries with care for this. The purée wants to be pleasantly sweet and may need a touch of sugar. The fruit sugar – fructose – is really good for enhancing the flavour of fruit compotes and purées and can be bought from most supermarkets or health food shops.

As an alternative, buy a good-quality strawberry purée. These are often intense in flavour and many only have a small added sugar content. The frozen purées available from specialist online shops are a great thing to have in the freezer for an impromptu dessert or cocktail.

SERVES 8

NOTE: Start this recipe 24 hours ahead

For the parfait
4 large free-range egg yolks
2 tbsp water
100g caster sugar
85g full-fat natural yoghurt
1 leaf of gelatine, soaked in cold water
200g strawberry purée
100ml double cream mixed with 2 tsp semi-
  skimmed milk
lemon juice to taste

To serve
300g ripe strawberries
1½ tbsp caster sugar
16 shortbread biscuits (see Basics p. 289)

1. Place the egg yolks in a small, heatproof bowl that will fit over a saucepan to make a bain-marie.

2. In a heavy-based pan, mix the water and sugar and warm gently until the sugar has dissolved, then increase the heat and bring the syrup to 110°C. Whisk the syrup gradually into the egg yolks and then place the bowl over a pan of simmering water. Whisk gently until the egg mix reaches 79°C. At this stage the mix will be thick, creamy and quite stiff. Remove from the heat and allow to cool to room temperature, whisking occasionally. Whisk the yoghurt into the egg mix.

3. Next, drain the gelatine and place with a few spoonfuls of the purée in a small pan and heat gently, stirring constantly to dissolve the gelatine. Whisk this back into the remaining purée and then whisk the purée into the yoghurt mix. Whip the cream and milk to very soft peaks and gently fold this through the fruit mix. Add lemon juice to taste. (The gelatine can be omitted, but using it makes the parfait slightly softer and easier to cut, as well as holding its shape better on the plate as it starts to defrost.)

4. Lightly oil a small loaf tin and line with a double thickness of cling film, using a clean tea towel to push the film tightly into the corners of the tin. Pour in the parfait mix and freeze overnight.

5. Remove the parfait from the freezer 20 minutes before serving. Hull the strawberries and cut into pieces if large. Mix with the sugar,

which will draw a little moisture from the berries and form a glaze. Slice the parfait as required, wrapping any leftovers tightly in cling film and returning to the freezer if you don't use it all at once.

6. Serve the sliced parfait with the berries and biscuits. More cream is, of course, always an option.

Gooseberry and elderflower cheesecake

The gooseberry seems to be abundant on allotments and loved by gardeners across the country but it is a crop that is dying out commercially.

The berries come in a number of guises that, when ripe, can be green, red, white or yellow, and divide into dessert and cooking varieties. The dessert berries are usually red in colour and are sweet enough to eat as they are.

As so often happens, if the seasons are in alignment, things that grow together go together. With luck, there should still be some elderflower around, and the combination of elderflower and gooseberry is a heady one, perfect for a sorbet or granita, or a tangy, fresh topping for a cheesecake.

SERVES 8–10

NOTE: Start this recipe 24 hours ahead to allow for setting time

For the base
65g unsalted butter
30g golden syrup
180g digestive biscuits, crushed

To keep the base crisp, try painting it with a thin layer of melted white chocolate. Chill for a few minutes to set the chocolate hard before pouring on your cheesecake cream. The chocolate will be too thin to notice but will act as a barrier to keep the filling's moisture out of the base.

For the gooseberry topping and jelly
100ml water
125g caster sugar
150ml elderflower cordial
400g gooseberries
1 leaf of gelatine, soaked in cold water

For the cream cheese filling
500g full-fat soft cream cheese
60g caster sugar
85ml semi-skimmed milk
1 vanilla pod, split and seeds scraped out,
    or ½ tsp vanilla paste
2 leaves of gelatine, soaked in cold water
200ml double cream mixed with 1½ tbsp semi-
    skimmed milk

1. Preheat the oven to 160°C.

2. To make the base, heat the butter and golden syrup in a small saucepan until it comes to the boil, stirring frequently. Mix the syrup into the biscuits and then press the mix into a 20 x 8cm stainless-steel ring that is sat on a baking tray lined with baking parchment or a Silpat mat. Bake the base for 6 minutes and then allow to cool completely.

3. For the gooseberry topping, top and tail the berries using small scissors or a sharp knife, reserving eight berries for garnish. Combine the water, sugar and cordial in a medium pan and bring to the boil, stirring occasionally. Add the berries and use a spoon to keep turning them over until they begin to soften slightly and change from bright green to a paler, more muted colour. Remove from the heat and drain, reserving the liquid. Chill the berries in a shallow plastic container that will hold them in a single layer.

4. To make the jelly, measure 100ml of the poaching liquid and add the soaked gelatine. Stir to dissolve the gelatine and then pass the liquid through a sieve into a small bowl. Refrigerate to set overnight.

5. For the cream cheese filling, combine the cream cheese with the sugar in a large bowl and set to one side. Heat the milk in a small pan with the vanilla pod and seeds or paste. Use three quarters of the warm milk to soften the cream cheese mix, and dissolve the soaked gelatine in the remainder. Pass the gelatine/milk mix through a fine sieve into the cream cheese and combine thoroughly with a whisk. Whip the cream and milk mix to very soft peaks and fold into the cream cheese mix.

6. Pour the mixture over the biscuit base and level with the back of a spoon. Press a sheet of cling film onto the surface of the cheesecake and use an 18cm circle of thick card to press down, causing a 1cm lip of the filling to rise up around the edges. This creates a neat well to hold the berries. Remove the card and film and chill the cheesecake to set overnight.

7. Once set, arrange the berries on top of the cake, covering the surface completely. Pile any extra berries in the centre. Gently warm the jelly, either in the microwave or by placing the bowl into hot water. Stir and break up the jelly until it is just liquid but still cool. Spoon over the fruit and garnish with thin slices of the reserved raw berries. Chill to set the jelly; this should only take 20–30 minutes. If you can find a couple of elderflower heads, they will make a great finishing touch.

07 | July

Hegmonath – hay month, when grass was cut to feed cattle later in the year

July is high summer. By now, the weather gods have invariably got the memo and we can look forward to reliably long, hot days with balmy evenings, perfect for beaches, barbecues and all manner of outdoor activities. Although Midsummer's Day has already come and gone, the best of the summer season is still stretching out in front of us.

It's a bumper harvest time, and our shops and markets overflow with fresh, home-grown produce. We're spoilt for choice in most departments and for the next few months putting together a three-course meal made entirely of local, home-grown or foraged seasonal produce should be a simple but rewarding challenge.

In what is usually our hottest month, light, fresh dishes are the order of the day, so simply cooked fish should feature frequently on the menu. There are soft fruits galore, too, and chilled or frozen desserts with the refreshing tang of raspberries, strawberries and cherries are the obvious choice.

Things are less straightforward on the vegetable patch as we wage war on the weeds and pests that also make the most of the harvest. Aggressive bindweed frequently threatens to strangle our genteel courgettes, and marauding greenfly flock to our chilli plants in huge numbers – our poor jalapeños become the aphid equivalent of Magaluf.

Ignoring the horticultural challenges, July is usually the very best of British summer in all its sunny, sweet glory. So whether it's sandcastles on the beach, picnics in the park or just running through the garden sprinkler in your underpants, get out there and make the most of it.

The peak of summer, when the chilly British waters, inland and coastal, have had a chance to warm up, is the best time to discover wild swimming, and with a little research you can enjoy an al fresco dip in some of our most secluded and beautiful countryside.

Wild swimming simply means swimming somewhere natural – in lakes, rivers or the sea – rather than a swimming pool. It has seen something of a resurgence in recent years as people seek a sense of adventure.

A number of books, web resources and apps now exist to help you take the plunge into wild swimming, and there will certainly be a suitable spot somewhere near you. Stick to recommended locations that will be free of strong currents, deep water and dangerous features like weirs.

You need very little kit – purists will make do with a towel and suitable swimming costume (in some spots you won't even need that!). However, even in the warmest summer months, British waters can be pretty bracing, so take plenty of warm clothes for afterwards. In many places you'll be a lot more comfortable wearing a wetsuit, and water shoes or wetsuit boots are also a good idea.

Whether it's a tarn in the Scottish Highlands, a waterfall in the Welsh mountains or a river running through a quintessential English village, a refreshing swim followed by a waterside picnic is the perfect way to spend a dreamy summer's afternoon.

B oth cuttlefish and squid come into season during the summer months. Cuttlefish will usually be found in our waters a little earlier (from late April to early May), with the squid following on shortly afterwards in June or July.

Possibly because of their association with Greek island holidays, people are often surprised to find that both species are regularly caught off our coastline in large numbers. In fact, you don't have to go far at all to find them – cuttlefish are caught in pots and you'll see anglers hooking squid from harbour walls on warm summer evenings (both species are cannibals so are usually caught using lures designed to look like smaller relatives).

Being cephalopods, the two fish also share a colourful characteristic – ink. Both rely on thick dark mucus, squirted from a sac between their gills, as a defence mechanism. That means not only that your fresh, tentacled beastie might look a bit soiled when you buy it off the fishmonger's slab, but also that you need to take care preparing it. Always do it in a metal sink or a large bowl, and never on a smart wooden work surface – if you rupture the ink sac you risk a serious stain. Squid ink is usually very black whereas the ink of the cuttlefish is nearer to dark brown (their Greek name is *sepia*). Neither looks good as a permanent kitchen feature.

The good news is that, if you can get the sac out without damaging it, the inky liquid is delicious and will add a classy monochrome touch and subtle fishy notes to many a dish.

Although squid is now very popular, you're still quite unlikely to chance upon a cuttlefish in most shops, so you may need to order one in. It's worth the effort though, and not just for the conspiratorial nod you'll get from the fishmonger as he hands over your special delivery.

To prepare cuttlefish or squid:

Give yourself plenty of time. You'll need a sharp knife, chopping board, a tea towel and a metal sink or large bowl . Make sure the board has a non-porous surface like glass or granite.

Start with the fish on a board in front of you. Cut off and keep the tentacles by slicing just in front of the eyes, then squeeze out and discard the hard 'beak' if that is still attached.

Firmly but steadily pull the remainder of the head away from the body. Most of the guts will come away with it. Discard all of this.

Now, put your hand inside the body and gently work out the rest of the innards and the cuttle (the large bone-like cartilage beloved of budgerigars)– or, in the case of squid, the transparent quill. Give the inside a quick rinse. Preferably all of this should be done without rupturing the ink sac, which you'll find inside the body towards the back end. If you can get it out whole, reserve the ink. (Some fish, especially those from online retailers, will come with the ink already removed and in a little sachet.)

On larger specimens, remove the tough individual suckers from the legs by rubbing the legs between your hands under running water.

Finally, remove the slippery skin from the body. It should peel off fairly easily, leaving bright white flesh. Use the tea towel to help you grip. The side wings will usually come off with the skin. Peel and keep those, too.

Although a little tricky the first time, you can't go too badly wrong and at the end of the process you are left with a pile of sweet, white, boneless meat. Depending on your chosen dish you can now either slice across the body tube to make those familiar calamari rings, 'butterfly' it by slicing lengthwise or leave it whole and stuff it with some delicious summery ingredients (rice, pine nuts, tomatoes and green herbs are common bedfellows in Mediterranean recipes).

Try: Sautéed squid with chorizo and piquillo pepper dressing (p. 160)

I t's undeniable that the raspberry isn't revered in quite the same way as its summer sibling, the strawberry. Yet these delightfully tart, tangy and juicy fruits deserve every bit as much love.

The reason they don't feature as frequently as they should on our summer menu is presumably twofold – firstly because the ripe fruits are too soft to transport easily and secondly because they spoil too quickly. Their delicate constitution and short shelf-life make them a nightmare for any supply chain that is longer than your garden.

You'll occasionally find supermarkets trying to overcome the problem by selling un-hulled fruit, a sure sign that the berries were picked before they were ripe. Whilst that might enhance their transportability, they invariably remain much too tart, so are best avoided.

There are a couple of ways to overcome this unfortunate state of fruity affairs. One is to visit a Pick Your Own farm (see June) and hand-pick your own punnet of berries on the day you're planning to eat them. The slightly more labour-intensive alternative is to grow your own. They are relatively easy to grow in any sized garden and work well in containers if you have limited space.

Pick bright red, plump berries, ideally on a dry day when they'll be at their fragrant best. Wash them as little as possible and only ever under a light trickle of water.

The earliest varieties come into season in June, with later crops producing fruit as late as October.

Try: Fresh raspberries with honey and oat ice cream (p. 171)

Food & Foraging | Samphire

From June into mid-July, marsh samphire, sometimes called sea asparagus, is in season.

The name derives from Saint Pierre (St Peter), the patron saint of fishermen, due to samphire's close connection with the sea. Unsurprisingly, it's one of the finest seasonal accompaniments to fish (including those mackerel we caught in the June chapter) and other seafood. Growing in our salt marshes and estuaries, its small, cactus-like shoots are succulent and crunchy, with a salty tang, picked up from the sea air.

Foraging for marsh samphire is easy and you'll find it in large beds in flat, muddy areas near to many coastlines. Just snip the top off fresh, young shoots. Gather only as much as you need and never pull up the whole plant (in common with other estuary plants, samphire roots help stabilize these valuable coastal ecosystems).

There is a second, less common plant called rock samphire, which is a completely different species. Its season starts slightly earlier in the summer – around May. But there's good reason for less experienced foragers not to go looking for this variety and the clue is in the name. It grows on rocky sea cliffs. Shakespeare's King Lear famously refers to the 'dreadful trade' of collecting rock samphire because of the dangers that collectors faced hanging from the rock faces.

You'll occasionally find both kinds in delicatessens, pickled – they make for a crunchy, vinegary treat. But, during the season, you're most likely to find fresh marsh samphire next to the cold slab in your local fishmonger's. To cook it, just steam or boil (without salt) for a couple of minutes, then top with some melted butter or a light olive oil.

| # The Dunmow Flitch (mid-July – various)

One longstanding and unique food-related event takes place in July every four years in the town of Great Dunmow, Essex.

The Dunmow Flitch Trials invite applications from couples the world over who have been married for at least a year, to satisfy a judging panel of six maidens and six bachelors that in 'twelvemonth and a day' they have 'not wisht themselves unmarried again'. If they can convince the jury that their claim is true they are awarded a side, or flitch, of bacon.

It's said that the original trials date back to 1104, when the lord and lady of the manor dressed as poor villagers and sought the blessing of the local prior a year and a day after their marriage. The prior was impressed by their devotion to each other and gave them a flitch of bacon. When they revealed their true identity the lord agreed to gift land to the priory on the condition that anyone else who could prove the same claim would be similarly rewarded.

The Dunmow Flitch Trials were well renowned and are even mentioned briefly in one of Chaucer's fourteenth-century *Canterbury Tales*, 'The Wife of Bath's Tale'. Formal records of claimants date back to the 1400s and although the custom lapsed for some time, it was revived in the Victorian period. Since the Second World War the trials have been held every four years in a marquee erected specially for the purpose. Successful couples are carried in the Flitch Chair to the market place, where they swear an oath kneeling on pointed stones to prove their devotion.

The trials are said to be the origin of the phrase 'bring home the bacon'.

Try: Braised bacon with butter beans and new season's carrots (p. 167)

| St Swithin's Day (15th July)

The fifteenth of July is St Swithin's Day. Folklore has it that whatever the weather on St Swithin's Day, it will continue for the next forty days. As the old poem tells:

St Swithin's day if thou dost rain,
For forty days it will remain;
St Swithin's day if thou be fair,
For forty days 'twill rain nae mair.

If you're only reading this page because it's pouring with rain outside, take heart; perhaps unsurprisingly, the myth is a long way off being meteorological fact. According to a study it has been debunked many times over – on virtually every recorded occasion when it has rained on St Swithin's Day, forty days of rain did *not* follow.

That said, it does happen occasionally. The longest number of consecutive rainy days recorded in Britain is eighty-nine, a record set on the Scottish island of Islay in 1923. (The Welsh village of Eglwyswrw – pronounced *Egg-lis-oo-roo*– came close to equalling the record between October 2015 and January 2016 but fell short by just five days.)

Sautéed squid with chorizo and piquillo pepper dressing

Cooked well, squid is tender, sweet and delicious. It is a case of extremes, though, and it needs either really high heat for a very short time or long, slow cooking at low temperatures. I prefer the really high heat approach; the smoky notes you get from chargrilling, or the crisp finish from a light flour coating and hot oil, are a delight. You still retain some of the texture of the squid but it doesn't become tough.

I can't remember where I first saw the idea of freezing squid to make it more tender but I do feel it works. Lay the cleaned, dry squid between layers of baking parchment, freeze overnight and then defrost in the fridge. There doesn't seem to be any loss of flavour but the result is a more delictae dish.

SERVES 4 AS A STARTER

For the squid

4 medium whole squid (500–600g), cleaned, bodies opened up, lightly scored and cut into rough squares and tentacles split into two or three

200ml buttermilk mixed with 50ml semi-skimmed milk

50g plain flour

50g semolina

125ml olive oil for frying

½ lemon

Maldon sea salt and freshly ground black pepper

For the dressing

100g piquillo peppers

2 tsp Dijon mustard

50ml good sherry vinegar

15g honey

1 tsp Maldon sea salt, finely ground

100ml grapeseed oil

50ml light, fruity extra virgin olive oil

For the chorizo

2 cooking chorizo sausages, cut in half lengthwise

To serve

40g rocket leaves

olive oil

1. Start by adding the squid to the buttermilk mix (this can be done 24 hours ahead and refrigerated).

2. Next, make the dressing. Place all the ingredients except the oils in a small food processor and blend to smooth purée. Gradually blend in the oils and then adjust the seasoning. Transfer the dressing to a plastic squeeze bottle.

3. Cook the halved chorizo in a dry non-stick pan, caramelizing the surface well. Turn to finish cooking and then drain on some paper towel.

4. Drain the squid well. Combine the flour and semolina and season heavily. Toss the squid pieces in the flour mix, coating evenly. Put the squid in a sieve, shake well to remove any excess flour. Using a non-stick pan, shallow fry the squid very quickly in smoking hot oil. Do this in batches to avoid overcrowding the pan, then drain on paper towel and season with lemon juice and sea salt.

5. To serve, lay a piece of chorizo on each plate, mound the squid beside it, toss the rocket with a little olive oil and a pinch of salt, add this to the plates and then squeeze big dots of the dressing onto the plate.

NOTE: This recipe makes more dressing than you need but keeps in the fridge and makes a good dip or sauce for a chorizo and egg sandwich!

Broad bean bruschetta

Inside their skins, baby broad beans are vibrant green, jewel-like and tender with a sweet and earthy flavour. Warm those tender morsels gently with a little butter and stock and you will have something very special. I do think it is worth the effort of slipping the beans from the skins to enhance both the flavour and texture.

This bruschetta is a simple dish to put together. Most of the work is in the shopping; really good bread, oil, butter and goat's cheese or curd will make this a special starter or snack.

SERVES 6 AS A STARTER OR SNACK

NOTE: To prepare the beans once they have been podded, blanch in boiling salted water for 1 minute and immediately transfer to iced water. Pinch the skin with your thumbnail and squeeze the beans out of their grey skin. Alternatively, use frozen baby broad beans; let them partially defrost then pop the bean from its skin.

500g podded broad beans, around 1.5–1.75kg unpodded
75ml vegetable stock (see Basics p. 284)
20g unsalted butter
120ml olive oil for the bread plus extra to garnish
6 large slices of rustic bread
1 clove of garlic, peeled
180g goat's curd or soft, fresh goat's cheese, beaten
pea shoots to garnish
good extra virgin olive oil
Maldon sea salt and freshly ground black pepper

1. Place the beans in a small pan with the vegetable stock and heat rapidly, reducing the stock by half. Crush the beans with the butter and olive oil, and season well.

2. Drizzle the bread slices with oil and sprinkle on a little salt. Chargrill and then rub with the garlic clove.

3. Divide the crushed beans between the chargrilled bread, and spoon the goat's curd on top. Dress with a few pea shoots and finish with a drizzle of your best olive oil.

Fillet of bass with samphire, braised gem lettuce and peas

Bass are highly sought after by both commercial fishermen and recreational anglers alike, but the fish are relatively scarce so strict limits are in place both on minimum size and the number caught. If you fish for bass recreationally, from 1 July until the end of the year, you are currently only allowed to keep one fish per day. In the first half of the year, any bass must be returned. The minimum size you can keep in the permitted period is 42 centimetres (16.5in). Generally, wild bass is considered to be unsustainable but farmed bass can be a sustainable option. There are also some hook and line fisheries that tick the sustainability box.

The availability of fresh, wild fish is completely subject to the vagaries of nature but, from the cook's point of view, it isn't all bad news. Very few fish recipes won't work with an alternative. As a rule of thumb, you can swap any of the flat fish, most of the oily sea fish, and replace one white fish with another. Bass is a pretty distinctive fish but a good alternative would be black bream.

SERVES 4 AS A MAIN COURSE

For the sauce
olive oil for frying
1 banana shallot, thinly sliced
1 clove of garlic, thinly sliced
50ml dry vermouth
100ml white wine
200ml vegetable stock (see Basics p. 284)

For the vegetables
140g fresh peas, podded weight
100g samphire
4 small Little Gem lettuce, outer leaves
    removed, halved lengthwise

For the fish
4 x 100g bass fillet portions
20g unsalted butter
70g unsalted butter for the sauce, cold, diced
Maldon sea salt and freshly ground black
    pepper
lemon juice

1. To make the sauce, heat 1 tbsp of oil in a sauté pan and add the shallot and garlic. Stir in a pinch of salt and cook for 3–4 minutes until the shallot have starts to soften. Add the alcohol and reduce until syrupy. Add the vegetable stock and reduce over a high heat by half. Set the mix aside for now.

2. Blanch the peas and samphire in boiling salted water for 1 minute, then transfer to a bowl of iced water to refresh.

3. Trim a 'V' notch out of the root end of the lettuce to remove most of the core but still keep the lettuce in one piece. Season the lettuce well on the cut side and rub with a little oil. Heat a non-stick pan and sear the lettuce on the cut side. You want a deep golden brown with the odd spot of black. Turn the lettuce over and add a splash of water to the pan. Cover with a lid or plate and remove from the heat. The idea is that the lettuce will wilt a little but still retain some crunch.

4. With a sharp knife, lightly score the skin on the bass with cuts about 1cm apart. Cut through the skin but only just into the flesh. Season the skin side with salt. Heat a couple of tablespoons of oil in a large, non-stick pan and place the bass in, skin side down, pressing down gently on the fillets to stop them curling. Cook for around 2 minutes until the skin has started to crisp. Season the flesh side with salt and pepper and add the butter to the pan. When the butter is foaming, turn the fillets skin side up and cook for a further minute. Test by pushing a cocktail stick into the thickest part of the flesh; if it goes in smoothly, the fish is done; if you can still feel the fibres tearing, give it a little longer. Remove the fish to some kitchen paper to drain.

5. While the fish is cooking, warm the sauce base and whisk in the butter. Adjust the seasoning with salt, pepper and lemon juice. Add the peas and samphire. Warm the vegetables through without letting the sauce boil.

6. To serve, place two pieces of lettuce in the centre of each of four shallow bowls and spoon the pea and samphire ragout around. Place a fillet of bass on top of the lettuce. This will eat well as it is, but crusty bread or baby new potatoes are a good addition.

Braised bacon with butter beans and new season's carrots

A bacon joint comes from the fore end of the pig; as opposed to gammon, which comes from the hind. It is likely to have more marbling and is a succulent, well-flavoured choice. It also tends to be slightly cheaper than gammon. Bacon joints are something you may have to visit a butcher for rather than a supermarket. Of course, a gammon joint can be used instead of bacon.

This is a great alternative to a traditional roast during the summer and makes full use of sweet new-season carrots. If you want to cook a smaller joint, I would just reduce the number of carrots but keep the other ingredients the same, and check 30 minutes earlier than suggested.

SERVES 6 AS A MAIN COURSE

1.5kg bacon joint such as collar or slipper
2 large onions
3 cloves of garlic
2 tbsp olive oil
1 tbsp mustard seeds
1 tsp chilli flakes
1 400g tin good-quality plum tomatoes
2 bay leaves
500ml water
18 new-season carrots, tops trimmed and washed
1 x 400g tin butter beans
10g bunch of flat-leaf parsley, leaves only
Maldon sea salt and freshly ground black pepper

To serve
A simple salad of Little Gem lettuce with a sharp cider vinegar dressing or the pickled courgettes using the recipe from the brined pork chops on pp. 210–11.

1. Preheat the oven to 140°C.

2. Place the bacon joint in a large saucepan and cover with cold water. Bring to the boil, drain and rinse with cold water.

3. While the bacon is coming to the boil, peel the onions and cut each into eight wedges. Thinly slice the garlic. In a large casserole or deep roasting tin that will hold the joint, heat the olive oil and add the onions, cook for 2 minutes and then add the garlic. Cook for a further minute before adding the mustard seeds. Stir and cook until the seeds begin to pop, then add the chilli followed by the tomatoes. Stir well and add the bay leaves and a good grind of black pepper. Do not add salt at this stage as the joint will be reasonably salty.

4. Place the bacon into the casserole or roasting tin, add the water and cover with foil or a lid. Cook in the oven for 1½ hours.

5. Carefully uncover the joint and scatter the carrots around, re-cover and cook for a further hour. Drain the tin of butter beans and tip them around the joint. Mix gently, cover once more and cook for 30 minutes and then cook uncovered for a final 30 minutes. If at any stage the dish looks dry, add a little more water. The carrots should be just tender and a carving fork will push easily into the meat. If either aren't done, give the dish another 15 minutes and check again.

6. Remove the bacon to rest in a warm place for 30 minutes, leaving the casserole or roasting tin in the oven with the oven turned off. The finished dish wants to have a fair bit of liquid but not be too runny; you can always pop it on the hob and reduce the liquid slightly to thicken up, if necessary.

7. When the bacon is rested, roughly chop the parsley and stir into the beans and carrots. Check and adjust the seasoning. Carve the bacon into thick slices and lay on large serving platter, spoon the beans and carrots around the bacon and serve.

White chocolate mousse with cherry compote

Stone fruits come into their own during the warmer months of summer but our climate still isn't really warm enough for the likes of peaches and nectarines, although there is now a small but significant crop of British apricots. Cherries, however, we do have, although the volume of cherry orchards is much lower than it used to be. The outlook is improving, though, and the harvest of cherries is at a thirty-year high according to some reports. Many cherries are now grown in polytunnels with modern varieties grafted onto dwarf root stock, which makes the harvesting much easier than on traditional varieties.

This contemporary recipe brings in some of the flavours of a classic gâteau, with the cherries being a good foil for the light, white chocolate mousse. Adding a few chocolate shavings and some small cubes of chocolate brownie to the dish jumps this right into Black Forest territory.

SERVES 6

For the mousse

220g good-quality white chocolate
130ml double cream
1 leaf of gelatine, soaked in cold water
210ml double cream plus 1½ tbsp semi-
  skimmed milk, whipped to very soft peaks

For the compote

400g cherries, halved and stoned (retain a few
  for garnish)
2–3 tbsp caster sugar, depending on the
  tartness of the cherries
50ml port
1 tsp good balsamic vinegar
½ tsp cornflour, dissolved in 1 tbsp cold water

To serve

dark and white chocolate shavings
30 small cubes of chocolate brownie or
  chocolate cake

1. For the mousse, melt the chocolate in a heatproof bowl either on a low setting in the microwave or over a pan of gently simmering water. Bring the cream (130ml) to a simmer, remove from the heat and add the soaked gelatine. Stir to dissolve the gelatine.

2. Gently whisk the cream mix into the white chocolate to form a ganache. Check that the temperature is around 35–40°C and then fold in the whipped cream/milk. Pour into glasses and allow to set in the fridge for at least 2 hours.

3. To make the compote, combine three-quarters of the cherries in a pan with the sugar, port and vinegar. Cook over a medium heat until the cherries are tender and the juices have thickened. If the cherries are cooked before the liquid has thickened, spoon them out into a bowl with a slotted spoon and continue to reduce the liquid. Once reduced, return the cherries to the pan. Turn off the heat and leave to sit for 30 minutes. More juice will be released from the fruit. Rewarm and thicken the juices with the cornflour. Chill and then add the raw cherries.

4. To serve, place 5 cubes of brownie into each glass, then spoon on the cherries allowing them to cascade down onto the mousse. Finish with a few chocolate shavings scraped from the back of a bar with a small knife.

Fresh raspberries with honey and oat ice cream

Summer berries offer us so many choices in the kitchen. They can play a supporting role to create balance or they can be the star of the show when they only need a little help to become a sublime dish. Sugar and cream help mellow the raspberries' tartness and toasted oats provide both flavour and some texture. This brings together the flavours of a classic cranachan, just in a different form.

Making your own ice cream is a simple process and has few rivals in terms of quality. It is the perfect impromptu dessert and will keep well in the freezer for several weeks.

SERVES 4 WITH ICE CREAM LEFT OVER

NOTE: Start the ice cream at least 12 hours ahead to allow time for chilling

For the ice cream
80g oatmeal
20g honey
2 tsp vegetable oil
450ml double cream
375ml semi-skimmed milk
1 vanilla pod
10 large, free-range egg yolks (160g)
80g caster sugar
75g runny honey
2 tbsp whisky

For the raspberries
150g fresh raspberries
1 tbsp caster sugar

To serve
2 tbsp of toasted oats reserved from making the ice cream
honey to drizzle

1. Preheat the oven to 160°C.

2. To make the ice cream, start by mixing the oats with the honey (20g) and oil in a small ovenproof pan or roasting tin. Bake for 10–15 minutes, stirring occasionally, until the oats are a deep golden brown. Allow to cool.

3. Combine the cream and milk in a heavy-based pan. Split the vanilla pod and scrape out the seeds; add the pod and the seeds to the cream mix. Bring to a simmer, whisk well and turn off the heat. Cover the pan and leave to infuse for 30 minutes.

4. Whisk the egg yolks in a bowl with the sugar and runny honey, reheat the cream mix and pour onto the yolks, whisking constantly. Return to the pan and place over a moderate heat. Bring the custard to 80°C, stirring constantly in a figure-of-eight motion as well as circles around the edge of the pan. It is a good idea to have a large bowl of very cold water to dip the base of the pan into should the custard start to scramble.

5. Once the custard is cooked, pass through a fine sieve into a clean plastic container. Chill over ice, then add the whisky and refrigerate overnight. The following day, churn in an ice cream machine. Reserve 2 tbsp of the oats and add the rest to the ice cream once it is firm then transfer to the freezer.

6. To make without an ice cream machine, freeze for 2 hours and then remove and whisk well, repeating until the ice cream is virtually solid. Chill the bowl of a food processor and add the ice cream. Blitz in the processor briefly, fold in the oats and then return to the freezer to set completely.

7. Transfer to the fridge 30 minutes before using.

8. For the raspberries, gently wash the raspberries and then purée a third of them with the sugar. Pass through a fine sieve and mix gently with the remaining raspberries. Add more sugar if required.

9. To serve, put two scoops of ice cream into small bowls, add a quarter of the raspberries and scatter some toasted oats on top. Drizzle with a little honey to finish.

o8 | August

Shearmonath – shearing month, when sheep were shorn

As seasonal food fans, we're not really allowed favourite months. Like twelve beloved children, we should cherish them all equally for their unique talents and attributes (yes, even February, who can't catch at all). But if you really, really pressed me to make a choice, August would have to be a contender for my secret favourite.

All month long, food is plentiful, with a huge selection of fruit, vegetables and fish all in season and bursting with summery goodness.

It's gloriously hard work keeping up with everything on the vegetable patch and in the orchard. We'll be tucking into tomatoes, beans, chillies, aubergines, cherries and apricots to name but a few. It's an impressive list and in a good year we'll have them all coming out of our ears.

Before the month is out, the hedgerows will be brimming with more elderberries and early blackberries than you can shake a jam thermometer at and we've even got some game as the grouse season begins mid-month. So there's undoubtedly something for everyone to enjoy.

In fact, the only negative thing I can find to say about August is that there's almost too much produce – we'll simply never eat it all. This is the first month we need to start thinking seriously about bottling some of the goodness, preserving the glut for the autumn and winter ahead.

In addition to the first-class food, we're still enjoying the long, hot days of summer and there's so much to do outdoors in the great British countryside that it's pretty much impossible to do it justice in one short chapter.

Not only are butterflies some of our most beautiful invertebrates, they are critically important to our ecosystem, both as pollinators of plants and as food for other species.

There are more than fifty indigenous species of butterfly found in the UK (and many more occasional foreign visitors) but, depending on exactly where you live and the time of year, the ten you're most likely to see in your garden are probably the brimstone, comma, small cabbage white, large cabbage white, green-veined white, meadow brown, painted lady, peacock, red admiral and the small tortoiseshell.

They prefer bright and warm weather (you're very unlikely to see them when it's raining), so look out for them in your garden on sunny days from late spring through to the early autumn.

Sadly, more than three-quarters of Britain's butterfly species have declined in the last forty years. Some of those declines are understood and linked to loss of habitat, but others have yet to be explained and highlight a worrying trend for our insect population generally.

Similar to the RSPB's Big Garden Birdwatch in late winter, Butterfly Conservation runs the Big Butterfly Count every summer, between July and August. It's another invaluable 'citizen science' project, designed to assess the health of our butterfly population, so be sure to take part.

You can do even more for butterfly conservation by creating the right environment in your garden, particularly by planting flowering shrubs and plants. By choosing species that flower at different times of the year you can ensure a constant food supply over many months. Your local garden centre will be able to give you specialist advice and the Royal Horticultural Society publishes a list of plants that they recommend specifically to attract butterflies, and, just as importantly, to provide protection for their caterpillars.

As well as flower nectar, butterflies love eating sweet, soft fruits like bananas, brown apples and strawberries. Towards the end of summer and into autumn, when there are fewer flowers in bloom, leave plates of sliced fruits in your garden to give them a welcome sugar boost.

G rowing apricots in the UK has long been seen as something of a challenge for gardeners. The little orange, stoned fruit is a native of hotter parts of the world, notably southern Europe and Asia, meaning our damp, cool growing conditions aren't an ideal match.

But apricots are a valuable crop, much enjoyed here, so in recent years growers have been working hard to develop cultivars more suited to our milder climes, with Moorpark and Tomcot varieties becoming the most popular.

Perfect growing conditions require a mild spring followed by a warm and wet summer. If we get that, the fresh fruits will be available from May to the end of summer with production peaking in July and August. With annual British production now exceeding 200 tonnes (largely from the south and south west), there's a reasonably good chance of finding British apricots in your local shops this month.

The home-grown fruit seems to have a slightly different flavour profile to continental imports, with a greater depth of flavour, more acidity in the skin and an unctuous texture. The longer, slower growth is likely to be the cause of these differences.

And here's an interesting fact for you – the Italian liqueur Amaretto is widely thought to be flavoured with almonds. In fact, it is an extract of apricot kernels.

Try: Honey-roast apricots with yoghurt sorbet (p. 193)

Food & Foraging | Tomatoes

As a nation, we consume nearly half a million tonnes of fresh tomatoes each year and import nearly 80 per cent of that. Our understandable love of the Mediterranean diet has led to a year-round demand that is (along with strawberries) sadly emblematic of the globalized food market.

There is undoubtedly a place for quality tinned tomatoes, purées and even, dare I say it, the odd squirt of ketchup, on our dinner plates, but out-of-season fresh tomatoes are right at the top of my food crimes charge sheet, as they are so often a far cry from the fragrant and sweetly flavoured fruits they should be. If you have ever stepped into a greenhouse full of home-grown tomatoes, you'll know the unmistakable, highly scented aroma that should accompany these fruits when they're ripe and on the vine. (For me, it takes me instantly back to my father's greenhouse and the very beginnings of my interest in seasonal food.) Yet, it seems, the average British shopper would rather live with a rock-hard, tasteless tom than explore any seasonal alternatives.

As it happens, with the benefit of polytunnel growing and the increasingly sunny weather on our south coast (notably the Isle of Wight), these days it's hardly a major sacrifice to stick to in-season tomatoes. Different varieties now yield fruit on a continuous basis from early June through to October – more than a third of the year – with production volume, variety and flavour all peaking around mid-August to early September.

It's definitely worth taking a diversion away from the classic red salad tomato to discover some of the resurgent heritage (or heirloom) varieties that are now being widely grown. The definition of 'heritage' is not a strict or legally controlled one but it's generally accepted that a fruit grown, without hybridization, for at least forty years can be classified as such. So, many varieties pre-date the supermarket supply chain and in a lot of cases taste superior to their modern commercial counterparts. Of course, some varieties went out of fashion for good reason so it doesn't necessarily follow that anything marketed as 'heritage' will be tastier!

Virtually any tomato dish will benefit from incorporating a range of sizes, textures and tastes. There are now literally hundreds to choose from, and with black, yellow, orange and even striped varieties widely available, there's certainly little excuse not to brighten up your summer salad (and Russell touches on a few of his favourites in the galette recipe).

Try: Tomato galette with rocket and Parmesan salad (p. 182)

The unearthly-looking spider crab first turns up on our shores in May (hence its Latin name, *Maia*) and can be found throughout the summer months. They congregate in huge clusters in shallow waters off our coastline, usually reaching a peak around August before disappearing in the early autumn. No one is totally sure what they are up to but it's likely to be a combination of mating and moulting. Importantly, however, they make for excellent eating.

Even in these more enlightened times, it can be difficult to get hold of spider crab. As a country, we catch about one-tenth of Europe's haul but hardly eat any of it, which is pretty inexplicable given the number of brown crabs we happily tuck into. Unfortunately for us, the vast majority (more than 90 per cent) of our spider crab catch gets exported to France. In the last few years, some of the more canny British fishmongers have caught on to the small but growing market here, so if you look hard enough you should be able to find some near you.

You can catch your own spider crab fairly easily and without a pot. At low tide, snorkelling off any sand or shingle beach will often be fruitful. You'll find them loitering around patches of rocks and seaweed but they're also out in the open more (and therefore easier to catch) than their brown relatives. Alternatively, if you don't fancy getting wet, any angler will tell you that spider crab will latch on to most baits left on the sea bed for long enough.

There are two types of crab you should avoid eating – any who have recently moulted and females carrying eggs. Both are easy to spot – you'll see the eggs on the underside of egg-carrying or 'berried' females, and recently-moulted specimens will have pristine shells. Look for older specimens covered in barnacles and seaweed (which they apply as a camouflage). In any event, it's usually better to eat the males because they have much larger claws, with more meat.

Russell's recipe includes notes on the humane treatment of crabs and shellfish. In most areas the minimum landing size for a spider crab is 13 centimetres (about 5 in). Frankly, your catch should be significantly bigger if you want any kind of meal from it.

Try: Spider crab linguini with chilli, garlic and parsley (p. 185)

(1 st August)

The first day of August is Lammas Day, loaf mass day, in Anglo Saxon. At the beginning of August, shortly after the main wheat harvest, farmers would bring bread or flour from the new crop to church. Tenant farmers would also be obliged to take a share of their flour to their landlord and the occasion was marked with the Feast of the First Fruits.

In modern times, Lammas Day has almost completely fallen away as a celebration in favour of Harvest Festival, which takes place a bit later in the year, around the autumn equinox (see September) but if you ever wanted proof (pun intended) of the importance of bread in British culture (pun also intended), consider this – the word 'lord' derives from the Old English '*hlaefweard*' or 'loaf-keeper' and 'lady' from '*hlaefdige*' or 'loaf-kneader'.

Try: Viennese tin loaf (p. 190)

| # The Glorious Twelfth (12th August)

There is surely no more famous seasonal food date than the 'Glorious Twelfth' of August, the first day of the grouse-shooting season.

Red grouse are one of the few truly wild game birds left in this country and they live exclusively on the moors of Scotland, Wales and northern England – together, home to more than three quarters of the world's remaining heather moorland habitat.

The shooting season for grouse kicks off every year on the twelfth (unless it falls on a Sunday, in which case it's the following day), after chicks hatched in the spring have reached maturity. Once shot, the first birds of the season are plucked from the moors and rushed to the kitchens of high-end restaurants who race to serve them to diners that same evening.

The season continues until 10 December and, even after the initial rush, prices for the birds usually remain stubbornly high, simply because of the entirely non-intensive way in which they are reared.

Although grouse moors are carefully (and, I should acknowledge, controversially) managed, nature plays a huge part in the success of this iconic species. A late, cold winter or wet spring can quickly kill off young birds, whereas an early warm, dry spell means insects emerge exactly as the chicks hatch, providing plenty of food. So, whilst estates will have a rough idea of how many birds they hold, only when shooting starts will they really know how they have fared over the winter. It makes estimating the supply of birds very difficult and numbers vary considerably from year to year.

Grouse meat is tender, rich and full of flavour, with more than a hint of the heather that the birds grew up in. It's a true delicacy that's worthy of the eight-month wait between seasons.

Try: One-grouse starter for four (p. 189)

Tomato galette with rocket and Parmesan salad

One of my strongest food memories from childhood, and a very similar one to Jon's, is of the intoxicating smell in my grandpa's small greenhouse. As you opened the door and the warm air flooded over you, the smell of ripening tomatoes and their vines was so intense. Wooden salt and pepper pots sat in the corner of the greenhouse ready for an impromptu snack! To this day, I can't pick up a tomato without smelling it.

There are some fascinating different varieties being grown commercially these days and they do have distinctive flavours. Ranging from the classic vine through to Marmande, Coeur du Boeuf, Lemon Tiger, Red Tiger, Pineapple Marmande and the San Marzano. These specialist varieties are more common now and are worth a place on the shopping list. The San Marzano is one of my favourite tomatoes and is perfect for this tart. It has a high flesh content so the pastry stays crisper, and it delivers on flavour too.

SERVES 6 AS A STARTER

For the sauce
1 clove of garlic, minced
2 tbsp extra virgin olive oil
200ml tomato passata
100ml vegetable stock

For the galette
6 large, ripe San Marzano tomatoes (or more if the cherry type)
1 small clove of garlic, minced
½ tsp chopped thyme
½ tsp chopped oregano
2 tbsp extra virgin olive oil
6 rough puff pastry discs 15cm x 4mm, docked and frozen (see Basics p. 288)
Maldon sea salt and freshly ground black pepper

To serve
40g small rocket leaves
extra virgin olive oil
Maldon sea salt
Parmesan shavings
good balsamic vinegar

1. Preheat oven to 180°C.

2. To make the sauce, sweat the garlic in the olive oil for a couple of minutes and then add the passata and stock. Reduce until thick and spreadable.

3. For the galette, slice the tomatoes into even slices around 5mm thick. Mix the garlic, thyme and oregano with 2 tbsp of olive oil. Spread the puff pastry discs with the tomato sauce, leaving a 1cm clear border, and then arrange the tomato slices over the top, overlapping each slice slightly. Drizzle with the garlic and herb oil and season well. Bake on a heavy baking sheet for 15–18 minutes until the pastry is golden and crispy. Remove to a cooling rack and allow to cool for 5 minutes before serving. Warm rather than piping hot is what you are looking for.

4. To serve, toss the rocket leaves with a little oil and salt, place small mounds in the centre of each tart and add some Parmesan shavings. Drizzle a little of the vinegar onto the tarts and finish with some olive oil.

NOTE: This recipe makes enough sauce for around 20 portions but leftover sauce can be used for pizza or stirred into pasta.

Spider crab linguini with chilli, garlic and parsley

Even without the crab this is a great bowl of pasta, but the sweet shellfish brings it to another level entirely. If you are buying live crabs they will need killing before cooking (see below) and take 10 minutes per kilo to cook once the water has come back to the boil.

Of course, you don't have to use spider crab or prepare your own for this recipe. The yield from a brown crab is greater than from spider crabs but the spider crab is perhaps sweeter. Ready-picked white crab meat is easily available and is a perfectly acceptable alternative.

SERVES 4 AS A MAIN COURSE

4 tbsp extra virgin olive oil, plus extra to serve
2 cloves of garlic, sliced
1 red chilli, minced
100ml white wine
300ml vegetable stock (see Basics p. 284)
120g unsalted butter
320g good-quality dried linguini
250g fresh white crab meat, picked
2 tbsp chopped flat-leaf parsley
lemon juice
Maldon sea salt and freshly ground black
    pepper

NOTE: If using a live crab put it in the freezer for about 1 hour to render it insensible before dispatching. This is considered the most humane way to kill them. From the freezer it will be in a semi-dormant state and should not be moving – if it is still visibly active, put it back in for another 30 minutes. Lay the crab on its back and lift back the tail – a hole should be visible. Push a pointed instrument such as a screwdriver firmly through the hole into the body at an angle of 85 degrees. Repeat the process through the front nerve centre where there is a shallow depression, this time at an angle of 65 degrees towards the centre of the crab.

1. For the pasta, bring a large pot of water to the boil and salt heavily. While the water is boiling, take a large, heavy-bottomed sauté pan and sweat off the garlic and chilli in 2 tbsp of olive oil. Add the wine and reduce to a syrup, then add the stock and reduce again to approximately 75ml. Whisk in the butter and set aside.

2. Cook the pasta until al dente, add to the sauce and warm through. Finish by adding the white crab, parsley and the remaining 2 tbsp of olive oil.

3. Check the seasoning and adjust with salt, pepper and lemon juice.

4. Divide between four pasta bowls and finish with a final drizzle of olive oil.

Crab and fennel tart

The first full-time job I had in a commercial kitchen was at the Alverton Manor Hotel in Truro, Cornwall. It was a steep learning curve but I was lucky that the head chef invested his time in me, and I had the opportunity to not only hone my skills, but to taste many amazing dishes. I can remember my first taste of a number of things: my first oyster (still not keen, if I'm honest!); the first veal sweetbread (which I still adore); and my first lobster – a take on a classic Thermidor but made with a light butter sauce, Parmesan, tomato and basil. Just divine. Thank you, Chef!

This crab tart takes some of those Thermidor flavours, too, as it has the mustard, creamy sauce and cheese from the classic with the addition of tomato and a little chilli. The recipe allows you to have all the components ready in the fridge to mix and cook in just a few minutes.

SERVES 4 AS A STARTER

For the tart base

1 tbsp olive oil
½ small onion, finely diced
¼ bulb of fennel, finely diced
1 clove of garlic, minced
½ medium red chilli, deseeded and diced
50ml dry vermouth
40ml tomato passata
150ml vegetable stock (see Basics p. 284)
100ml double cream
1 tsp Dijon mustard
3 large, free-range egg yolks

To assemble

200g white crab meat, carefully picked through
   to check for shell
30g Parmesan, grated
4 x 10cm blind-baked rough puff pastry cases
   (see Basics p. 288)
1 tbsp chopped chives

To serve

1 courgette, peeled into thin ribbons, seeds and
   core discarded
2 tbsp pickled fennel (see Basics p. 286)
1 tbsp cider vinaigrette (see Basics p. 287)
50g mixed salad leaves

1. Preheat oven to 160°C.

2. In a heavy-based pan, heat the olive oil and then add the onion, fennel, garlic and chilli. Season with a pinch of salt and sweat the vegetables until tender. Add the vermouth and reduce until syrupy. Add the passata and cook out for a couple of minutes, then pour in the vegetable stock and allow to reduce by half. Add the cream and mustard and again reduce by half. Season to taste and then pour into a shallow container. Cover with cling film, pressing down onto the surface of the mix. Chill completely then beat in the egg yolks. Cover and return to the fridge.

3. When you are ready to serve, mix the tart base with the crab meat and chives and fill the tart cases. Place on a baking sheet and scatter the Parmesan over the top. Bake for 15 minutes until golden and just set. To serve, mix the courgette ribbons with the pickled fennel, dress with the vinaigrette and season. Toss the leaves through at the last minute and serve alongside the tarts.

One-grouse starter for four

Grouse is a very unique game bird with a strong flavour and rich dark meat; it also has a reputation for being pricey.

If it is something that you fancy trying but don't want to spend a large amount of money on, this recipe may be the one for you, as with a bit of work it makes one grouse go a long way.

SERVES 4 AS A STARTER

For the grouse
1 whole grouse, boned out as described below
2 tbsp olive oil
20g unsalted butter
2 sprigs of thyme
2 rashers smoked, streaky bacon, cut in half
Maldon sea salt and freshly ground black
   pepper

For the sausage
meat from the grouse legs
approx 75g boneless, skinless, diced chicken
   breast (the weight with the grouse-leg meat
   should total 120g)
½ tsp Maldon sea salt, finely ground (2g)
50ml double cream
liver from the grouse (if available), finely chopped
freshly ground black pepper

For the blackberries
200ml white wine pickling liquid (see Basics
   p. 286)
16 blackberries

For the sauté potato
1 baking potato, peeled and cut into 1cm dice
2 tbsp olive oil
10g unsalted butter
freshly ground black pepper

To serve
12 sprigs of watercress
2 tsp of the pickling liquid mixed with 2 tsp of
   olive oil to make a dressing

1. Preheat the oven to 180°C.

2. For the grouse, start by removing the
wishbone and then remove the legs and wings.
With a pair of kitchen scissors, cut out the
backbone to leave the two breasts as a crown.
Pull the skin off the legs and cut the meat from
the bone. Cut into a fine dice and chill.

3. To make the sausage, blend the diced grouse-
leg meat and the chicken in a small food

processor with the salt until it forms a paste, then
blend in the cream. Process as quickly as possible
to keep everything cold. Scrape into a bowl and
stir in the liver (if using) along with a good grind
of black pepper.

4. Lay a 30 cm x 40 cm sheet of cling film on
the work top with the narrow edge towards you.
Spoon on the grouse mousse on to the clingfilm
in a line, leaving a 5cm gap at each edge. Roll up
to form a tight sausage. Twist and tie the ends
to seal.

5. Heat the pickling liquid to a simmer, pour
over the blackberries and set aside.

6. Cook the potato at a simmer in salted water
until nearly tender. Drain in a sieve and place
back over the pan to steam dry.

7. Heat the olive oil for the grouse in a small
frying pan. Season the grouse and place in the
pan laying on one breast. Cook for 2 minutes
until nicely coloured, turn and repeat on the
other breast. Add the butter and thyme and
baste well. Lay the bacon rashers over the crown
and put the pan in the oven for 8–10 minutes.
Remove from the oven and transfer the grouse
to a plate to rest. Put the bacon back in the oven
to crisp up.

8. Place the sausage in a pan and cover with
water, bring to the simmer and cook for
approximately 6 minutes (core temperature
80°C) while the grouse is resting.

9. In a small, non-stick frying pan, heat the
oil and butter for the potato until the butter
is foaming, then add the potato. Season and
cook, turning frequently, until golden. Drain on
kitchen paper.

10. To serve, carve the breasts from the
grouse crown, trim and cut each breast in half
lengthwise. Unwrap the sausage and cut into
twelve even slices. Place a piece of breast and
three sausage slices in the centre of each of the
four plates, and lay a piece of crispy bacon across
the top. Scatter the blackberries and potatoes
around. Finish with the watercress and a drizzle
of the dressing.

Viennese tin loaf

There is something really special about baking bread; perhaps it is the combination of the science and the art or craft. This type of loaf is enriched with a little egg yolk and butter, which produces a thin, crisp crust with an even-textured, soft crumb. It lends itself to a sandwich, toasts beautifully and, if made into rolls, is great for a dinner breadbasket. There is a hint of sweetness but overall this is a neutral loaf. There isn't the buttery nature of brioche or the tang of sourdough so it makes for a very versatile offering.

Fresh yeast is, to my mind, preferable if you can find it, but if not use half the quantity of dried active yeast hydrated in the same way as described for fresh.

MAKES 2 LOAVES OR APPROXIMATELY 40 ROLLS

600g strong bread flour
340g plain flour
1½ tbsp Maldon sea salt, finely ground (22g)
30g fresh yeast
1½ tbsp caster sugar (20g)
540ml water (540g)
2½ large, free-range egg yolks (40g)
80g unsalted butter, melted

1. Preheat the oven to 200°C.

2. Sift the flours and salt into the mixer bowl. In a separate bowl, combine the yeast, sugar and 100ml of the water. Leave for 10 minutes until the mix starts to bubble. Whisk the egg yolks into the remaining water and add to the flour. Start mixing on a slow speed, then add the melted butter and the yeast mix. Mix on a low speed for 15 minutes, scrape down the dough hook and mix at a slightly higher speed for a further 5 minutes. On a Kitchen Aid mixer, speed 2 and then 4 is about right.

3. Cover the bowl with cling film and a tea towel. Leave to double in size. The time will vary according to room temperature. At 20°C it will be around 1 hour.

4. Divide the dough into two and shape into loaves for two 1lb loaf tins, or shape into 40g rolls to cook as batch rolls. Cover with oiled cling film and a tea towel. Again, allow to double in size.

5. Dust the tops of the loaves with flour. Bake for 10 minutes with a dish of water in the oven to create steam. Reduce the temperature to 160°C and cook for a further 15–20 minutes. Tip the loaves out of the tins and tap the bottom of the loaf – it should sound hollow. If not, return to the oven for a further 5 minutes. Once cooked, remove from the tins and place on a wire cooling rack. Resist the temptation to cut the loaves for 20 minutes if you can!

Honey-roast apricots with yoghurt sorbet

The apricot is one of my favourite summer fruits. I like all the stone fruits but apricots are particularly special because, unlike peaches and nectarines, we now get a good crop in Britain.

It is great to make the most of our home-grown fresh fruit while it is available, but high-quality dried apricots are a really useful store-cupboard item for both sweet and savoury dishes. Gently poached in a vanilla-flavoured syrup and then allowed plenty of time to plump up, they are a delight.

SERVES 6

NOTE: Start the yoghurt sorbet 24 hours ahead to allow time for the sorbet to freeze

For the yoghurt sorbet
1 vanilla pod
100g caster sugar
100ml water
500g full-fat natural yoghurt mixed with 100ml semi-skimmed milk
20g glycerine

For the almond streusel crumb
50g ground almonds
50g light muscovado sugar
50g soft patisserie flour
½ tsp (scant) Maldon sea salt, finely ground
50g unsalted butter

For the apricots
40g runny honey
30g unsalted butter
2 tsp lemon juice
1 vanilla pod (it can be one you have used the seeds from in another recipe)
12 fresh apricots, halved and stoned

1. Preheat oven to 160°C.

2. Start the sorbet a day or more ahead of time. Begin by making a vanilla syrup; split and scrape the vanilla pod, and add to a heavy-based pan with the sugar and water. Heat gently until the sugar has dissolved, then bring to the boil and cook for 2 minutes. Cool and strain. Whisk the syrup into the yoghurt and milk mix and use a stick blender or whisk to mix in the glycerine. Chill overnight and then blend again before churning. Churn in an ice cream machine and then transfer to a plastic container or tin and freeze.

3. Next, make the streusel crumb. In a small bowl, sift together the dry ingredients. Rub in the butter and bring together into a rough dough. Press out on to a Silpat mat or baking parchment, placing another piece of parchment on top to prevent sticking, and roll out to a thickness of around 5mm. Slide onto a tray and bake for 10–12 minutes until golden brown. Allow to cool on the tray. This is a simple way of adding crunch to many desserts and it will keep in an airtight tin for around a week.

4. Turn the oven up to 230°C. In a small roasting tin, heat the honey, butter and lemon until the mixture just starts to simmer. Add the vanilla pod. Toss the apricot halves in the honey mix to coat thoroughly. Roast at 230°C for 10 minutes, basting every few minutes with the honey mix. The roasting time may vary according to how ripe the fruit is.

5. To serve, allow four apricot halves per portion. Place in a small bowl with a little of the buttery juices, top with a ball of the sorbet and sprinkle the streusel over the top.

09 | September

Haervestmonath – harvest month, when the main crops were brought in

The arrival of September, the first month of our autumn season, is inevitably a bittersweet affair. Our good friend summer is just so much fun that it's always with a touch of sadness we say farewell. But then, just as we're getting a bit gloomy about the whole thing, autumn knocks on the door, asking if we can come out to play in a beautiful new landscape of bright colours, crisp mornings and intense flavours.

September is kind enough to ease us in to the new season gently and, even compared to August, it's a bountiful month. The light, sweet tastes of summer start to make way for the richer, earthier flavours of autumn. So, we'll probably see the last of the strawberries and cherries being replaced by the first squashes and nuts.

The hedgerows are packed full of foraging treats, too, with plump blackberries, sharp damsons and tart crab apples all abundant. You're certain to have something interesting and edible growing wild near you.

Not only do the late-summer fruits and early-autumn nuts create a delightful gluttony of produce, but the weather in September is pretty reliable, too. In fact, if you look at the recent historical rainfall data in the UK there's little to choose between August and September. So, with a bit of luck, there's plenty of good weather still to come and we can be out and about (and fairly dry) for a good few weeks yet.

Enjoy your September; it's usually an absolute humdinger of a month and a splendid curtain-raiser to autumn.

Out & About
scrumping

Food & Foraging
sweetcorn, damsons and sloes,
  blackberries

Feasts & Festivals
Pannage Season
Harvest Festival

Vegetables
globe artichokes, marrow, peppers,
  sweetcorn

Fruit
apples, pears

Fish
lobster, scallops

Meat
autumn lamb, rabbit

Hedgerow Harvest
blackberries, crab apples, damsons

Recipes
Sweetcorn and potato chowder
Lobster and charred sweetcorn risotto
Blue cheese beignets with spiced damson dip
Brined pork chops with roasted red pepper and
  courgette salad
Blackberry and caramelized apple trifle
Bramley apple and sultana chutney

'S crump' was originally the name for a slightly withered apple that had fallen from the tree – the best fruit for making cider or 'scrumpy'. But it evolved to become a colloquial term for stealing fruit of any kind, particularly apples.

I'm not seriously suggesting you go pilfering from your neighbour's orchard this month. But September is usually the start of the apple season and is definitely the time to start thinking about broadening your appley horizons. With more than 2,500 named varieties of British apple there's no excuse not to try some new ones and your local farmers' market is the ideal place to start.

It's also a good time to look for apple trees in your local hedgerow. Depending on the species, they might be either a genuinely wild species or grown from pips discarded by past travellers. Your earliest and most likely find, however, is a crab apple. Although unsuited to eating raw, these small, sour and woody relatives of our orchard apples are high in pectin, making them an ideal base for preserves and jellies.

There's a famous age-old Anglo-Saxon verse called 'The Nine Herbs Charm' – something of a cross between a poem, a spell and an old wives' tale. The charm was mentioned in it were used as a recipe for a salve to treat a variety of illnesses, poisoning and infection. It references nine herbs, many of which are now known to have genuine medicinal properties (including mugwort and camomile), but the seventh ingredient mentioned is *wergulu* – an Old English name for the crab apple.

Try: Bramley apple and sultana chutney (p. 215)

F rom mid-August to the end of September, the arrival of the first succulent sweetcorn is perhaps the earliest strong hint that summer will soon be at an end. This tall variety of maize ripens in the late-season sun, its kernels turning from pale white to golden yellow as autumn approaches.

With corn, freshness is everything. In common with other sweet vegetables like asparagus and peas, once harvested it's a race against time to get it to your plate and it's definitely worth buying at an early-morning farmers' market for that recently picked guarantee. If you're not planning to eat it on the same day as you buy it, strip the kernels off the cob with a sharp knife and freeze them to preserve the sweetness.

Look for plump, firm cobs, wrapped tightly in fresh green leaves and with dark brown silky tendrils attached to the husk. A creamy white liquid should ooze from cut grains. If the liquid is watery then the corn isn't yet ripe.

It's difficult to beat freshly barbecued corn on the cob, smeared in butter with a grinding of black pepper, but its robust kernels make it a versatile ingredient, just as suited to flash-frying as slow cooking.

Try:
Sweetcorn and potato chowder (p. 204)
Lobster and charred sweetcorn risotto (p. 207)

F rom September to mid-October, damson trees produce clusters of small, dusty violet plums. Few hedgerow finds are more exciting or productive than a tree in full fruit, and in a good year you'll be able to gather several kilos in minutes.

Sloes, another relative of our domestic plum, usually arrive a few weeks later and can be found as late as November. They are the fruits of the blackthorn which we saw flowering back in early spring. Their thorny branches make this wild harvest a slightly more hazardous, though no less rewarding experience.

Both shrubs are fairly common in well-established hedgerows and their small, juicy fruits are easily identified. I'd counsel against any kind of taste test. Even in their prime, bitter tannins mean both damsons and sloes can be tart enough to make your eyes water. But damsons are the sweeter of the two and lend themselves particularly well to that home-made classic, damson jam, as they are naturally high in pectin. Sloes invariably require rather more sugar to be palatable but also make a decent jelly to accompany cold meats.

It's traditional to wait until the first frost before picking sloes – some say it improves the flavour. However, since your main problem is likely to be finding a suitable bush and harvesting it before anyone else does, you're usually better off picking them as soon as they look purple, plump and ripe. Give them a squeeze, and as long as there is plenty of juicy softness, they are ready. Both fruits can be used to make excellent flavoured gin. There are few finer winter tipples and I'm rarely without a flask of one or the other during the shooting season. After many years of trial and error (and a comprehensive tasting session that we arranged in a Dorset pub the year before this book was written) I settled on the following ratio of fruits to sugar and spirit. (Every countryman or woman will have their own preferred recipe but I find this produces a reliably drinkable drop with plenty of fruitiness, without being cloyingly sweet)

Take 450g of fruit, 200g caster sugar (250g for sloes) and about 750ml of gin. Lightly wash the fruit and prick each one a couple of times with a needle or fork. Place into a litre jar or empty gin bottle. Pour in the sugar and top up with as much of the gin as it takes to fill the bottle. Screw the lid on and give it all a good shake. Store in a cool, dark cupboard and give the bottle another couple of turns every week for at least two months, then strain out the fruit and return the liquid to the bottle. The result is a sweet, ruby red spirit. Delicious neat, it will also add a fruity kick to mulled wine and, added to champagne or a good sparkling wine, it makes a classy Christmas cocktail (see December). Don't feel obliged to polish it off in one go – it will keep for years and significantly improves with age.

Try: Blue cheese beignets with spiced damson dip (p. 209)

Food & Foraging | Blackberries

The discovery of plump, darkest-purple blackberries in a September hedgerow can transform a genteel country walk into a juice-splattered scoffing session. They're probably most families' earliest experience of foraging and, whether you're in town or the countryside, you're certain to have some growing within a short stroll of home at this time of year.

Of course, you risk the odd thorny scratch when collecting blackberries, but they should be worn as badges of honour – it's unavoidable if you want to reach those truly prize specimens.

The juiciest berries (and those that ripen earliest) are usually the ones at the tip of each stem, with those further down ripening as the month progresses. If possible, take fruits above waist height (to avoid any tainted by animals) and, especially if you're picking along a busy roadside, it's worth a quick rinse before tucking in. (As with July's raspberries and any other soft fruits, wash them gently as it is easy to damage the ripest berries under a high-pressure tap.)

Blackberries start to spoil quickly so are best eaten on the day they are picked. However, unlike some other soft fruits, they do freeze reasonably well. If you manage a bumper haul and are planning to make jam or crumble at a later date, spread the berries out on a baking tray and freeze them before bagging up.

According to folklore, Michaelmas (the Feast of St Michael) is the last day that blackberries should be picked. It was said that, because Michael kicked Lucifer out of heaven, the devil spits (or worse) on the fruits and they will soon be spoiled or even poisonous. Michaelmas now falls on 29 September but in the old calendar it was 10 October, and while, of course, they never turn toxic, the fruits do tend to be past their best by mid-autumn. Because of this, it's also traditional to end a Michaelmas feast with a pie made with the last blackberries of the season.

Try: Blackberry and caramelized apple trifle (p. 213)

Harvest Festival (late September)

September has long been seen as the end of summer, the beginning of autumn and the start of the harvest season. Many of the most important crops, particularly grains, were (and still are) gathered this month. In fact, the word 'harvest' or '*haerfest*' simply means 'autumn' in Old English.

In pre-Christian times, the autumn equinox on 22 or 23 September was celebrated as Mabon. It was the second of three harvest celebrations (the other two being Lammas in August and Samhain in October), and the most important in terms of preparing for the colder months ahead. It was the culmination of a year's hard work and cause for celebration – a good harvest could literally make the difference between life and death over a long winter – and the feast that followed was one of the most significant events of the agricultural year.

Doubtless since the Christian faith became predominant in Britain, prayers of thanksgiving have been offered up during September, but the formal Harvest Festival is actually a relatively modern creation. In 1843 Robert Hawker, a Cornish vicar of some repute, announced a special service of thanks for the harvest. The idea caught on and was quickly adopted by other churches across the country.

Harvest Festival now takes place on the first Sunday after the harvest moon – the full moon closest to the autumn equinox. (The next full moon is called the hunter's moon, probably given its name because bright moonlight was helpful to hunters gathering wild meat ahead of the winter months.)

Connected to the Harvest Festival, many churches and local communities still host harvest suppers, also known as mell suppers. The mell (or neck) was the last patch of wheat in the farmer's fields. The ceremonial 'Cutting of the Mell' signified the end of the labours and the beginning of the celebratory feast hosted by the landowner to thank his workers. The removal of this final sheaf also signalled that local people were free to gather any leftover wheat from the fields. The practice, known as 'gleaning', was a valuable resource for poorer families at the time.

Feasts & Festivals | Pannage Season (September)

Because many of our livestock-farming methods now operate efficiently all year round, with the exception of spring lamb (see March), we don't usually think of reared meat as being seasonal. But in leafy Hampshire there is a particular porky produce that is worth looking out for throughout the autumn months – and it all starts in September with an ancient land management system that is still relevant today.

It's autumn in the New Forest and the scene has hardly changed since the twelfth centure. Traditional breeds of pig are roaming freely on the Hampshire heathland, foraging and snuffling through leafy undergrowth. They are hunting primarily for acorns, but beech nuts, chestnuts and crab apples are also highlights of the free porcine picnic. It's a practice dating back many hundreds of years, to when certain inhabitants of the forest, known as 'commoners', claimed their right to graze pigs in the national park. But it's more than just an age-old custom – as well as getting a free meal, the pigs are doing good for the more famous residents of the forest, because acorns are poisonous to the wild ponies and cattle.

The practice is known as 'pannage' or the 'Common of Mast' and it takes place every autumn, usually starting in September. The local forest wardens or verderers, together with the Forestry Commission, decide when the pannage season will begin, depending on the weather and when the acorns start dropping. The season usually lasts for sixty days, ending in November. In some years, however, trees produce unusually large numbers of acorns and nuts. This mysterious event is known as 'masting' and the cause of it is not completely understood. But in mast years the pannage season is usually extended to December to ensure all of the acorns can be eaten.

At the end of the season, the pigs are 'finished' on a diet of whey and barley before going to slaughter. The resulting meat, pannage pork, is truly unique, with a coarse-grained texture and unusually dark appearance. It can be almost black if the pig has had a particularly acorn-rich diet. You'll find pannage pork in specialist butchers for about two months after the end of the season.

Try: Brined pork chops with roasted red pepper and courgette salad (p. 211)

Sweetcorn and potato chowder

Sweetcorn was one of the crops grown on the farm in Cornwall where I grew up and I remember it as a private maze, a hunting ground for rabbits, and fun to harvest. Sweetcorn is widely available, but one thing I have noticed is that a lot of corn sold today is marked as 'super sweet'. Personally, I would avoid these varieties as they can border on sickly and I find that they don't balance well in most dishes.

This chowder recipe is a comforting bowl of soup just as it is, but it can also form the base for something more substantial. Steam open some clams in the broth or add some chunky pieces of white fish. Alternatively, slice roast partridge breasts onto the soup for something entirely different – this is how I served it at the restaurant, with a good drizzle of reduced game stock to finish it off.

SERVES 4 AS A STARTER

150g pancetta lardons
2 cloves of garlic, crushed
2 large shallots, diced
100ml white wine
500ml vegetable stock (see Basics p. 284)
250g waxy potatoes, diced, prepared weight
500g sweetcorn kernels, fresh or frozen
20g unsalted butter
Maldon sea salt and freshly ground black
  pepper

1. Sweat off the lardons until the fat starts to render out and then add the garlic and shallots. Continue to cook until the shallots are soft. Add the white wine and reduce to a syrup, then add the vegetable stock and reduce by half. Add the diced potato and cook at a gentle simmer until barely tender.

2. While the potato is cooking, place half the sweetcorn in a pan, cover with water and add a pinch of salt and the butter. Simmer for 5 minutes and then purée in a food processor. Pass the purée through a fine sieve and add the purée and the remaining corn to thepan with the potato and stock. Season to taste with salt and pepper.

Lobster and charred sweetcorn risotto

Sweet, succulent shellfish folded into creamy rice with the added texture and flavour of charred corn, this really does have a touch of luxury to it but it is also a good way of making a lobster go a long way. Ideally you want to buy a live lobster to be able to control the cooking. When you add the meat to the risotto, it should only be partly cooked; that way it can poach gently in the hot rice, keeping it moist and tender. If you are going to use cooked lobster it only wants to warm through, so add the meat when the rice is cooked, turn off the heat and then follow the rest of the last step.

SERVES 4 AS A MAIN COURSE

1 live lobster, 600–700g

For a quick lobster stock

50ml olive oil

shell, head and legs from the lobster, roughly
   chopped

100ml white wine or dry vermouth

1 small onion, roughly chopped

1 clove of garlic, smashed

50ml tomato passata

pinch of saffron

1 tsp fennel seeds

1 roasted red pepper (from a jar is fine)

2l water

For the corn

2 cobs of sweetcorn, 1 if very large

olive oil

Maldon sea salt, finely ground

For the risotto

50ml olive oil

1 medium onion, finely diced

1 clove of garlic, finely sliced

250g risotto rice, preferably Vialone Nano

125ml white wine

approximately 1.5l lobster stock or vegetable
   stock (see Basics p. 284)

50g unsalted butter

lemon juice

1 tbsp chopped chives

Maldon sea salt

1. Place the lobster in the freezer for about 1 hour to render it insensible, if there are still signs of movement, freeze for another 30 minutes. Use a large, heavy, sharp knife to pierce the lobster, pushing swiftly through the cross on its head. Meanwhile, bring a large pan of water to the boil. Salt the water heavily and get ready a roasting tin with a good amount of ice and a few centimetres of cold water to chill the lobster after cooking.

2. Cook the lobster in the boiling water for 3 minutes, then transfer to the pan of ice and allow to cool, turning occasionally. Once the lobster is cool enough to handle, it can be shelled. Twist and pull the tail away from the body, twist off the claws and the legs. Turn the tail upside down in your hand and, with a pair of kitchen scissors, cut down the centre of the shell. Carefully prise the shell back with your thumbs, working from the head end towards the tail to release the meat. Make a small cut on the top side at the very end of the tail to reveal the end of the intestinal tract, pull it out and discard.

3. Twist the claws from the jointed arms and crack them with the back of a heavy knife, before prising out the meat. There is a plastic-like piece of cartilage in each claw that needs pulling out and discarding. Separate the joints on the arms and remove the meat using a lobster pick. Pick the meat from the bigger joints on the legs. Cut the meat from the the claws and tail into chunks and chill. Roughly cut up the shell and head.

4. To make the stock, heat the oil in a large pan and add all the lobster shell. Cook, stirring until any moisture has evaporated and the shell starts to fry. Add the wine and reduce to a syrup. Add the remaining ingredients. Bring to the boil and then reduce the heat to a simmer. Cook for 45 minutes, then strain into a clean pan.

5. Rub the corn cobs with a little oil and then season with salt. Heat a griddle pan and char the corn, turning and pressing down until there are blackened spots all over the cob. Allow to cool and then carefully slice the kernels from the cob.

6. To make the risotto, sweat the onion and garlic in the oil until completely soft. Add the rice and cook for 2–3 minutes until translucent. Add the wine and cook until absorbed.

7. In the meantime, bring the stock back to a simmer. Add the hot stock a ladleful at a time, stirring to break down the outer layer of the rice. The rice should have some bite still and a creamy, starchy texture. If you run out of stock, you can use hot water to finish the cooking.

8. When the rice is very nearly cooked, stir in the corn and the lobster meat. Bring back to a simmer and then turn off the heat. Scatter the butter over the surface and leave to rest for 5 minutes. Put back on a low heat and stir to mix. Season with salt and lemon juice. Check one of the largest pieces of lobster to see if it is cooked and opaque in the centre. Stir in the chives.

Blue cheese beignets with
spiced damson dip

The damson, once moderated with heat and sugar, has such an incredible depth of flavour, it certainly makes for something spectacular in the autumn. Cooked into jam, made into pies or crumbles or turned into damson cheese, it will provide rich flavours for both sweet and savoury dishes. A damson sauce for wild duck is excellent and a damson jam tart makes a sweet, sticky teatime treat.

I have gone down the savoury route for this recipe, taking some cues from the old-fashioned fruit cheeses. Quince cheese is perhaps the most common, either in its British guise or the slightly more textured Spanish version, membrillo. A slice with a strong cheddar or crumbly blue is a perfect pairing.

The buns are based on a classic choux pastry recipe with the addition of the cheese and some mustard.

MAKES APPROXIMATELY 40 BUNS

For the damson dip

1 cinnamon stick, broken up
10 black peppercorns, crushed
1 bay leaf
1 tsp dried chilli flakes
75ml red wine
200g damsons
50g caster sugar
Maldon sea salt and freshly ground black
  pepper

For the buns

125ml water
125ml milk
100g unsalted butter, cold, diced
2 tsp Maldon sea salt, finely ground
1 tsp caster sugar
140g plain flour
4 large, free-range eggs, beaten (220g)
1½ tbsp Dijon mustard
100g crumbly blue cheese (Devon Blue, Stilton,
  Bath Blue or similar), coarsely grated
25g Parmesan, grated
freshly ground black pepper
15g Parmesan, finely grated

1. Preheat oven to 200˚C.

2. Tie all the spices for the dip in a square of muslin. Combine the wine, damsons and sugar in a heavy-based pan and heat gently until the sugar has dissolved. Add the spice bag and cook on a gentle simmer until the fruit has broken down and the stones are released.

3. Squeeze all the liquid from the spice bag and then rub the fruit through a coarse sieve. Pick out all the stones and add any pulp back to the liquid. Check the consistency and season with salt and pepper. The dip wants to be like runny jam so it clings to the buns but isn't too thick. If it is too thin, just return to the heat and simmer a bit more.

4. To make the buns, put the water, milk, butter, salt and sugar in a pan and bring to the boil. Boil for 1 minute and then add the flour all in one go. Cook for a further minute, beating the mix hard with a wooden spoon. The mix should become shiny and fairly dry-looking.

5. Remove from the heat, allow to cool for a couple of minutes and beat in half the egg. Add the remaining egg gradually until you have a smooth paste. Add the mustard, blue cheese and the 25g of Parmesan along with a good grind of black pepper. Transfer the mix to a piping bag with a 1cm nozzle.

6. Pipe 2cm balls onto a tray lined with baking parchment or a Silpat mat. Bake for 15–18 minutes until crisp and a deep golden brown. Sprinkle the finely grated Parmesan over the buns and return to the oven for 2 minutes. This will give a crisp, savoury top to the buns.

Brined pork chops with roasted red pepper and courgette salad

Jon has talked about the pannage pork from the New Forest but you don't have to use that for this recipe, just make sure to buy the best free-range pork you can get. A reasonable amount of fat is a good sign and the meat should be fairly dry and firm.

Brining meat gets the flavours right into the muscle and also helps to make for more succulent eating. The science bit is that a 5.5 per cent brine solution partially dissolves some of the protein structure and increases the amount of water the muscle cells can hold. The water that flows from the brine into the cells also contains salt and any flavourings in the brine. The meat still loses moisture when cooked but this is partly offset by the extra it has absorbed from the brine. If the science of cooking fascinates you, then Harold McGee's *On Food and Cooking* is well worth adding to the book collection.

SERVES 4 AS A MAIN COURSE

NOTE: Allow 12 hours for the pork to brine

For the brine

1l water
55g Maldon sea salt
100ml cider
1 clove of garlic
2 sprigs of sage
2 sprigs of thyme

For the pepper and courgette salad

2 red peppers
2 medium courgettes
1 tsp Maldon sea salt, finely ground
50ml pickling liquid (see Basics p. 286)

For the chops

4 thick pork chops, rind removed
freshly ground black pepper
2 tbsp olive oil
30g unsalted butter
2 sprigs of sage
1 clove of garlic

To serve

60g watercress
2 tbsp cider vinaigrette (see Basics p. 287)
Maldon sea salt and freshly ground black
  pepper

1. To make the brine, heat half the water to a simmer and add the salt. Stir well until the salt has dissolved. Add the cider, garlic and herbs and bring to the boil. Remove from the heat and add the remaining water. Chill until completely cold.

2. Place the chops in a mixing bowl or deep plastic tub and pour the cold brine over the top. Refrigerate for 12 hours.

3. For the salad, char the peppers under a hot grill until blistered with patches of black all over. Remove and place in a plastic bag for 10 minutes to steam. Rub off the charred skin and deseed the peppers. Cut into 1cm-wide strips. Use a speed peeler to slice ribbons from the courgettes, working around and discarding the seedy core. Place the ribbons in a bowl and toss with the salt. Leave for 10 minutes then rinse off and dry with some kitchen paper. Pour on the pickling liquid and leave for 30 minutes. Drain, and mix in the peppers.

4. Remove the chops from the brine and pat dry with kitchen paper. Season with just black pepper. Heat a heavy-based pan and add the oil. Stand the chops in the pan on the fat to give some colour and start to render the fat. Once the fat is golden, lay the chops down and seal well. Turn and seal the other side. Add the butter, sage and garlic, baste well and turn occasionally. They will take around 4–6 minutes in total. The meat wants to be just cooked through; a core temperature of 62–68°C is a good range. Allow the pork to rest in a warm place for 10 minutes.

5. To serve, toss the watercress with the pepper and courgette mix, and dress with the cider vinaigrette. Check and adjust the seasoning. Serve the chops with the salad, pouring any juices from the meat over the chops.

Blackberry and caramelized apple trifle

For those of us who grew up in the 1970s the word 'trifle' seems to refer to two dishes bearing the same name: one made from scratch with fresh ingredients, and one where everything came out of tins and packets.

When you make a trifle from scratch, it is a real treat, albeit one that takes a little time. You can tackle things in stages, though, and you do want to give the jelly time to set before adding the custard.

SERVES 10–12

NOTE: Start this recipe 24 hours ahead to allow for setting time

For the sponge (you will only need half for one trifle but it will freeze well)
4 large, free-range eggs
115g caster sugar
125g plain flour, sifted
80g unsalted butter, melted and cooled

For the caramelized apple
20g unsalted butter
4 Cox or Braeburn apples, peeled, cored and each cut into 8 wedges
2 tbsp caster sugar

For the brandy syrup
45ml cider brandy or brandy
45ml water
45g caster sugar

For the jelly

300ml apple juice
6 leaves of gelatine, soaked in cold water
300ml sieved blackberry purée
sugar and lemon juice to taste

For the custard

465ml double cream
90ml semi-skimmed milk
2 vanilla pods
9 large, free-range egg yolks
125g caster sugar
2¼ leaves of gelatine, soaked in cold water.

To garnish

100ml double cream plus 2 tsp semi-skimmed
   milk
12 blackberries
gold lustre powder and flaked almonds if you
   choose

1. Preheat oven to 160°C.

2. Start by making the sponge. In a stand mixer with whisk, or with an electric whisk, beat the whole eggs with the caster sugar until well aerated – this will take around 10–12 minutes on a high speed. Take the sifted flour and sift it again onto the surface of the egg, then fold in using a balloon whisk. When the flour is half incorporated, add the cooled butter and fold that in. Pour the batter into a greased and floured 30cm x 20cm Bakewell tin. Bake for 10–12 minutes until well risen and firm to a light press. Turn out onto a wire rack to cool.

3. Next, caramelize the apple. Heat half the butter in a non-stick frying pan and add half the apple. Sprinkle on half the sugar and cook over a moderately high heat, shaking the pan and turning the apple frequently. When the apple is a deep golden colour, transfer to a plate to cool. Wipe out the pan with kitchen paper and repeat with the remaining apple.

4. Mix all the ingredients for the brandy syrup together, stirring until the sugar is dissolved.

5. Trim the outside edges from the sponge, reserve half and cut the remaining half cut in two lengthwise, then slice into 1.5cm-thick slices.

Line the bottom of a glass trifle bowl with slices of the sponge, coming about one-third of the way up the sides. You want a double thickness in the centre to get the right balance of boozy sponge to the other layers. Brush the sponge all over with the brandy syrup and then lay in the apple. Place in the fridge to chill.

6. For the jelly, heat half the apple juice in a small pan. Squeeze the excess water from the gelatine and stir it into the hot apple juice. Make sure all the gelatine has dissolved and then pass through a fine sieve into a jug. Whisk in the remaining apple juice and the blackberry purée. Add sugar and lemon juice to taste. Place in the fridge to chill for 30 minutes. The jelly wants to be just starting to set on the edges. Give the jelly a good whisk and pour over the apples. Return the bowl to the fridge to set overnight.

7. To make the custard, combine the cream and milk in a large heavy-based saucepan. Split the vanilla pods and scrape out the seeds, adding the seeds and pods to the cream. Heat the mix, stirring occasionally, until it just comes to a simmer. Take off the heat, cover and leave to infuse for 30 minutes.

8. Whisk the yolks with the sugar in a large bowl. Reheat the cream and gradually whisk into the yolks. Return the custard to the pan and cook out on a medium heat, stirring constantly in a 'figure-of-eight' motion as well as circles around the edge of the pan. Continue to cook until the custard has thickened but not started to scramble. Squeeze the excess water from the gelatine and whisk into the custard. Pour into a clean bowl and cover the surface with cling film. Cool to room temperature. Give the custard a good stir and then pour onto the jelly layer, shaking the trifle bowl to even the surface. Return to the fridge to set for at least 4 hours.

9. To garnish, whip the cream and milk to soft peaks and transfer to a piping bag fitted with a large star nozzle. Pipe rosettes of cream onto the custard and then add the blackberries. If you really want to go to town, brush a little gold powder on the berries and add some flaked almonds before serving.

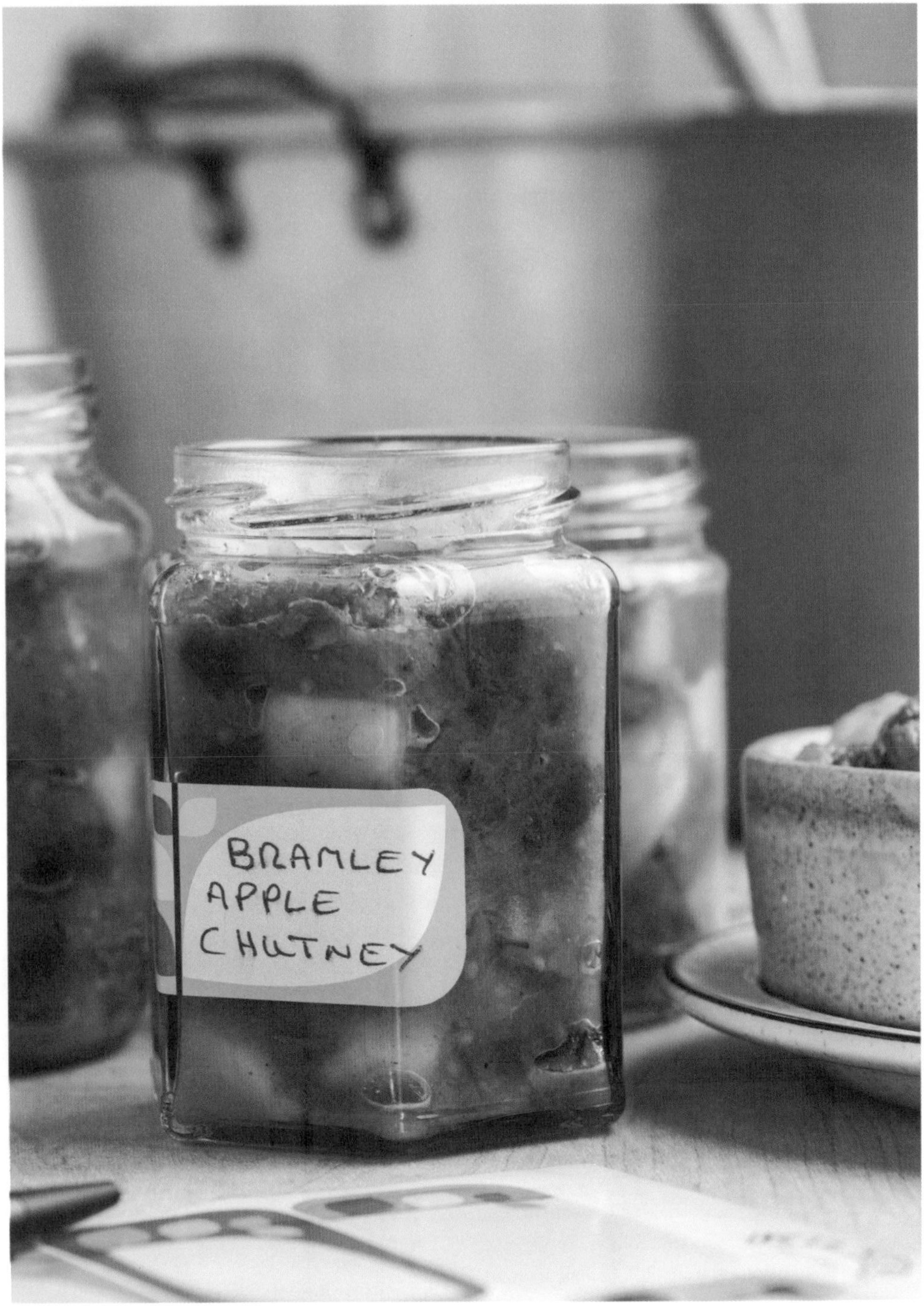
BRAMLEY
APPLE
CHUTNEY

Bramley apple and sultana chutney

The Bramley is one of the earlier British apples to be harvested. The season generally starts in late August with Discoveries and ends in November with Braeburns. It is the quintessential cooking apple, used extensively in pies and crumbles across the country. Its flesh is tart and breaks down into a fluffy texture when cooked, making it perfect for many desserts, but it also lends itself to delicious chutneys.

Don't forget to keep a jar or two for later in the game season, as it is a good match with a game terrine. For me, though, it's a chutney that goes perfectly on a cheese board. A piece of good, mature cheddar, maybe some walnut bread or home-made digestive biscuits, and you have a great way to finish a meal.

MAKES 3 OR 4 STANDARD JARS

2 tbsp olive oil

1 onion, diced

1 tsp ground cumin

1 tsp ground ginger

1 tsp yellow mustard seeds

1kg Bramley apples, peeled, cored, cut into 8 and sliced

120g sultanas or raisins

140ml cider vinegar

55g caster sugar

55g dark soft brown sugar

Maldon sea salt and freshly ground black pepper

1. Sweat the onion in the olive oil until soft. Add the spices and cook, stirring for one minute. Add the remaining ingredients and stir together well. Season with salt and pepper. Bring to the boil and then simmer, stirring occasionally, until thick and fairly dry.

2. Chill a small sample and taste. Adjust the seasoning and the sweet/sour balance by adding a little more sugar or vinegar as required. Both the acidity in the apples and the type of vinegar will make a difference. The flavour is quite dramatically different when the chutney is cold, so it is worth taking the time to chill the sample before tasting it.

3. Decant the chutney into sterile jars while it is still hot. The chutney does eat well as soon as it is cold but gets even better if you can manage to keep it for a month or two!

10 | October

Winmonath – wine month, when grapes were harvested

I f September was the curtain-raiser to autumn then October is definitely the main feature.

This month, our green and pleasant land puts on a show of brilliant oranges, browns, golds and reds in a visual and epicurean spectacular.

The long, hot days of summer are definitely behind us now but they've left an embarrassment of edible riches. With winter just beyond the horizon, October is a month when preserving our bounty for the colder months is even more important. Chutneys, jams and pickles are all promoted to the top of our seasonal to-do list.

On the vegetable patch, there's more than enough to keep us busy, too: marrows, pumpkins and squashes all thrive at this time of year; while in the orchard, those delicate soft fruits have all now given way to hardier, but certainly no less delicious, apples and pears.

But perhaps the most exciting thing about October is that Mother Nature invariably flings opens the door of her wild larder and invites us to stuff ourselves silly. It's one of the best months to be outdoors foraging, with hedgerows fit to burst with ripe berries and nuts, and the mild, damp conditions mean mushrooms abound on forest floors. We can literally take our pick from hundreds of wonderfully named fungi, including puffballs, penny buns and chicken of the woods. Scallops and mussels are plump and plentiful and there is game aplenty as pheasant joins duck, partridge and grouse on the autumnal menu.

October's weather also helps make it a great month to be outdoors. Hopes of a seriously hot day have all but vanished, but it's surprisingly common to have a sustained spell of sunshine towards the middle of the month (it's known as 'St Luke's little summer', named after the saint's day which falls on the eighteenth). The days are getting noticeably shorter by now, but with all of this food around we can appreciate a little extra time in the kitchen.

So, with respectable weather and no shortage of produce to choose from, we can look forward to filling our boots in October.

O ur ancient hedgerows are a haven for Britain's wildlife. These complex ecosystems act as an important refuge for all kinds of creatures. For the forager, they're brimming with fruits and nuts in early autumn and for the aesthete, they are also undoubtedly at their most beautiful this month.

The word 'hedge' comes from '*haeg*', the Anglo-Saxon name for the hawthorn. One of the reasons the hawthorn was so commonly planted is that its wood burns slowly and produces lots of heat; it was the perfect fuel for stoves and fires.

Hedgerows traditionally marked the boundaries between estates and parishes. Some are the remnants of ancient woodlands, but most were planted by landowners keen to protect their territory and to prevent livestock escaping. In particular, the Inclosure Acts of the eighteenth and nineteenth centuries led to hedges being planted all over the country.

You might think they're a common sight, but after the Second World War thousands of miles – up to one-third – of Britain's hedgerows were lost as a result of modern agricultural methods. The industrialization of food and mechanized farming meant a demand for bigger fields in which large machinery could easily operate. These days we have a deeper understanding of the hedgerow's importance as a habitat and they are protected by law.

Hedgerows are home to hundreds of different plant and animal species. They also provide safe corridors for wildlife to move between larger areas of woodland. So, following a hedge line can make a particularly interesting and attractive autumnal ramble, revealing no end of trees, shrubs, small mammals, insects and birds.

The colours you'll see at this time of year are the result of a three-way chemical ebb and flow that takes place every autumn. During the summer, two chemicals are produced for photosynthesis (the process by which plants 'breathe', converting water and carbon dioxide into sugar and oxygen). The first chemical, chlorophyll, is green, and the second, carotene, is yellow. To produce chlorophyll, trees need both warmth and light, so when the cooler days and longer nights of autumn arrive, chlorophyll production slows. As the green chemical fades away, the yellow carotene remains. Anthocyanins, a third chemical group, are produced when sugars in the leaf become concentrated and trapped in the leaves as the tree prepares for winter. This is the red that you see – it also pigments apples and grapes.

While you're enjoying your ramble, try working out the age of your local hedgerow. Hooper's Hedgerow Hypothesis works on the rule that one new large species will establish itself in a hedge every century. Pace out a thirty-metre stretch of hedge, count the number of different woody species you find and multiply that number by 100 – you'll have the approximate age, of your hedge. The oldest man-made hedgerows in the UK are thought to have been planted nearly a thousand years ago.

Food & Foraging | Beetroot

Many of us will have suffered at the hands of school dinner ladies serving up vinegary pickled purple mush, made no more appealing by the obligatory crinkle-cutting. In the worst cases, it will have been enough to put you off this root for years. But if you haven't tried it recently, rediscovering the sweet, earthy flavours of good-quality, fresh beetroot will be a revelation.

Crunchy, raw beetroot adds exciting flavour, texture and colour to salads – don't forget to include its young leaves, which are also edible. Roasted whole, beets develop an even more intense, sweet flavour and are particularly adaptable – as happy accompanying a joint of roast meat as they are being blitzed into an alternative hummus or even grated into a 'healthy' chocolate brownie.

Larger roots can become slightly bitter as they age so, if you have a choice, stick with younger ones, about the size of a golf ball or plum. The peeled and vacuum-packed (but un-pickled) varieties available in many supermarkets are actually not bad if you'd rather avoid Purple Hand Syndrome, an unsightly but otherwise harmless affliction suffered by those of us who are too cheap to pay for anyone else to do the peeling.

Beetroot has seen a recent boom and bust as a result of its unfortunate labelling as another 'superfood' (a personal bugbear that I touched on back in March). In fact, there are some reliable studies that suggest a number of health benefits connected with eating beetroot, but to list any of them here would be to do a disservice to all the other healthy, nutritious and vitamin-packed autumn vegetables.

In season from mid-summer through to the winter months, October is the peak of beetroot productivity, when flavours are sky high but prices rock bottom.

Try: Beetroot, mascarpone and horseradish tart (p. 226)

Food & Foraging | Medlars and quince

Lots of our native fruits are in season this month, with apples and pears being the nation's autumnal favourites. But if you fancy something a little different, there are two old English cousins that you should look out for in October – medlars and quince.

In Elizabethan times, before many of our now-common fruit varieties were introduced, medlars and quince were both staples of the British diet. Few other fruits were available in late autumn and so most orchards would have at least one tree of each.

The medlar fruit looks something like a cross between a russet apple and a rosehip. Their odd appearance led to the less than complimentary nickname of the 'dog's bottom' tree. The ripe fruits remain hard and green so, before they can be eaten, they need 'bletting' – to be allowed to rot slightly. Most crops are harvested and stored in sawdust or bran while the bletting process takes place. However, some growers prefer to leave their crops on the tree where the process is aided by the autumn frosts. Either way, raw, they remain something of an acquired taste – a bit like a custardy, slightly mouldy apple. Don't let that put you off: they make a spectacular chutney.

Quinces look like lumpy, hairy pears. Much like medlars, if you bite into a raw one, you'll be sorely (or sourly) disappointed. Most are very bitter and unpleasantly grainy. But these golden, furry fruits have a real depth of flavour and are another high-pectin fruit, making them ideal for making puddings, jams and jellies. In fact, the word 'marmalade' is a derivation of 'marmello', the Portuguese word for quince.

Both fruits are referenced extensively in British literature. At least four of Shakespeare's plays mention medlars (although it's not clear if he actually liked them – nearly all of his references are negative and in some places very rude). And, of course, in Edward Lear's famous poem, the Owl and the Pussycat 'dined on mince, and slices of quince' (which they proceeded to eat with a runcible spoon, whatever that is. Presumably a Victorian precursor to the spork).

Despite their former glories and some recent resurgence thanks to the heritage food movement, you're unlikely to find either fruit in the supermarket – apples and pears, along with more exotic fruits, have largely replaced them in our diet. Instead, keep an eye out at farmers' markets, and if you fancy recreating your own Elizabethan orchard, you can now buy saplings of both trees at larger garden centres.

Try: Quince paste (p. 236)

O ctober's chapter would certainly be incomplete without a mention of mushrooms. Although the season for most British mushrooms runs from the end of summer throughout the autumn, October provides the best opportunity to find and gather a good haul of edible ones. The UK has something like 15,000 types of wild fungi but you can narrow it down to around fifty with serious culinary appeal that are in season this month.

However, it would also be remiss not to include a serious health warning. A large number of mushrooms are toxic – some just enough to give you an upset stomach, others enough to kill you in under an hour. The golden rule is simply never, ever to eat anything unless you're absolutely certain of its identification. In Croatia, where mushroom hunting is very popular, they have an adage that is worth keeping in mind:'All mushrooms are edible, but some only once.'

So, the first thing to do before you even think about foraging for mushrooms is to get yourself a comprehensive mushroom guide. The best books now come with laminated field guides that you can take with you on your woodland ramble. You'll also need a mesh bag or lightweight wicker basket (a bucket will do but it's helpful to have something with gaps that bugs and loose soil can fall through, and avoid using plastic bags because the mushrooms will sweat), a magnifying glass to help with identification and a small knife to cut mushrooms. Never pull a whole mushroom out of the ground. You can buy specialist mushrooming knives, but any small folding knife will be fine.

• Mushrooms like damp, cool woodland and the edges of fields. As a general rule, you're unlikely to find them on very sandy soil.

• They often grow around rotting trees and piles of cut wood.

• Where you find one, you'll often find others. Mark your original find with a stick and explore the surrounding area. Mushroom spores are blown by the wind, so they will often grow in a line with the prevailing wind direction.

• September and October are the classic months for mushrooms but, as we saw earlier in the book, some very well-known and highly prized mushrooms like St George's and morels emerge in the spring.

• Don't forget to look up as well as down – some of the tastiest species like chicken of the woods grow amongst tree branches.

My top five edible fungi are all in season this month and are readily identifiable:

Field mushrooms (August to November) – A classic mushroom in shape and colour – creamy white and commonly found on field edges. Makes excellent eating.

Ceps (August to November) – A real forager's favourite, also known as the penny bun or porcini. Easily identified and extremely tasty. Found in most UK woodlands.

Giant puffballs (July to November) – Often spotted from a distance as these can reach monster proportions of up to 80 centimetres (2.6ft)! Found on woodland edges or in fields, sometimes hiding amongst nettles or tall grass. Can simply be sliced and fried ,or hollowed out and stuffed with other autumnal goodies.

Girolles (June to November) – One of the most highly prized autumn mushrooms. Beautiful bright yellow caps which add a wonderfully meaty texture to dishes. Can be rather harder to find but worth the effort.

Oyster mushrooms (all year) – A silvery grey-capped mushroom that grows in clusters, most often on beech trees. Fairly easily found most of the year round.

Don't ever feel you have to pick and eat your finds. It can be huge fun just spotting and identifying mushrooms. If your expedition has given you mushroom mania, a trip to a larger farmers' market should satisfy your cravings – you'll find a great selection of wild and cultivated mushrooms to experiment safely with.

Try: Partridge and wild mushroom terrine (pp. 230–2)

Feasts & Festivals | Punky Night (last Thursday of October)

Just before Halloween, usually on the last Thursday of October, an age-old ritual takes place in the village of Hinton St George in Somerset. The story behind the festival is recorded in local legend.

A local fair took place during the day at nearby Chiselborough, some 3 ½ miles to the east of Hinton. The men of the village would always attend the fair to do business but inevitably they failed to return home at the end of the day, having done a bit too much 'business' in the local hostelries. The wives of the village would then have to go looking for them (or, if some versions are to be believed, to scare them into coming home!) and would carry home-made lanterns carved out of roots and turnips known as 'punkies'.

The annual 'event' became something of a local joke, soon to be preserved in folklore as Punky Night.

These days it is a (comparatively) sober affair, with the children of the village parading through the streets with lanterns and singing the celebratory song:

It's Punky Night tonight;
It's Punky Night tonight;
Give us a candle, give us a light;
It's Punky Night tonight.

It's Punky Night tonight;
It's Punky Night tonight;
Adam and Eve wouldn't believe;
It's Punky Night tonight.

Try: Spice-roasted squash with couscous (p. 229)

A lthough there is some debate over the exact order of events, it's pretty clear that a mixture of pagan and Christian customs came together to create the modern celebration of all things ghostly that we know as Halloween.

The ancient Celtic festival of Samhain (pronounced *Sah-win*, meaning 'Summer's End') and its Welsh equivalent, Calan Gaeaf (New Winter Year) are generally accepted as the roots of Halloween. For the Celts it was a distinctly sombre affair. It marked the end of the harvest, the beginning of winter and a shift to the 'darker half' of the year.

The season marked the transition from a time of plenty to one of potential hardship and hunger, so it's hardly surprising that it was surrounded by themes of darkness and death. It was thought to be a time when a bridge between the worlds of the living and the dead was created so evil spirits or supernatural beings like fairies and goblins could enter to wreak havoc, spreading sickness or damaging crops. Flames were thought to ward off evil, so they were commonly used in rituals and festivities around Samhain. Hollowed-out turnips and pumpkins were lit with candles and decorated with scary faces to ward off malignant spirits, whilst spare places were set at dining tables to welcome friendly ones.

In the Christian calendar, All Hallows' Eve was the beginning of a period known as Allhallowtide. All Hallows' (or All Saints') Day was celebrated on 1 November and All Souls' Day on the 2nd. The three-day period was a time to pray for the dead. Over time, All Hallows' Eve was shortened to 'Halloween' and 31 October became a date of remembrance.

In the Celtic countries especially, the festivities around this time included a custom known as 'guising', when people dressed up in costume to sing songs or recite poems in exchange for food and drink. The costumes were intended to confuse evil spirits. At the same time, the Christian practice of 'souling' took place on All Hallows' Eve, when people would receive food and drink in exchange for praying for departed souls on All Souls' Day. Both customs involved going from house to house and, combined with an element of pranking that could be blamed on mischievous spirits, they became intertwined in the practice of trick-or-treating (although that phrase wasn't invented until the early twentieth century).

Over time, the mixture of pagan festivities, church customs and a general understanding that harder times were on the horizon, evolved into the event we now know as Halloween. It's an excellent example of how the natural seasons dictate our celebrations; all across Europe cultures celebrate late autumn with a combination of the macabre, feasting and a light take on that gravest of subjects – death. It is indeed a time when a bridge is created between two worlds – the autumn season of abundance and the winter of adversity.

Try: Sticky toffee apple pudding (p. 239)

Beetroot, mascarpone and horseradish tart

The beetroot season is a fairly long one, running from July until January and it really is worth buying them fresh and cooking them yourself. Roasting is my favourite way of cooking them, as it gives a consistent result and seems to intensify the flavour. Disposable gloves are worth using when you peel them – they certainly create some mess!

The rough puff pastry is worth making yourself, as having control over the quality of the butter and flour is key. If you do want to buy some ready-made pastry, look out for something that is made with real butter; the products from the Dorset Pastry Company are well worth a look.

SERVES 4 AS A STARTER

For the beetroot
8 medium beetroot
2 tsp olive oil
good balsamic vinegar
Maldon sea salt

For the tarts
4 x 15cm rough puff discs around 4mm thick, chilled (see Basics p. 288)
2 tsp horseradish cream
60g mascarpone
2 spring onions, sliced
20g Parmesan, grated
Maldon sea salt and freshly ground black pepper

1. Preheat oven to 160°C.

2. Wash the beetroot thoroughly and trim off the roots and stalks. Place in the centre of a large sheet of foil and drizzle with the oil. Season with salt. Cover with a second sheet of foil and fold all the edges up to seal. Scrunch another sheet of foil up to create a trivet to put the packet on. This avoids direct contact with the roasting tin and stops the beetroot overcooking on the bottom. Roast for 30–50 minutes depending on size. A cocktail stick should pierce the beets with only slight resistance.

3. Allow to cool slightly and then peel. Dress with good balsamic, a little oil and salt while still warm.

4. Blitz half the beetroot to a purée in a small food processor and season well. Cut the remaining beetroot into neat wedges, about ten from each beet.

5. Place the pastry discs on squares of non-stick baking parchment a little bigger than the pastry. Use a cutter or small knife to mark a border 1cm in from the edges of the discs. Prick the centres all over with a fork and then spread on a thin layer of beetroot purée. Arrange the beetroot slices over the top. Mix the horseradish with the mascarpone and season to taste. Drop small spoonfuls over the tarts. Scatter the spring onions and Parmesan on top and season with a little salt and pepper. Increase the oven temperature to 180°C and bake for 15-20 minutes.

6. Serve with a small salad mounded in the centre of each tart and drizzle with good balsamic vinegar and olive oil.

Spice-roasted squash with couscous

I would maintain that my cookery book collection isn't vast, although others may beg to differ... It is, however, a constant source of enjoyment and inspiration. The books I buy have changed according to circumstances and what I find particularly interesting at the time, and I usually read them from cover to cover as I would a novel. After that first reading, I tend to just dip in and out to look something up or search for a particular recipe. My collection ranges far and wide from technical tomes on the vagaries of chocolate to classics such as the *Good Housekeeping Cookery Book*. All have their place but a few have opened my eyes to a different cuisine, new methods or previously unused ingredients. One such book is *Persiana*, the first cookery book from the very talented Sabrina Ghayour, the inspiration for this recipe. All of Sabrina's books are worth adding to your collection.

SERVES 3–4 AS A MAIN COURSE

For the squash

2 red onions, cut into wedges

1 small butternut squash, peeled, deseeded and cut into rough 3cm cubes

2 tbsp olive oil

4 piquillo peppers or roasted red peppers from a tin or jar, deseeded and roughly chopped

3 cloves of garlic, smashed

1 tsp cumin

1 tsp sumac

1 pinch dried chilli flakes

200g chestnut mushrooms, halved

Maldon sea salt and freshly ground black pepper

For the couscous

1 tbsp olive oil

3 spring onions, sliced

160g couscous

220ml boiling water

15g unsalted butter

Maldon sea salt and freshly ground black pepper

To serve

30g natural yoghurt

2 tsp pomegranate molasses

1. Preheat the oven to 170°C.

2. For the squash, mix the red onions and squash together in a roasting tin with 1 tbsp of the olive oil, season lightly and roast for 20 minutes, stirring after 10 minutes.

3. In the meantime, heat the remaining oil in a small non-stick frying pan, add the peppers and garlic and sauté for 2 minutes, making sure the garlic doesn't burn. Add the spices and a little seasoning and cook until the spices are fragrant. Transfer to a blender and blitz to a rough purée, or chop finely with a cook's knife. Add a splash of water if needed to get the paste to blend.

4. After the first 20 minutes, add the mushrooms to the roasting tin and cook for another 10–15 minutes until the vegetables are nearly tender. Stir in the pepper mix and cook for a final 10 minutes. Check the seasoning and adjust if required.

5. For the couscous, heat the oil in a saucepan and add the spring onions. Cook, stirring, for 30 seconds, then stir in the couscous and remove from the heat. Stir in the boiling water or stock and a generous pinch of salt. Put a lid on the pan and leave to steam for 10 minutes, giving it a stir with a fork once or twice during this time. Add the butter to the couscous and fork it through, breaking up any clumps as you go. Check and adjust the seasoning.

6. Divide the squash and couscous between bowls, spoon the yoghurt on top and drizzle with the molasses.

Partridge and wild mushroom terrine

A partridge makes a perfect portion as a main course for one simply roasted with some seasonal vegetables but, like most game, it works very well as a terrine, too. The controlled cooking and the addition of some good, fatty, streaky bacon keeps the terrine succulent, and a mixture of mushrooms adds another flavour dimension.

As with all shot game, examine the meat carefully for any stray shot or bits of feather. On the breasts, lift up the fillet to check under it.

SERVES 6–8 AS A STARTER

4 rashers smoked, streaky bacon, roughly chopped
8 boneless, skinless partridge thighs
1 tbsp olive oil
2 banana shallots, peeled, halved lengthwise and thinly sliced
75g chestnut mushrooms, cut into bite-sized pieces
75g wild mushrooms such as girolles, cut into bite-sized pieces
1 clove of garlic, minced
50ml medium Madeira
2 tbsp double cream
8 boneless, skinless partridge breasts
Maldon sea salt and freshly ground black pepper
6 slices prosciutto

1. Preheat oven to 100°C.

2. Start by mincing the bacon and partridge thighs together, running them through the mincer twice. If you don't have a mincer but do have a food processor, dice the meat, chill in the freezer for 30 minutes and then pulse in the food processor. Place the meat in a bowl in the fridge.

3. Heat the oil in a small frying pan, add the shallots with a pinch of salt and cook over a moderate heat until the shallots start to soften. Add the mushrooms and cook until they have wilted and any water has been driven off. Once the mix starts to fry again, add the garlic and cook for 1 minute. Add the Madeira and reduce completely. Transfer the mix to a plate and chill.

4. When the mushrooms are cold, beat them into the farce made with the leg meat. Beat the cream into the farce and season well. Fry a teaspoon of the mix to taste, check the seasoning and adjust as required. The mix should taste robustly flavoured when it is warm, as it will be less so when cold.

5. Wipe your worktop with damp kitchen paper and lay out sheets of cling film to make a rectangle 40cm x 60cm with the short side towards you. Repeat, laying the film in the opposite direction to give a double thickness.

6. Lay four of the partridge breasts in a line 10cm in from the edge of the film, skin side down and slightly overlapping to form a neat

Continued on page p. 232

Continued from p. 230

rectangle, then season lightly. Using a spoon and a palette knife, spread the farce evenly over the top of the breasts and then lay the remaining four breasts on top of this, skin side up. Fold the cling film up over the partridge and gently shape into a cylinder. Roll up tightly, pulling towards you to get some tension. The film should stick to the damp surface. When the terrine is completely rolled, twist the ends up tightly. Next, wrap in a sheet of foil, again twisting the ends up tightly and pushing inwards to get as compact a cylinder as possible.

7. Lay the terrine in a deep roasting tin and cover with cold water. Heat on the hob to a temperature of 80°C, cover with foil and transfer to the oven. Cook for approximately. 1 hour. Test the internal temperature with a probe at the end of the cooking time; it should be between 70–75°C. If you have a steam oven, the terrine could be steamed as an alternative.

8. Allow the terrine to cool for 20 minutes and then transfer to iced water. Ideally use a roasting tin of iced water that can then be put in the fridge. Allow to chill completely.

9. Lay out sheets of cling film as you did when shaping the terrine. Starting 10cm in from the short edge, lay two of the prosciutto slices lengthwise left to right, overlapping them slightly. Lay the other four slices running away from you, starting at the far edge of the first two slices, to give a rectangle roughly 30cm x 25cm. Unwrap the chilled terrine and put any jelly and juices in a small pan. Reduce this liquid down to a syrup and brush over the ham; this will help to stick the ham to the terrine. Lay the terrine on the ham close to the long edge and, with the help of the cling film, wrap the ham tightly around the terrine. The terrine will end up in the middle of the cling film sheet. Straighten the film out and carefully roll the terrine back to the edge of the film. Wrap as tightly as possible in the film and twist the ends tightly. Tie the ends to keep everything in place and chill the terrine.

10. To serve, slice the terrine, allowing two slices per person. It will be easier to slice through the cling film and remove this afterwards. Allow the terrine time to come to room temperature before serving. Pickled mushrooms, apple chutney, cornichons, sourdough toast, brioche – all would make good partners for the terrine alongside a few simply dressed leaves.

Leek and mushroom cobnut crumble

Hazelnuts, filberts and cobnuts – they all are, in essence, the same thing. A cobnut (or filbert) is a cultivated hazelnut that is usually sold fresh rather than dried. The vibrant green leafy husks and the green shells are the hallmark of the cobnut. The nuts will be ready to pick in September and October but the cultivated cobnut can also make an appearance in the supermarkets and greengrocers, as early as August.

The flavour of cobnuts changes significantly as the nut matures. When just picked they are sweet, fresh and creamy, but as they mature or when they are roasted the flavour becomes deeper, with hints of caramel and a more earthy flavour. The cobnuts really do add an extra dimension to this simple crumble.

SERVES 4 AS A MAIN COURSE OR 6–8 AS A SIDE DISH

For the filling
2 tbsp olive oil
3 banana shallots , cut in half lengthwise and sliced
2 cloves of garlic, crushed
500g chestnut mushrooms, sliced
500g trimmed leeks, sliced into ½-cm slices
500ml vegetable stock (Basics p. 284)
100ml dry white wine
1 tsp Dijon mustard
75g crème fraîche
1 tsp cornflour, slaked in 1 tbsp cold water
Maldon sea salt and freshly ground black pepper

For the crumble
100g plain flour
1 tsp Maldon sea salt, finely ground
50g oatmeal
65g unsalted butter
50g cobnuts, chopped
50g Parmesan, grated
freshly ground black pepper

To serve
a crisp salad with a sweet mustardy dressing or some pork chops, a crisp-skinned chicken or a roasted pheasant.

1. Preheat the oven to 170°C.

2. Sweat the shallots and garlic in the olive oil until tender. Add the mushrooms and cook over a high heat for a couple of minutes. Stir in the leeks and add 100ml of the stock. Place a lid on the pan and reduce the heat, cooking for approximately 5 minutes until the leeks are tender. Remove the lid of the pan and cook over a high heat until the mix is fairly dry.

3. In a separate saucepan, reduce the wine to a syrup and then add the remaining stock. Reduce to around 250ml then add the mustard, crème fraîche and season to taste. Thicken with enough cornflour to achieve a thick double cream consistency. Add the sauce to the leek mix and check the seasoning. Transfer to an ovenproof dish or dishes.

4. For the crumble mix, sift the flour and salt into a bowl and stir in the oats. Rub in the butter and then mix in the cobnuts and Parmesan. Season with black pepper. Scatter the crumble mix over the leek base and bake for 20–30 minutes until the top is golden brown.

Quince paste

For me, the quince has two starring roles. Firstly, as quince paste (or membrillo) that goes so wonderfully with hard mature cheeses, or stirred into a meat-based sauce in much the same way as you would use redcurrant jelly. Secondly, I like to pickle or poach the fruit to use as an accompaniment to cold meat in the case of the pickle, or with game for the poached fruit.

What is the difference between quince jelly and quince paste or membrillo? Well, as with many food questions, the answer is rarely clear-cut but my best shot is that a jelly is made from the juice strained from the cooked pulp whereas a paste contains the pulp and juice. Texture is the main difference, with a jelly being lighter and smooth. Good enough reason to make some of both, I reckon!

MAKES APPROXIMATELY 1KG

1kg whole quince, washed
700g granulated sugar per kg of pulp
½ lemon, juice only
citric acid to taste
Maldon sea salt, finely ground

1. Roughly chop the quince and place in a large pan, cover with water and bring to the boil. Simmer until the quince is completely tender and starting to break up. This will take around an hour or more, so top up with water if necessary.

2. Carefully mash the contents of the pan with a potato masher to make a rough purée. Rub through a coarse sieve into a bowl and then whizz in a food processor until smooth. Quince have quite a lot of gritty bits, so it is worth passing the purée through a fine chinois to remove them.

3. Weigh the purée you have left and return to the pan with the appropriate quantity of sugar and the lemon juice. Bring to a boil and cook until a probe or jam thermometer registers 105°C. Dip a spoon into the jelly and allow to cool before tasting. Add citric acid to balance the sweetness and a small quantity of salt to enhance the flavour – note that it should in no way taste salty. Pour into sterile plastic boxes to set. I used takeaway-style containers, sterilized with boiling water, and filled them halfway.

4. Store in the fridge for the longest shelf-life.

Sticky toffee apple pudding

The sticky toffee pudding is, undeniably, a modern icon. Widely linked with Francis Coulson and the Sharrow Bay Hotel in the 1970s, its origins may go back further than that, possibly even to a different country. The British have, however, taken it to their hearts and it still graces many menus today.

   This recipe takes some of the sticky toffee elements but brings in the freshness and acidity of new-season apple. I like the balance this gives, as well as the different texture, and a little salt in the sauce just adds to the taste sensations. Being rooted in the West Country, clotted cream is my accompaniment of choice, but custard, cream, crème fraîche or ice cream all work well.

SERVES 8–10

For the toffee sauce
225ml double cream plus 1½ tbsp milk
1 strip of lemon zest
½ tsp Maldon sea salt, finely ground
100g caster sugar
50g golden syrup
lemon juice to taste

For the apples
10g butter
3 sharp apples, peeled, cored and cut into
    8 wedges
1½ tbsp caster sugar

For the sponge
200g unsalted butter, softened
150g golden caster sugar
50g light muscovado sugar
200g self-raising flour
½ tsp Maldon sea salt, finely ground
½ tsp mixed spice or cinnamon
3 large, free-range eggs, beaten

1. Preheat the oven to 160°C.

2. To make the toffee sauce, warm the cream and milk in a small saucepan with the lemon zest and salt. Allow to infuse for 20 minutes and then bring just to a simmer. Turn off the heat.

3. In a heavy-based pan, combine the sugar and syrup. Cook to a medium to dark caramel (170°C on a sugar thermometer). Carefully add the hot cream mix and cook over a low heat, stirring gently until the caramel has dissolved. Adjust the flavour with the lemon juice and pass through a sieve into a bowl. Press a sheet of cling film directly onto the surface and let cool.

4. For the apples, melt the butter in a non-stick frying pan, add the apple wedges and sprinkle with the sugar. Mix well to coat and fry until lightly caramelized. Transfer to a plate to cool.

5. To make the sponge, cream the butter and sugars together in the bowl of a mixer, beating until pale and fluffy. Sift together the flour, salt and spice. Gradually add the beaten egg to the butter mix, alternating with spoonfuls of the flour. Once all the egg is incorporated, mix in the remaining flour.

6. Grease and lightly flour a 2l ovenproof bowl. Lay two-thirds of the apple wedges in the bottom and pour half of the cold toffee sauce on top. Chill for 30 minutes and then cover with the sponge mix. Bake for 15 minutes then reduce the temperature to 150°C for a further 40–50 minutes until risen, golden, and firm to the touch in the centre of the sponge. Allow to rest for 10 minutes and then very carefully invert onto a serving plate.

7. Serve with the remaining caramelized apple wedges and warmed toffee sauce.

11 | November

Blodmonath – blood month, when animals were slaughtered for the winter months

November often catches us slightly by surprise, October can be pleasantly bright and mild, but a mere four weeks later it's ten degrees colder outside and, with the clocks changing back, dark at five o'clock. Quite a contrast. We're in the final month of autumn now and, as we say goodbye to the very last of the warm days, we can start to look forward to the frosts and snow of winter. Regardless of the weather, there's plenty to keep us entertained, both outside and in the kitchen.

For meat eaters, November should be all about game, with partridge, pheasant and venison abundant this month. Prices for the feathered game have usually come down from their early-season highs, making it affordable and increasingly accessible to all. You'll need some vegetables to go with it, and thankfully November is one of the best months for hardy roots. Parsnips and celeriac in particular should be on your shopping list. And although not quite as generous as in October, the hedgerows are still worth plundering, as rosehips and chestnuts make welcome late additions to the wild larder.

If you're outdoors at dusk this month, keep an eye out for murmurations of starlings which usually begin in November. From now until the spring our non-migratory residents are joined by their relatives from colder climates, with up to 100,000 birds flocking together in these hypnotic aerial pre-roosting displays. They're a truly spectacular phenomenon and a reminder that life definitely doesn't stop just because it's getting a bit chilly and dark out there. Indeed, we start the month with one of our biggest seasonal celebrations on 5 November, so let's wrap up warm, get outside and get the sausages sizzling.

Out & About | Seal Spotting

There are two types of seal in the British Isles – the grey seal and the common (or harbour) seal. The UK is home to about a third of the world's common seal population and nearly half of all grey seals, so our coast is a vitally important habitat for both species. They inhabit much of our shoreline and so, with a bit of planning beforehand, you've got a great chance of spotting these beautiful, charismatic creatures.

One of the best times to see seals is when they 'haul up' on to land for the breeding and pupping seasons. The grey pupping season starts at the end of August or early September in the UK's warmest waters (Cornwall and the Isles of Scilly), and gets progressively later as you go further north, so the Scottish seals are the last to produce pups – in late December. Early November is a good time in many places, particularly on calm, bright days.

Take a pair of binoculars and walk quietly along the coastline. Look for them on the rocks and flat, open areas in the early morning and evening, as well as scanning the sea surface for their bobbing heads as they 'bottle' upright in the water.

Grey seals are the larger of the two species (in fact, they are the largest wild carnivore in Britain), with long snouts and parallel nostrils. The smaller common seals have V-shaped nostrils that nearly meet at the bottom of their snouts.

If you do spot one, just find a comfy spot and sit still to watch it. Always keep your distance, even if you think it is sleeping or sick. Impossibly cute, furry white seal pups may often appear to be abandoned, but usually their mothers will be close by or hunting for food. If you think you've seen an abandoned pup or sick seal, call the British Divers Marine Life Rescue or the RSPCA.

Some of Britain's best places to spot seals include:

• **Blakeney, Norfolk** – take a boat trip from the quay to one of the UK's largest colonies of both grey and common seals. Also a particularly good spot in June for the common seal season.

• **The Orkney Islands, Scotland** – with some 30,000 seals in residence you have a great chance of spotting them on any shoreline stroll.

• **Lundy Island, Devon** – accessible only by boat, this unspoilt island off the North Devon coast is home to a large breeding colony.

• **Cornwall** – seals can be spotted all year round in the warm(ish) waters off the Cornish coast. Cornwall is also home to the Cornish Seal Sanctuary at Gweek.

• **The Llyn Peninsula, Wales** – the North Wales peninsula is an important refuge for seals living in the Irish Sea (and where I spent many a childhood holiday spotting these wonderful animals).

T he sweet, nutty flavour of parsnip is a fantastic accompaniment to a Sunday roast, but this versatile vegetable is capable of a great deal more besides. No harder to prepare than carrots, they are plentiful and great value at this time of year, as well as being able to withstand the most bitter of our weather – a really dependable, winter champion.

Oddly, to this day parsnips remain essentially relegated to animal fodder on the continent. I have a great deal of respect for the culinary histories of France and Italy but those two great food nations definitely get it wrong when it comes to this delightful root. They will occasionally allow it a small cameo in a peasant stew, but rarely permit it to partner anything as lavish as a joint of beef.

Historically, it would seem that the potato is to blame for the parsnip's demise. The arrival of this fashionable competitor to the continent in the 1500s ensured the parsnip was destined to become a bit player in European cuisine. Still, the Brits, always ones to cheer on the plucky underdog, stuck with it and were way too canny to let it all go to the cows. Unlike some other abundant ingredients, the parsnip's popularity in Britain survived wartime rationing when it was promoted as a substitute for more exotic sweet ingredients including, ambitiously, bananas.

Parsnips are grown most of the year round but are traditionally at their best after the first frost, which intensifies their sweetness by converting starches into sugar. A good parsnip will be packed full of flavour and will pair well with a number of heavyweight spices, particularly cumin. Roasted, the high sugar content caramelizes to form a crunchy golden skin (without the need for honey, which is so frequently suggested as a glaze).

If the first frosts haven't arrived before November, they will certainly be here some time in December, so make the most of this robust root from now until the spring.

Try: Parsnip croquettes (p. 254)

Food & Foraging | Venison

The word 'venison' used to refer to all wild, non-feathered meats (*venatio* being the Latin for 'hunt') and would have included animals such as wild boar and goat. But it's now used almost exclusively to refer to deer meat.

In days gone by, as a result of its aristocratic connections, deer was very much a rich man's food. Only the offal was affordable to commoners (the 'pluck' or offal of the animal was also called the 'umble', the origin of 'humble pie'). These days, however, venison is widely available and inexpensive.

With six species of deer in Britain (Chinese water, fallow, muntjac, red, roe and sika) and different seasons for stags or bucks (males) and hinds or does (females), there isn't a month of the year when you won't find venison of some kind available from your local butcher. Even better, while, from an ethical perspective, wild venison ticks all the boxes, deer aren't reared intensively in Britain so you can also eat farmed or park (from an enclosed estate) meat with a clean conscience.

Hinds, especially of the smaller species, tend to have a slightly less gamey flavour than bigger stags, and November is the month when the females of our three most commonly eaten species (the red, fallow and roe) are in season. It means a plentiful supply of good-value meat. In addition, venison partners particularly well with a number of other ingredients, savoury and sweet, that are in season this month (think rosemary, cobnuts, juniper and pears).

So, while there's no 'bad' month for venison, from November through to February is most certainly a very good time of year for this lean, iron-rich and well-flavoured meat.

Try:
Venison, cobnut and apple salad (p. 250)
Venison, celeriac and mushroom suet pudding (pp. 253)

Food & Foraging | Chestnuts

I s the mention of any other ingredient so comforting and evocative as chestnuts? A cosy fire, dark nights and a general sense of snug nostalgia all spring instantly to mind.

Late October through to late December is the season of the sweet chestnut and the time to get foraging, before the squirrels do.

A native of the Mediterranean, many of the original chestnut trees in the UK were planted by the Romans, and the Latin name 'castan' can be found in various guises across Europe, including Wales (also *castan*) France (*châtaigne*) and our own derivation, 'chestnut'.

Curiously for a food now so quintessentially seasonal and British, few of the chestnuts sold in the UK are actually grown here. The chances are, if you buy chestnuts in the UK (even from a farmers' market) they will have come from abroad, most likely France. There's no obvious reason for this, but presumably the twenty-year growing period makes it, at the very least, a long-term investment for the average landowner.

You may well have lobbed the odd stick into a chestnut tree in the hope of dislodging a spiky prize or two but (and I say this having once had a 'discussion' with the Royal Parks Police on the matter) it's best not to do this unless you own the tree. In any event, picking them up from the ground will ensure they are ripe. Damp is the enemy of the chestnut as they will quickly rot so, once foraged, make sure you store them in a dry, well-ventilated place.

For a wintery treat, you can't do much better than a traditionally roasted chestnut. If you have a fireplace, get a crackling fire going and throw a handful of chestnuts into a roasting pan (cut a small cross in the top of each nut first, to prevent any unwanted explosions and a dash across the living room to stamp out burning embers). After about ten minutes, depending on the heat of your fire, your nuts should be beautifully roasted and easy to peel. If you don't have a hearth, you can just as easily roast them in the oven at 200°C for about twenty minutes (again, cutting them first). If you find a seriously large haul, you can also grind the roasted nuts into chestnut flour, which makes a tasty base for pancakes and shortbread.

Try: Seared scallops with chestnut, apple and pancetta (p. 257)

| Stir-up Sunday
(fifth Sunday before Christmas)

S tir-up Sunday is the last Sunday before Advent (which starts on the fourth Sunday before Christmas). Traditionally, it's the day to make Christmas pudding, leaving plenty of time for all of those rich, festive flavours to mingle before the big day.

But 'stir up' has nothing to do with stirring of the Christmas pudding. In fact, it comes from the opening words of the *Book of Common Prayer*, dating back to 1549, and on the Sunday in question, church services start with the words 'Stir up, we beseech thee, O Lord, the wills of thy faithful people. . .'

It's only because most Christmas pudding recipes require the mixture to stand for several weeks that the day became connected with cooking; the words were a useful prompt to any housewife or servant who hadn't yet got their act together.

Try: Sue Brown's Christmas pudding (p. 261)

Feasts & Festivals | Bonfire Night (5th November)

For more than four centuries the British Isles have commemorated the failed plot to blow up the Houses of Parliament and assassinate Protestant King James I on 5 November, 1605. Guy Fawkes and his fellow conspirators had planned to replace the king with a Catholic head of state but, as we all know, the plot flopped and Fawkes and his accomplices were arrested and executed.

These days most of us will attend a well-organized local firework display, but in years gone-by the night was one of lawless celebration. Gunpowder Treason Day (as it was officially recognized) was marked by wild parties, bonfires in the street and anti-Catholic demonstrations. The celebrations grew out of control and the night was seen in many parts as an excuse to riot, free of the rule of law. The lawlessness continued well into the twentieth century in some parts of the country. A clamp-down on the riotous activities was needed and eventually succeeded, bringing the festivities nearer to the family event we enjoy today.

Many towns and villages have developed their own peculiar ways of marking the date. In Ottery St Mary in Devon, a spectacular, fire-filled celebration takes place. The custom of 'tar barrelling' is not for the faint-hearted and, frankly, it's a wonder that this particular event survives in today's health-and-safety conscious world.

Barrels and the West Country are inextricably connected because of the area's cider-making heritage and at some point in history (probably shortly after Guy Fawkes tried to send King James to all four corners of his kingdom simultaneously), it was decided that filling some barrels with burning pitch and carrying them through the streets of this small village was a good idea.

The main event involves seventeen tar-infused barrels, each sponsored by a local pub. Each barrel is lit outside its sponsoring pub and hoisted on to the shoulders of its first carrier, who then runs down the road with it, passing it on to others until it begins to fall apart. At this point it is thrown to the ground and left to burn out. The event lasts several hours and makes for a hot, frenetic and fun evening, with the last barrel being carried into the village square around midnight.

The inhabitants of another Devon village, Shebbear (where, incidentally, my father went to school) have a similarly peculiar but rather safer custom. On the small village green, a large rock, known as the Devil's Stone, is turned over. According to the local lore, the Devil's Stone dropped out of his pocket as he fell from heaven. Turning the one-tonne monolith (which is said to be of a stone not found anywhere else in Europe) and ringing the local church bells keep him from coming back to wreak disaster on the village.

Try: Venison dog and chilli-pickled cabbage (pp. 258–9)

Venison, cobnut and apple salad

Venison should be prolific at this time of year, and its rich, gamey flavour pairs well with the sweet and sour of the apple and the creamy crunch of the cobnuts in this dish. I have a real fondness for warm salads – the different textures, tastes and flavours provide some real excitement and they look gorgeous on a big platter to share. You can cook the venison ahead of time and chill it down, but do let it come properly back to room temperature and make sure the apples are warm before serving. Ideally, though, I would have the venison freshly cooked and well rested. Warm not hot is the key, and do pour any juices from the resting and carving over the salad.

SERVES 6 AS A STARTER

For the venison

300g trimmed venison loin

3 tbsp olive oil

20g unsalted butter

Maldon sea salt and freshly ground black
    pepper

For the apples

20g unsalted butter

3 sharp, firm apples, peeled, cored and cut into
    8 pieces each

2 tbsp caster sugar

2 tbsp cider vinegar

Maldon sea salt

To serve

60g cobnuts or blanched hazelnuts

1 bag watercress, picked, washed and spun
    dry

2 tbsp cider vinaigrette (see Basics p. 287)

30g Pecorino Romano, shaved

Maldon sea salt and freshly ground black
    pepper

1. Preheat oven to 200°C.

2. Season the venison loin with salt and pepper. In a large frying pan or roasting tin, heat the oil on a medium to high heat. Sear the venison all over, caramelizing well, then add the butter and baste. Transfer to the oven for 2 minutes, turning the loin half way through. Remove to a cooling rack, rest for 10 minutes and chill if not serving immediately. Allow to come up to room temperature before serving.

3. Using a non-stick frying pan, cook the apple in two batches. Heat half the butter until it stops foaming, add the first batch of apple and sprinkle with half the sugar. Cook over a high heat until well caramelized, then finish with 1 tbsp of vinegar and a sprinkle of salt, continuing to cook until the vinegar has evaporated. Put to one side to cool slightly and repeat with the remaining ingredients.

4. To serve, slice the nuts thinly and season with a little salt. Slice the venison loin and season lightly. Dress the watercress with the vinaigrette and toss with the apple. Divide the salad between the plates and arrange the venison on top. Scatter with the cobnuts and finish with the pecorino.

Venison, celeriac and mushroom suet pudding

Baking suet pastry gives a very different feel to this pudding than steaming would. I like them either way but the crisp texture of baked suet pastry contrasts so nicely with the soft meat and tender celeriac in this dish.

SERVES 4 HUNGRY PEOPLE OR WOULD MAKE 6 PUDDINGS AT A PUSH!

For the filling

500g diced venison, 1½–2cm pieces
olive oil
200ml red wine
2 rashers smoked, streaky bacon, cut into
   lardons
1 onion, diced
2 cloves of garlic, sliced
100g chestnut mushrooms, trimmed and
   quartered
350ml beef or venison stock (Basics pp. 284–5)
muslin bouquet garni of 2 bay leaves, 6 sprigs
   of thyme and 6 juniper berries
1 small celeriac, peeled and cut into 1cm cubes
   (250g)
1 tsp cornflour, slaked in 1 tbsp cold water
Maldon sea salt and freshly ground black
   pepper

For the suet pastry

250g plain flour
1½ tsp Maldon sea salt, finely ground
125g suet
cold water to mix (approximately 180ml)

1. Preheat the oven to 140˚C.

2. Season the venison with salt and pepper. Heat some oil in a heavy-based frying pan and seal the venison over a high heat, caramelizing well. Do this in a couple of batches. Tip the venison into a casserole dish and deglaze the pan with a little of the wine. Add this liquid to the venison. Wipe out the pan, add a little more oil and cook the lardons until the fat starts to render, then add the onion and garlic. Cook for around 10 minutes, stirring often, until the onion is soft. Add the mushrooms, raise the heat and cook until the mushrooms start to colour. Add this mix to the venison.

3. Pour the remaining wine into the pan and reduce to a syrup, then add the stock and bring to a simmer. Pour over the venison, mix well, add the bouquet garni and cover. Cook in the oven for 1 hour. Add the celeriac and cook for a further 20 minutes. Check that the meat and celeriac
are tender.

4. Drain the majority of the cooking liquid into a clean saucepan and reduce to approximately 150ml. Thicken with the cornflour, adding gradually, to give a thick double-cream consistency. Remove the bouquet garni from the venison, squeezing out any liquid. Add the sauce and adjust the seasoning. Allow to cool.

5. For the pastry, sift the flour and salt into a bowl and stir in the suet. Gradually add cold water, mixing with a blunt knife until a soft dough is formed. Flour the work surface and knead the dough quickly into a ball. Cut three-quarters of the dough and roll out to around 4mm thick. Cut out rough circles, 20cm in diameter. Roll the remaining pastry with the trim and cut out 12cm circles for the lids.

6. To assemble, butter four 10cm aluminium pudding basins and line with the larger pastry circles. Trim the excess, leaving around 1cm overhang. Fill the basins with the venison mix. Brush the lids with water and place over the filling. Squeeze the two layers of pastry together and trim off the excess. Brush around the rim of the pudding with water and roll the sealed edge inwards to create a double seal around the rim.

7. Turn the oven up to 180°C. Place the puddings on a heavy baking tray and bake for 20-30 minutes. The pastry should be crisp and golden and the filling hot right through. The puddings should tip out easily but may need the point of a knife run between the pastry and the basin.

8. Serve with seasonal greens, roasted carrots and mash.

Parsnip croquettes

Root vegetables have a unique range of flavours and textures that can be the main part of a meal or a great side dish. The one thing most roots do have in common is a touch of sweetness that is often enhanced by some frost. They also make excellent purées which freeze well, so it is worth making a decent-sized batch.

These croquettes make an alternative side dish to serve with roasted meat and game.

MAKES 10–12 CROQUETTES

For the parsnip pureé

300g parsnips, peeled, cored and cut into
   chunks
20g unsalted butter
6 whole black peppercorns
Maldon sea salt
NOTE: this may make more than required for
   the croquettes

For the filling

20g unsalted butter
2 tbsp plain flour
130ml semi-skimmed milk
25g Parmesan, grated
1 tsp Dijon mustard
Maldon sea salt and freshly ground black
   pepper

For the panné

100g seasoned flour
1 large, free-range egg, beaten with 2 tbsp milk
   and strained
75g panko breadcrumbs

vegetable oil for deep-frying

1. To make the parsnip pureé, put the parsnips in a large pan, cover with cold water and add the butter and peppercorns. Bring to the boil and then reduce the heat to a simmer. Cook until the parsnips are completely tender. Remove the parsnips with a slotted spoon and transfer to a blender, making sure none of the peppercorns are included. Reduce the remaining cooking liquid to a buttery syrup, strain and then add to the parsnips. Process until completely smooth and season well with Maldon sea salt.

2. To make the croquettes, melt the butter in a heavy-based pan, then add the flour to make a roux and gradually incorporate the milk to make a smooth, thick sauce. Add the Parmesan and mustard, and season well with salt and pepper. Beat in 200g of the parsnip pureé and check the seasoning, adjusting if necessary.

3. Transfer the mix to a piping bag with a large plain nozzle. Pipe the mix out onto a tray lined with baking parchment to form croquettes approximately 70mm long. Neaten the ends with a palette knife dipped in water. Freeze for 1 hour, turning the pieces after 30 minutes so they firm up evenly.

4. Coat the croquettes first in the seasoned flour, then the egg wash. Drain each croquette well before transferring to the breadcrumbs and, once coated, roll gently to shape. Transfer to a tray and refrigerate for 1 hour before deep-frying in vegetable oil at 165°C until golden brown and hot right through (approximately 5 minutes).

Seared scallops with chestnut, apple and pancetta

The scallop has to be one of the sweetest things to come out of the sea and is a good choice for anyone who is a little wary of shellfish. More people are put off food by texture than anything else, and some shellfish can be challenging on that score. I don't really enjoy the bright orange roe or coral of a scallop but many people do – it is, however, worth cooking the roe and the white muscle separately as they cook at very different rates.

Seared in a hot pan, the natural sugars in a scallop caramelize beautifully and a minute or two on each side should be plenty to give that deeply flavoured exterior and melting, tender interior. All that sweetness benefits from earthy flavours and acidity to balance things out. Some raw chestnut adds crunch, pancetta gives a salty kick and apple provides the acidity.

SERVES 4 AS A STARTER

For the dressing
2 tbsp olive oil
1 tbsp apple juice
1 tsp cider vinegar
1 tsp Dijon mustard
Maldon sea salt and freshly ground black
    pepper

For the salad
½ sharp, crisp apple
4 raw chestnuts, peeled and skinned
4 thin rashers of pancetta

For the scallops
2 tbsp olive oil for frying
12 large scallops, laid on kitchen paper to dry
Maldon sea salt

To serve
25g rocket leaves

1. For the dressing, whisk together the oil, apple juice, vinegar and mustard in a small bowl. Season to taste with salt and pepper.

2. Next, slice the cheeks off the apple and then cut the flesh into thin batons. Cut two of the chestnuts into 3mm dice. Toss the apple and chestnut through the dressing.

3. Heat the grill and cook the pancetta for 2–3 minutes on each side until crisp and golden. Set aside on some kitchen paper to drain.

4. Heat the olive oil in a heavy non-stick pan, season the scallops on one side only and lay carefully, seasoned side down, in the pan. Cook for around 1–2 minutes until well caramelized. Season the top side and turn over. Cook for a further 1–2 minutes. The scallops should be rare in the centre still. Transfer to some kitchen paper to drain.

5. To serve, drain any excess dressing from the apple and chestnut mix and reserve. Add the rocket leaves to the apple and chestnut mix and toss together gently. Check and adjust the seasoning. Divide the salad between the plates and arrange the scallops next to the salad. Place a strip of pancetta on the salad, drizzle the reserved dressing around and finish with thin shavings from the remaining chestnuts.

Venison dog with chilli-pickled cabbage

The sausage in all its various guises is the perfect way to use up tougher and fattier cuts of meat and is especially useful if you are dealing with whole carcasses or larger joints such as a whole saddle. Making your own sausages won't be for everyone but I have enjoyed experimenting over the years and often used a sausage as an element on a dish at the restaurant. If you fancy having a try at home, you don't really need any fancy kit for the odd batch and sausage casings are available online or your butcher will probably be able to supply them.

Bonfire night would be the perfect time to make some hot dogs and half the fun of a hot dog is choosing what will accompany it. Venison is abundant at this time of year and a little bit of chilli won't go amiss on a cold November night.

MAKES APPROXIMATELY 12 HOT DOGS

NOTE: Make the hot dog sausages and cabbage 24 hours ahead to allow for chilling

For the hot dog sausages
3m natural sausage casings *
500g diced venison, 1½–2cm pieces
200g diced pork shoulder, 1½–2cm pieces
150g pork back fat
2 tsp dried mustard powder
2 tsp smoked paprika
1 tsp freshly ground black pepper
1½ tsp garlic powder
15 juniper berries, finely ground
1 tsp ground coriander
2½ tsp Maldon sea salt, finely ground (12g)
20g dried breadcrumbs
150ml iced water

* To fill the skins, a cloth piping bag, a Jubilee clip and a 22mm to 15mm copper pipe reducer will do the job. Use the Jubilee clip to hold the pipe reducer tightly in the piping bag instead of a nozzle. The 15mm section is long enough to slide on about a metre of sausage skins.

For poaching the hot dogs
2 tsp Maldon sea salt
4 sprigs of thyme

For the chilli-pickled cabbage
100ml red wine
100g caster sugar
100ml red wine vinegar
4 juniper berries, crushed
4 black peppercorns
1½ tsp Maldon sea salt
1 tbsp olive oil
1 clove of garlic, minced
200g red cabbage, finely shredded
1 red chilli, finely sliced

To serve
12 brioche hot dog buns
condiments of your choice

1. Start by putting the sausage skins in cold water to soak. Next, working in small batches to keep everything cold, mince the venison, pork shoulder and the back fat using the coarse plate on the mincer. (If you don't have a mincer, you should be able to get the pork and venison ready-minced and the back fat can be finely diced by hand with a sharp knife.) Next, mix the meats and fat together with all the seasonings and the breadcrumbs, and pass through the mincer once more. (If you aren't mincing the meat yourself just make sure the seasonings are well mixed in.) Place the mince on a baking tray and chill in the freezer for 45 minutes.

2. Divide the mix into four and blend in a food processor to a smooth paste using a quarter of the iced water in each batch. Chilling the processor bowl and blade prior to using will help to keep everything cold.

3. Take a small portion of the mix and fry it in a small pan so that you can taste to check the seasoning. Adjust if necessary.

4. Transfer the mix to a piping bag fitted with the pipe reducer as described above. Find one end of the sausage casing and push it over the nozzle. Feed on one-third of the casings, or as much as you can easily fit on. Holding the casing in one hand, squeeze the piping bag with the other to fill the skins. Repeat with the remaining casings. An extra pair of hands can come in useful with this. Next, twist the sausages at 20cm intervals to form the individual links. Place the sausages on a tray and wrap with cling film. Chill overnight.

5. To cook, place the sausages in a large pan and cover with cold water. Add the thyme and salt. Heat the water to around 80˚C and then reduce the heat to keep the water temperature around this for 7 minutes. The sausages should reach a core temperature of 75˚C. Transfer to iced water to chill completely and then drain and refrigerate until required.

6. To make the pickled cabbage, combine the wine, sugar and vinegar in a pan with the juniper, peppercorns and salt. Bring to the boil and then remove from the heat. In a separate pan, heat the oil, add the garlic and cook gently until the garlic just takes on some colour. Add the cabbage and, using a sieve to catch the juniper and peppercorns, pour the vinegar mix over the top. Bring back to the boil, remove from the heat and stir in the chilli. Allow to cool and then refrigerate for at least 24 hours.

7. To serve, grill or fry the sausages until hot through, toast the buns and split to hold the sausages. Drain the pickled cabbage thoroughly and dress with a little oil, checking the seasoning and adjusting if required. Pile some pickle into the buns and top with a sausage. Finish with condiments of your choice. Maybe a little harissa mayo? Mustard, cheese, ketchup. . . all of them?

Sue Brown's Christmas pudding

I don't honestly know the origins of this recipe but I do have a tatty, grease-spattered recipe book that contains many of the recipes Mum used to make, including this one. She loved cooking as much as I do and there were always tins of home-made cakes and biscuits in her kitchen. We often talked about food and shared recipes, without her help we would never have got the restaurant off the ground.

This recipe is just labelled 'Christmas pudding, Maiden Green recipe'. It was the one she made in huge numbers for the farm shop. I have probably taken a few liberties with the recipe and I had to convert it from imperial but I know she would have been really happy to see it appear here.

'Stir-up Sunday' is the traditional day for making Christmas puddings but, whenever you do it, it's a good time to raise a glass to all those who taught us to cook, who encouraged us and shared their passion and their tables with us.

MAKES A 1.2 KG PUDDING

NOTE: Start this recipe 24 hours ahead to allow time for the fruit to soak.

2 tbsp sherry
2 tbsp brandy
20g black treacle
1 lemon, zest and juice
100g sultanas
150g raisins
50g dates, chopped
50g dried apricots, chopped
1½ large, free-range eggs (100g)
60g plain flour
1 tsp Maldon sea salt, finely ground
2 tbsp mixed spice
120g fresh breadcrumbs
45g suet
90g Bramley apple, grated
50g carrot, grated
100g dark muscovado sugar
150g soft dark brown sugar

1. In a large mixing bowl, combine the sherry, brandy, treacle, lemon juice and zest. Add all the dried fruit and mix well. Cover and leave to steep overnight. The following day, mix in the egg and then sift the flour, salt and mixed spice on top. Mix thoroughly and then stir in the remaining ingredients.

2. Put the mix into a 16–17cm pudding basin, packing it down well. If using a plastic basin, snap on a plastic lid; otherwise use a sheet of baking parchment topped with a sheet of foil. Lay the foil on the parchment and make a pleat in the centre to allow for some expansion, and then tie around the basin's rim with string. Place in a large pan of boiling water with the water coming halfway up the basin. Cover the pan with foil or place a lid on. Steam for 6 hours, checking the water level frequently. Top up with boiling water as necessary.

3. Once the pudding is cooked, remove from the pan and allow to cool completely before wrapping up in foil and storing somewhere cool until required. If you have used a traditional pudding basin, replace the baking parchment and foil while the pudding is hot and then wrap tightly in cling film when completely cold.

4. To reheat, steam again for 2 hours or the pudding can be heated in a microwave.

12 | December

Heligmonath – the holy month

It's December and that means we've put the central heating on, taken our warmest coats out of the cupboard and decided that, however fashionable we think we are, it's OK to wear mittens. The last of the leaves will lose their fight against gravity this month and we'll see countrywide frosts biting hard.

So, the mellow fruitfulness of autumn has definitely given way to the numb-fingerness of winter, and you might be tempted to think that means a lack of good food. But fear not, seasonal-food friends, there's more than enough to go around.

While the icy weather does mean that there's no point trying to do much in the garden or on the vegetable patch, the flip side is that many of those vegetables that have made it this far will quite happily sit tight, fresh and flavoursome, for the rest of the season. There's a giant natural larder of frost-resistant turnips, swedes, parsnips, cabbages, chicory, carrots, artichokes and sprouts (who could forget the sprouts?) just waiting to be eaten.

To accompany the vegetables there's plenty of good meat, and December is one of the best-value months for pheasant, duck and goose. And, as always, there's plenty of fish to choose from, with cod, oysters, scallops and prawns all excellent quality at this time of year.

Is all this really any surprise? For centuries now, even in the bleak midwinter, as the year draws to a close and near to the shortest day, families across the country have been managing to put together one of the biggest seasonal feasts of them all.

The tradition of burning a large log in the hearth on Christmas Eve dates back many hundreds of years. Although the yule log is probably Norse in origin, it was whole-heartedly adopted here, initially for the solstice festival of Yuletide and later for Christmas, at a time of year when warmth and light were essential for making a welcoming house for guests.

Many supposed ceremonies and myths surround the yule log and, in particular, its entry to the house. In some counties it was important that the youngest member of the family brought it across the threshold. Others said it was vital that the log should be sprinkled with cider or mead. Few of these rules could be said to be universal, with two exceptions. First, it was certainly considered bad luck to let the fire die out before Christmas Day. (Although it's frequently suggested that the log would burn throughout the Twelve Days of Christmas, it's not difficult to see how this would have been impossible in all but the very largest of houses.) The second golden rule was that the end of the log should be kept to kindle the next year's Christmas fire.

In the West Country (particularly Devon and Somerset) a variation on this theme still forms part of Christmas Eve festivities. An ashen faggot – a bundle of ash twigs – is ceremoniously burned. The bundle is said to represent the meagre fire gathered and lit either by the shepherds who visited the baby Jesus in the stable or by Mary. (Various Norse myths suggest that the ash tree has magical properties so there may well be an amalgamation of more than one tradition here.) As with the yule log, a fire is lit from the remnants of last year's bundle, usually by the oldest person in the room. Nine 'withies' of green ash or willow are used to bind the new bundle, which is placed on the fire. Once the withies have all burnt through, the party guests each take a piece to form part of their own bundles for the next year. In some instances, everyone present takes a drink as each of the nine withies burns through. In others, the unmarried women present each choose a withy and the one whose burns through first will, it's said, be the next to be married.

These days the true tradition has all but died out in favour of edible alternatives, but if you want to rekindle it, Christmas Eve is definitely the time to go in search of your yule log. Pagan tradition dictates that, when looking for a log, you should listen for the call of the trees to be guided to it and you should only take one that a tree has 'given', rather than cutting a live branch. There is certainly some practical sense in this because a freshly cut log will never burn well.

Christmas Eve is a peaceful and magical time for a woodland walk. So even if there's no fire in your house, go for a wander. Maybe you'll still hear the call of your yule log, even if it's a very small one.

Food & Foraging | Clementines

I am, without apology, going to allow one more imported citrus fruit into this book. It just seems churlish to talk about our festive celebrations without mentioning clementines.

For decades the last item to be plucked from many an excited child's Christmas stocking has been one of these cheery orange fruits. Even the most hard-line home-grown food enthusiast would have to concede that a potato or beetroot would probably not cut the mustard.

Why clementines at Christmas? Many writers suggest that the fruits are used as an allegory for gold in medieval paintings of St Nicholas of Myra (the fourth-century Christian bishop, known for his generosity and who at some point morphed into Santa Claus). It's equally likely that these glossy, seedless fruits just provide a welcome burst of zesty refreshment at a quiet time of year for British fruits.

Of course, clementines were also once seen as a particularly exotic fruit in Britain and undoubtedly a rare treat for many – a timely reminder, as we approach the end of the year (and this book), of how the global food trade has changed our lives.

Allegory or not, clementines are a firm fixture on our winter menu and it's hardly a surprise they have remained popular.

Patient gardeners will know that it is possible to grow clementines in the UK under cover of a heated greenhouse and lots of tending but, frankly, it's hard-going and proof that, occasionally, it makes sense to look abroad for a few of our ingredients. These days, most of our Christmas clementines are harvested in North African countries like Tunisia, and in southern Spain where their season runs from November through to late January.

Try: Clementine and sultana frangipane tarts (p. 280)

C eleriac is a greatly under-appreciated vegetable that really should be a star of our winter season. They grow well in our climate and are widely available from October through to February. Yet it seems the majority of shoppers find it hard to see past their outward appearance.

To be fair, they are pretty ugly. Even once spruced up for the supermarket shelf, the celeriac is a knobbly, lumpy brute of a root – like a muddy, deflated football that you might see in the park (usually in the dribbling jaws of a Staffordshire bull terrier.)

It wasn't always this way. Celeriac, or celery root as it is known in some parts, has a noble past. In ancient Greece it was revered – it featured on some Greek coins and, alongside 'real' celery (they are related), it was used as a medicine. It took a couple more centuries for Europeans to realize its culinary value but it remains popular on the continent to this day.

Celeriac has a depth of nutty, sweet flavour and none of the watery, bitter quality that you can find with its stalky relative. You'll need to start by peeling it and rinsing off any remaining soil. Store it in a bowl of water with a squeeze of lemon juice to stop it turning grey. Then all you have to do is decide how to cook it. It really is spectacularly versatile and lends itself to mashing, as a warming winter soup or simply eaten raw in that crisp, mustardy classic, remoulade.

Try: Rare roast beef with celeriac remoulade (p. 272)

Across the British countryside, the familiar croak of pheasants in late summer signals the release of birds into the wild and the imminent start of the game season.

Feathered game is one of the most traditionally seasonal elements of the British diet. The very fact that game can only be shot at particular times of the year means it is strictly (and legally) a seasonal treat. We saw the partridge and duck season begin at the start of September and pheasants join them on the menu from 1 October. Early-season birds can be a little underweight so I usually prefer to wait until they have filled out after a few more weeks of feeding and flying in the field.

There is a tongue-in-cheek Victorian saying that reflects the economics of shooting – 'Up goes a guinea, bang goes sixpence and down comes half a crown.' Although the currency may have changed, the broad principles remain the same. Shooters, referred to as 'guns' will pay considerable sums to shoot pheasant, but the shoot will then sell an entire bird in the feather to a game dealer for well under a pound. That means that, even once gutted and plucked, you rarely need to pay more than a fiver for a bird large enough to feed two people (and make a decent stock from the carcass). Prices drop even further mid-season as shoots across the country produce a glut of birds, and all of that puts December bang in the middle of great value and taste.

I've written about the ethics of pheasant shooting elsewhere and decided not to reproduce that in this book, simply for lack of space to do the difficult topic justice. Suffice to say that I firmly believe, when done properly, game shooting for food is defensible from an ethical standpoint. Indeed, for many reasons, it is a positively good thing. It promotes healthy eating and a respect for the countryside, for its wildlife and the birds we shoot. It can create jobs, supply us with good-quality meat and have animal welfare standards on a par with the best meat-farming practices. As with so much of our food chain, it's when shooting becomes big business that things can go wrong. A focus only on profit or the number of birds shot in a day completely severs the essential link between shooting and food and, quite reasonably, raises objections.

When buying game of any kind, speak to your butcher or game dealer about it. Don't be afraid to ask where it came from and what he knows about the reputation of the supplier. Buyers of high-quality meat want to talk about it – and, ultimately, charge you a premium for it – so you should have a willing audience.

Try: Pot-roasted pheasant with cider and apple (p. 275)

| # Winter Solstice (21st to 23rd December)

Back in March we saw the vernal equinox firing the start gun for spring, June gave us Midsummer, and the autumn equinox in September was marked by Harvest Festival celebrations. In December, we complete our game of solar Happy Families with the shortest day – the winter solstice – which falls between the 21 and 23 December.

The optimists amongst you will realize that, it's not just the darkest day of the year (which perhaps isn't a cause for celebration) but an important seasonal turning point, after which the days once again start getting longer.

In the past, the winter solstice was a date of significance for most of the country's cultures. It marked (at various times in our history) the festivals of Yule, Saturnalia (Saturn being a god of agriculture) and Sol Invictus, the feast of the 'unconquered sun'.

Since adoption of the Gregorian calendar, when Christmas was bumped forward a few days, and the growth of Christmas as our predominant national celebration, the solstice tends to be overlooked. But the celestial event and all of the celebrations that surrounded it have long played an important role in reminding us that, even in the depths of a cold, dark winter, better, warmer times lie ahead.

Despite Saturn's best efforts, the solstice is hardly a time of agricultural bounty, but tradition has it that the shortest day of the year is the date to plant garlic that will be harvested, exactly six months later, at the summer solstice.

Feasts & Festivals | Christmas Day (25th December)

A s we edge towards the end of the calendar year, deep in the middle of the winter, the country hosts what has undoubtedly become our most popular seasonal feast. A long-standing debate continues to rage as to exactly why the twenty-fifth was the chosen day to celebrate Christmas, since there is no mention of the date of Jesus's birthday in the Bible.

It is well established that the day – the winter solstice, under the old Julian system – was already a big one in the party calendar. The festivals of Saturnalia and Sol Invictus were celebrated by many Romans, so it could have made sense to usurp the same day for the new religious celebration of Christmas.

However, biblical scholars argue that Christians at the time would have wanted to distance themselves from the old religions and debauched pagan festivities, so it wouldn't have been particularly logical for them to deliberately choose the same date. Further, there is good evidence to show that the choice of date was a decision of the very early Church rather than (as is often suggested) the manipulative and more powerful institution of the Middle Ages. There are records of the Roman Emperor Constantine (the first Christian Emperor) celebrating Christmas on the twenty-fifth in 336, and some texts even suggest that neither Sol Invictus nor Saturnalia were actually celebrated on the solstice but on surrounding dates. So, despite conviction on both sidesof the debate, it's far from clear.

In any event, for many centuries Christmas was not seen as the main Christian celebration, with Easter being far more widely observed (and for some time marking the new year, rather than 1 January, such was its importance). Over time, the winter festival became more widely adopted and eventually celebrated as the biggest event in our calendar.

We have the Victorians, and the German Prince Albert in particular, to thank for many of today's Christmas traditions. Before their time neither Christmas cards nor trees were commonplace. In fact, Charlotte (the German wife of George III) was probably the first to introduce the tradition of bringing an entire tree indoors but there is little doubt that Albert popularized the concept and, following publication of an engraved Christmas message in 1848 showing the royal family celebrating around their tree, it soon became ubiquitous.

As with so many of our customs, practices and celebrations, Christmas is a little of one religion and a bit more of another. Add some local customs and imported family traditions and, before you know it, it's what we've always done but no one can quite emember why.

And in this diverse, eclectic, eccentric country that we're lucky enough to call home, there's something very appropriate about that. Happy Christmas!

Try: A Well Seasoned Winter (p. 282)

Rare roast beef with celeriac remoulade

This isn't quite the famed carpaccio from Harry's Bar in Venice but something a little more robust. It is a perfect use for the fillet tail, usually much cheaper than a centre-cut piece of fillet. The celeriac remoulade provides some heft to the dish but also gives a creamy foil to the rare meat. We are pushing the seasonal envelope slightly with watercress in December, so swap for mustard leaves or mizuna if the cress is over.

You can either serve this as an elegant starter, individually plated, or use a big platter or wooden board for a sharing dish.

SERVES 8 AS A STARTER

For the beef
600g trimmed fillet tail
2 tbsp olive oil for frying
Maldon sea salt and freshly ground black
   pepper

For the remoulade
750g whole celeriac
2 tsp Maldon sea salt
2 tbsp water
3 tbsp mayonnaise
1 tbsp crème fraîche
2 tsp wholegrain mustard
2 tsp good olive oil
1 tsp lemon juice plus extra to taste
Maldon sea salt and freshly ground black
   pepper

To serve
1 bunch of watercress, picked and washed
Parmesan shavings
extra virgin olive oil

1. Preheat the oven to 180°C.

2. Season the fillet tails heavily with coarsely ground pepper and salt. Press in well by rolling the fillet on a tray to create a thin crust of seasoning. Heat the oil in a heavy-based frying pan and sear the beef to achieve a well-caramelized crust. Finish in the oven for a couple of minutes if necessary. Remove to a cooling rack and allow to rest.

3. Peel the celeriac and cut in half. Roughly square off the pieces and then slice into 2mm-thick slices. Cut the slices across to form matchsticks 2mm square at each end. In a bowl, mix the celeriac, salt and water. Leave to salt for an hour to soften the celeriac slightly. Rinse off and squeeze dry in a clean tea towel.

4. Mix the remaining ingredients together and add the celeriac, coating thoroughly. Adjust the seasoning to taste with salt, pepper, lemon juice and more mustard if desired.

5. To serve, slice the beef thinly, and lay a line of remoulade down the centre of each plate. Scatter some watercress over it and arrange the beef slices across the top. Finish with the Parmesan shavings and a drizzle of your best olive oil.

Pot-roasted pheasant with cider and apple

As Jon has pointed out, a brace of oven-ready pheasants is unlikely to cost more than £10 – much less on occasions – and will certainly make a good meal for four, (and the thighs can be used to make a pâté or pie for another day.)

As with most game, it is very lean, though, and care needs to be taken with the cooking to keep the flesh moist. Most game birds are better cooked a touch pink to keep them from drying out and, whilst the accuracy of the cooking is important, it's always better to aim for under rather than over.

Pot-roasting is a great technique for smallish birds such as pheasant as the meat cooks gently in the steam and is flavoured by the aromatic liquids and the caramelization from the initial sear in a pan. Fat from good streaky bacon also helps and, as with any meat cookery, the final stage of resting is absolutely vital.

SERVES 4 AS A MAIN COURSE

2 pheasant crowns
2 tbsp rapeseed oil
1 onion, peeled and cut into 8 wedges
2 cloves of garlic, sliced
150ml cider
200ml chicken or pheasant stock (see Basics
    p. 285)
4 slices smoked, streaky bacon, stretched with
    the back of a knife and cut in half
2 Braeburn apples, peeled, cored and cut into
    8 wedges
75ml double cream
1 tsp wholegrain mustard
1 tsp cornflour slaked in 1 tbsp cold water
Maldon sea salt and freshly ground black
    pepper

1. Preheat the oven to 160°C.

2. Rub the pheasant skin with 1 tsp of oil and season well. Heat a heavy-based frying pan and very quickly seal the pheasants on the skin side. Remove the pheasants and use the same pan to soften the onions in the remaining oil, adding a pinch of salt.

3. Add the garlic and cook for a few minutes longer. Pour in the cider and reduce completely. Add the stock and bring to a simmer.

4. Tip the onion mix into a large casserole which will hold the pheasants fairly tightly. Place the sealed pheasants in the casserole, cover the birds with the strips of bacon, scatter the apple around and seal with a tight-fitting lid. Cook in the oven for 25–30 minutes.

5. Remove the pheasant to rest in a warm place. Take off the bacon and crisp under a hot grill. Drain the liquid from the casserole into a pan, add the cream and mustard and place over a high heat to reduce slightly. Thicken with the cornflour, adding gradually as you may not need it all – a thick double-cream consistency is what you are looking for. Adjust the seasoning and add the sauce back to the apple and onion mix.

6. Carve the breasts from the pheasant, checking for shot as you do so. Divide the sauce with the apple and onion between the plates, top with the pheasant andfinish with the bacon.

7. Serve with creamy mash and some buttered greens.

Lamb sausage roll with garlic and mustard mayonnaise

Both my wife, Eléna, and I have the same childhood memory of a Tupperware box of sausage rolls appearing on the kitchen worktop a few days before Christmas. What we both marvel at now is that they would have sat in a warm kitchen for at least a week before the last ones disappeared! Neither of us remember any ill effects from the lackadaisical storage but it does seem odd now, given the greater fear and more enlightened view of food hygiene. One thing I am sure of is that the fridge is the enemy of pastry products as it dulls the flavours and spoils the texture. Storing sausage rolls on the kitchen counter probably isn't wise, though, so I suggest you just eat the sausage rolls the day you make them!

MAKES 8 LARGE ROLLS

For the sausage rolls
250g lamb mince, 20% fat
½ tsp Maldon sea salt, finely ground
¼ tsp freshly ground black pepper
½ quantity rough puff pastry (see Basics p. 288)
1 large, free-range egg yolk, beaten with 1 tbsp cold water

For the garlic and mustard mayonnaise
1 small clove of garlic, smashed and covered in boiling water.
30g mayonnaise
30g crème fraîche
1 tsp Dijon mustard
1 dsp finely sliced chives
pinch of Maldon sea salt

1. Preheat oven to 180°C.

2. In a mixing bowl, break up the lamb mince and season. Cut the seasoning through the mince with a knife and then work in thoroughly with clean hands. On a chopping board, squeeze and roll the mix into a sausage around 40cm long. Wrap the lamb tightly in cling film and then in foil. Allow enough film and foil to twist the ends up to compress the lamb mince. Place in the fridge to chill for at least an hour.

3. Roll out the puff pastry into a 40cm x 16cm rectangle. Brush the pastry all over with the egg wash. Unwrap the chilled lamb sausage and roll up in the pastry. Seal well at the join. Transfer to a baking tray lined with baking parchment, with the join in the pastry underneath. Press down gently to flatten the bottom slightly. Return to the fridge to chill for 30 minutes. Once chilled, cut into eight individual portions, score the top of the pastry three times on each roll and brush with the remaining egg wash. Place back on the tray and bake for 15–18 minutes until the pastry is crisp and golden and the centre of the meat reads 70°C on a temperature probe. Alternatively insert a small sharp knife into the centre of the meat for a few seconds, remove and carefully touch onto your bottom lip, it should be too hot to hold it there. Transfer the sausage rolls to a cooling rack and leave to rest for at least 15 minutes before serving.

4. To make the mayonnaise, drain the garlic and crush to a paste using a pinch of salt and the back of a cook's knife. Mix with the remaining ingredients and adjust the seasoning. A good dollop of ketchup is, of course, a perfectly acceptable alternative!

Beenleigh Blue cheesecake with sweet and sour pears

British cheeses really are something to celebrate and we should do all we can to support and protect the industry. A good cheese course can be about one single perfect cheese or a large number of different cheeses. If you are going to serve a selection at home, though, I would keep it small and try to give a mix of textures, milks and strengths. Beenleigh Blue, a Quicke's cheddar, Bath Soft and the cider-brandy-washed Katherine would make a well-balanced and entirely British but West-Country-biased selection.

The actual blue cheese you use for this cheesecake isn't as important as choosing something with a similar texture to Beenleigh Blue – nothing too soft and creamy. The sweet and sour pears provide a fruity and sharp note to balance the richness of the dish, much as grapes and chutney would on a cheese board.

SERVES 8–10

NOTE: Start 24 hours ahead to allow setting time

For the cheesecake base
50g salted butter
2 tbsp rapeseed oil
15g dark maple syrup
100g digestive biscuits, crushed
80g oatcakes, crushed
½ tsp Maldon sea salt, finely ground

For the cheesecake topping
300g soft cream cheese
100ml semi-skimmed milk
2 leaves of gelatine, soaked in cold water
450g blue cheese, coarsely grated
2 tsp lemon juice
10g honey
140ml double cream plus 1 tbsp semi-skimmed
    milk, lightly whipped
Maldon sea salt and freshly ground black
    pepper

For the pears
20g unsalted butter
4 firm Williams pears or similar, peeled, cored
    and cut into 6 wedges
2 tbsp caster sugar
50ml cider vinegar
50ml apple juice
Maldon sea salt and freshly ground black
    pepper

To serve
½ ripe pear, cored, thinly sliced
1 tsp cider vinaigrette (see Basics p. 287)
winter salad leaves

1. Preheat the oven to 160°C.

2. To make the base, heat the butter, oil and maple syrup in a small saucepan until it comes together, stirring frequently. Mix the butter into the biscuits along with the salt and then press the mix into a 20cm x 8cm stainless-steel ring that is sat on a baking tray lined with baking parchment or a Silpat mat. Bake the base for 6 minutes and then allow to cool completely.

3. To make the topping, soften the cream cheese with half of the milk. Squeeze any excess water from the gelatine and then heat in a small pan with the remaining milk to dissolve. Pass the gelatine mix through a fine sieve into the cream cheese and whisk in.

4. Beat in the grated blue cheese. Stir in the lemon juice and honey and season. Fold in the lightly whipped cream and pour the mix onto the base. Smooth out the mix with a palette knife, finishing with abstract swirls and dabs to make an attractive pattern. Return to the fridge to set overnight.

5. For the pears, heat a large non-stick frying pan and add half the butter. When the butter stops foaming, add half the pears and toss in the butter. Sprinkle over half the sugar and season well. Cook over a high heat until a deep caramel colour is achieved. Add half of the vinegar and half of the apple juice. Allow the mix to bubble for a few seconds and reduce slightly. Transfer the pears to a plate and repeat with the second half of the ingredients. Chill until required but allow to return to room temperature before using.

6. Serve the cheesecake with a garnish of thinly-sliced raw pear dressed in a little vinaigrette on top, the sweet and sour pear wedges, a drizzle of the juice and some winter leaves, maybe mizuna, or mustard leaves.

Clementine and sultana frangipane tarts

They are as enchanting as any bauble on a Christmas tree: the shine, the vibrant orange colour and, occasionally, the contrast of green leaves. The clementine is, to my mind, inextricably linked with the festive season, and so one thought led to another and an alternative to a mince pie came to the fore. Baked as small tarts or as one large tart to slice, this brings together so many of my seasonal favourites. Add some clotted cream or spiced brandy butter, a little of the fresh fruit and just a touch of the clementine confit, and dessert is sorted. Or, of course, as the cook, you can indulge in some quality control straight from the cooling rack. . .

I make no apologies for this being a complex recipe and, in mitigation, all the elements could be made separately over a number of days and then assembled before baking. The confit will keep for several weeks, the frangipane and pastry freeze well and you could even blind-bake the pastry cases the day before you cook the tarts.

MAKES 12 SMALL TARTS USING A DEEP MUFFIN TIN

For the clementine confit
(makes much more than required but has many other uses)
8 clementines
500g granulated sugar
500ml water
2 cinnamon sticks
10 black peppercorns

For the frangipane
100g unsalted butter
100g dark muscovado sugar
1½ large, free-range eggs (100g)
1 tbsp self-raising flour
100g roasted almonds, blitzed to a powder
1 tsp mixed spice
pinch of finely ground Maldon salt

For the sultanas
100g sultanas
100ml cider

To assemble
½ quantity sweet pastry (see Basics pp. 288–9)

1. Preheat oven to 170°C.

2. To make the clementine confit, start by blanching the clementines. Cover with cold water, bring to a boil then simmer gently for 10 minutes, then drain and refresh in cold water. Repeat three more times.

3. In a clean saucepan, combine the sugar, water and spices and bring to the boil, stirring to dissolve the sugar. Prick the blanched clementines several times with a cocktail stick, add to the syrup and cover with baking parchment. Use a saucer or small plate to keep the clementines submerged and simmer very gently for around 1½ hours. Using a slotted spoon, transfer to a blender and purée until completely smooth. Use a little of the cooking syrup if necessary. You are looking for a consistency similar to lemon curd.

4. For the frangipane, cream together the butter and sugar. Gradually beat in the egg, adding the flour in stages along with it. Fold in the almonds, mixed spice and salt and combine thoroughly. Transfer to a piping bag.

5. Simmer the sultanas in the cider until all the liquid is reduced/has been absorbed. Allow to cool.

6. Roll out the sweet pastry to approximately 4mm thick and use to line your chosen tart tin. Chill and then blind-bake until just set and a light golden colour.

7. Add enough clementine confit to the sultanas to create something akin to mincemeat. Place a generous teaspoonful in the tart shells if individual, or spread across the base of the tart if making a large one. Pipe on the frangipane and bake for around 20 minutes until the frangipane is risen and firm when pressed lightly.

8. Allow to cool slightly in the tin and then remove to a cooling rack. Store in a sealed container at room temperature.

A Well Seasoned Winter

Jon has been utterly dedicated and meticulous in his search for the perfect sloe or damson gin recipe and I know that extensive testing has been undertaken. I felt it only right and proper that I should put some effort into a festive cocktail recipe using the wonderful product of his labours. I have, of course, been equally dedicated in the testing department!

I can't think of many better ways to start a meal or celebration than with a glass of something sparkling and some canapés, so maybe try the Parmesan shortbreads with your cocktail.

Cheers all!

A FESTIVE COCKTAIL

SERVES 8

ice to half-fill a cocktail shaker
150ml sloe or damson gin
60ml amaretto
50ml fresh orange juice
½ orange, zest only
1cm piece fresh ginger
1 bottle of champagne or sparkling wine

1. Half-fill a cocktail shaker with ice and add the gin, amaretto and orange juice. Grate in the orange zest and the ginger. Shake briefly and then strain into your glasses. Carefully top up with the champagne or sparkling wine.

PARMESAN SHORTBREAD

MAKES AROUND 50 BISCUITS

120g plain flour
½ tsp Maldon sea salt, finely ground
120g Parmesan, grated
90g unsalted butter, cold, diced
1 large, free-range egg yolk
1 tbsp wholegrain mustard

1. Preheat oven to 170°C.

2. Using a food processor, mix together the dry ingredients, then pulse in the butter, egg and mustard to form a dough.

3. Roll into a sausage around 3.5cm in diameter, wrap tightly in cling film and refrigerate for half an hour.

4. Cut into 5mm-thick rounds and bake until golden brown (approximately 12 minutes).

NOTE: The mix freezes well so divide in half and freeze the remainder if required.

Basics

Vegetable stock

If there was a single item that could have been called the life blood of our restaurant kitchen, this would have been it. I can't imagine how many thousands of litres of vegetable stock we must have made over the years! It was a key component in so many dishes and certainly features in several recipes in this book.

In its dilute state, the flavour is clean and fairly delicate with obvious aniseed notes. Reduce it down and the flavours intensify, the savoury notes of the onion are revealed and the sweetness of all the vegetables plays its part. I truly love this stock and can't imagine cooking without it.

MAKES APPROXIMATELY 1½L

NOTE: Make 24 hours in advance if possible

2 bulbs of fennel
1 stick celery
1 large leek
1 medium onion
1 small bunch flat-leaf parsley
2 tsp fennel seeds
1 star anise

1. Slice and wash all the vegetables and place in a large pan. Add the parsley, fennel seeds and star anise. Just cover with water, bring to a boil and then simmer for 30 minutes. Store with the vegetables in until required.

Beef stock

A good stock is a fantastic base for many dishes, and making your own gives you absolute control of what goes in and how it is made. This is a perfect example of the 'rubbish in, rubbish out' scenario – you have to use good ingredients and cook a stock with care to make a tasty end product. I have seen all sorts of crimes committed in the making of stock, including the leftover sausages and bacon from a breakfast service being dumped into the stock pot!

MAKES APPROXIMATELY 6L

3kg small-cut mixed marrow and rib bones
500g beef trim or beef shin
1 large onion, cut in half, skin on
1 large leek, cut in half
2 sticks celery, cut in half
2 carrots, peeled

1. Preheat the oven to 180˚C.

2. Roast the bones until well coloured, turning frequently – this will take around 30–40 minutes. Add the beef trim or shin after 15 minutes.

3. Wash the vegetables, place in a deep pan and add the bones and beef. Cover with water so that it comes 5cm above the bones and bring just to the boil. Immediately skim well to remove any fat, foam or impurities that have come to the surface.

4. Reduce to a simmer and cook for 4 hours, skimming frequently and topping up with cold water as required.

5. Pass the stock through a colander and then a fine sieve. Ideally, strain through muslin and chill. Remove any surface fat when solidified.

1 large carrot, peeled and cut into 4
2 sticks of celery, cut into 4 pieces
2 bay leaves
8 peppercorns

1. Roast the bones until well coloured, turning frequently – this will take 20–30 minutes.

2. Wash the vegetables and place in a deep pan, add the bones. Cover with water so that it comes 5cm above the bones and bring just to the boil. Immediately skim well to remove any fat, foam or impurities that have come to the surface.

Chicken stock

Although lighter than a beef stock, chicken stock still adds great depth of flavour to sauces, casseroles, pasta dishes and risottos. I often buy a whole chicken and bone it out to give breasts, thighs and drumsticks then chop the bones to make stock – getting a batch made and in the freezer is worth it.

A stock cube is never really a good alternative to fresh stock but the situation has improved hugely over recent years and both the fresh, chilled stocks on sale in supermarkets and some stock concentrates are a viable alternative. I would recommend the retail range from Essential Cuisine that is available online.

Home-made stock can be reduced down and frozen in small pots or ice cube trays, which makes it much more practical.

MAKES APPROXIMATELY 2L

1 kg chicken bones
1 large onion, peeled and roughly diced
1 large leek, sliced into 4cm pieces

Red wine sauce

I think of this as a base for many sauces and also as a way of boosting or rounding out flavours. In itself, the sauce has quite a simple flavour. This means that you can choose to add flavours later according to your recipe.

For example, a small quantity added to reduced chicken stock and infused with some thyme would make a flavoursome sauce for many chicken dishes. Equally, a little of the sauce will mellow the flavour of a game stock.

Make a batch and allow to set in the fridge, then cut into cubes, wrap well and freeze until whenever you need it.

MAKES APPROXIMATELY 600ML

1 tbsp olive oil
2 banana shallots, peeled and sliced
4 cloves of garlic, smashed
1 small bunch of thyme
375ml red wine
125ml ruby port
1 quantity beef stock (see Basics pp. 284–5)
Maldon sea salt

1. Heat the oil in a large pan and sweat the shallots and garlic with a pinch of salt. Cook until they soften completely and allow to take on a little colour.

2. Add the thyme and then the alcohols and reduce to a light syrup. Add the stock and bring to the boil, then turn down to a simmer. Allow the sauce to reduce to about one litre and then start tasting. While the stock is reducing, skim off any foam and impurities that rise to the surface.

3. The sauce should have a deep, savoury, meaty flavour, balanced by the acidity of the wine with subtle notes of herbs and garlic. When the sauce has the required depth of flavour, season with salt and pass through a fine chinois or sieve into a plastic container. Chill as quickly as possible.

Pickling liquid for fennel, carrots, shallots, etc.

Lightly pickled vegetables can add a real punch to a salad, make a great accompaniment to cheeses or charcuterie and can be used to bring a twang of acidity to balance a dish. Tougher or harsher vegetables benefit from salting first and then pickling so with the fennel, for example, peel the tough fibres away from the outside of the bulb, then halve and remove the core. Slice as finely as possible with a sharp knife or on a mandolin. Mix with a dessert spoon of Maldon salt and leave for an hour. Drain and wash off thoroughly. Squeeze dry and then pour over the boiling pickling liquid. For something like the carrots, I would add them to the pan of boiling pickling liquid, bring it back to the boil and then immediately remove from the heat.

Store your pickles in sterilized jars in the fridge and they will keep for a couple of months. To use, drain off what you need and dress with a little good oil and some seasoning.

You can ring the changes by swapping the vinegar and the wine in this recipe, I like red wine and red wine vinegar for pickled shallot rings, cider vinegar and dry cider for fennel, and cava vinegar with orange juice for the carrots, so feel free to experiment!

125ml white wine
125ml white wine vinegar
125g caster sugar
1 tsp mustard seeds
1 clove of garlic, smashed
2 sprigs of thyme
1 tsp whole black peppercorns
½ tsp Maldon sea salt

1. Combine all the ingredients in a small pan and bring to the boil. Add the raw vegetables, return to the boil and immediately remove from the heat. Allow to cool at room temperature and then transfer to sterile jars.

Cider Vinaigrette

This would be my 'go to' house dressing. I like the subtle flavour of the cider vinegar as a good all-rounder. Finding good quality vinegars is something well worth doing and a few drops can lift a sauce or add that all important acidity to balance a dish.

5g lecithin powder
1 tsp honey
1 tsp Dijon mustard
100ml apple juice, reduced to 50ml
150ml light olive oil
125ml grape seed oil
75ml good cider vinegar
Maldon sea salt and freshly ground black pepper

1. Mix the lecithin with a tablespoon of hot water in a jug, whisk in the honey, mustard and apple juice. Add a generous pinch of salt and a few grinds of black pepper. Using a hand blender, gradually add the oils. If the dressing gets too thick, add some of the vinegar as you mix. Once all the oil has been incorporated, add the remaining vinegar and season to taste.

Simple flatbreads

There are so many uses for flatbreads; they are perfect for scooping up a dhal, wrapping around pulled pork or dipping into hummus. However you choose to use them, they are quick and easy to make, requiring little kneading or resting and no proving.

As with any bread, quality flour does make a difference and the mixture of white bread flour and wholemeal adds both flavour and texture.

MAKES 8 FLATBREADS (20CM)

200g strong white bread flour
100g wholemeal flour
1½ tsp Maldon sea salt, finely ground
150ml semi-skimmed milk
100g plain full-fat yoghurt (ordinary, not Greek)
a little oil for the griddle

1. Weigh the flours and the salt and tip into a medium bowl. Using a whisk, give everything a good mix together. Make a well in the centre and add the milk and yoghurt. Bring the mix together into a soft dough.

2. Tip out onto a floured surface and knead for 2–3 minutes until well combined. Try to add as little flour as possible. Flour the bowl lightly and place the dough back in the bowl and cover with cling film. Rest for 15 minutes, although longer won't hurt.

3. Flour the work top and roll the dough into a cylinder. Cut into eight even pieces. Roll each piece into a ball and then flatten into a rough disc with your fingertips. Allow to rest for a couple of minutes and then roll out to 2–3mm thick.

4. Heat the oil in a cast-iron griddle pan or a non-stick frying pan and cook the flatbreads for about 90 seconds on each side. They should be slightly blistered but still pliable. Wrap in a clean tea towel to keep them warm as you cook the others.

Pasta dough

I wonder how many pasta machines there are languishing in the far recesses of kitchen cupboards? Plenty, if the conversations I have with people at dinners or cookery demonstrations are typical. They are one of those kitchen gadgets that people seem reluctant or unsure how to use. But there is something satisfying about trays of home-made pasta; the curled ribbons or neatly formed parcels containing delicious fillings hold so much promise of good food to come.

So, it's time to dust that machine off and have a go. I'm sure you will master the technique and the resulting meals will be ample reward for the effort.

MAKES 3–4 MAIN-COURSE PORTIONS OF PASTA RIBBONS

180g type '00' pasta flour
20g fine semolina
1½ tsp Maldon sea salt, finely ground (7g)
1 whole large, free-range egg, plus
   approximately 4 yolks (total weight 115g)
1 tsp olive oil

1. Sift the flour, semolina and salt into the bowl of a food processor. Whisk the egg and yolks with the olive oil.

2. Start the motor running on the food processor and pour in the egg mix in a steady stream. Stop the motor and scrape in the last of the egg with a rubber spatula. Pulse the mix until a fine breadcrumb texture is achieved.

3. Squeeze a small quantity of the dough together to check the consistency. You want a firm dough that is pliable and can be squashed between the fingers but is not overly soft or sticky. Tip the dough out onto a clean work surface and knead together. Rub the dough lightly with oil, wrap in cling film and rest in the fridge for 30 minutes.

4. Roll out using a pasta machine and then cut to the desired shape. Part of the secret is folding and turning the dough at the thickest setting until the pasta is silky smooth. Only then do you want to adjust the setting and start thinning the pasta. You want to be just able to see your fingers through the dough.

5. Use to make stuffed pastas or cut into ribbons or sheets. Place the cut or shaped pasta on a tray dusted with semolina and store unwrapped in the fridge until ready to use.

Rough puff pastry

225g plain flour
1 tsp Maldon salt, finely ground
240g unsalted butter, well chilled
135ml iced water

1. Sift the flour and salt into a mound on the work surface. Hold the butter with the wrapper and dip into the flour repeatedly as you grate it on a coarse grater. Stop every now and then to toss the butter gently in the flour.

2. Make a well in the centre and pour in the iced water. Bring the dough together with your fingertips and the aid of a pastry scraper. Pat the dough into a rough block and roll into a 40cm x 25cm rectangle. Brush off any excess flour and fold the top down by a third and then the bottom up by a third. Rotate the dough by 90 degrees and roll out again using more flour for dusting.

3. Repeat the folds and use the rolling pin to tap the dough into a neat block. Wrap in cling film and chill for 30 minutes.

4. Repeat the rolling, folding and resting twice more. Chill for at least an hour before using. The pastry freezes well if wrapped tightly in cling film.

Sweet pastry

This rich, sweet, buttery pastry is one I have been using for around twenty years and the exact recipe was a born out of a shortage of ingredients! This makes a fairly large quantity but it is worth making the whole batch and freezing what you don't need immediately. Wrapped tightly in a double layer of cling film, it will keep frozen for two months and for a week in the fridge.

MAKES 4 TART CASES (26CM)

225g unsalted butter
170g caster sugar
4 large, free-range egg yolks
4 tbsp cold water
110g cornflour
335g soft plain flour
1 tsp Maldon sea salt, finely ground

1. Cream the butter and caster sugar together, until the mixture starts to go pale. Combine the egg yolks and the water and beat gradually into the butter mix. Mix the flours and the salt and sift onto the butter mix. Use a rubber spatula to fold the flour in; you are aiming for dough that is homogenous but has been worked as little as possible. Turn the dough onto a floured surface and bring together into a cylinder. Wrap in cling film and chill for at least 30 minutes before using.

Shortbread

This is a classic recipe based on one from the book, *The Roux Brothers on Patisserie*. Published in 1986, this book is still utterly relevant today and is packed with excellent recipes for many classics.

Made by hand, I find this has a more delicate texture than making in a machine. The quantity is fairly large

but the dough does freeze well.

You could roll the dough out thicker and bake in a sheet, then cut into fingers while still warm – cooking times will be longer, though.

A WHOLE BATCH WILL MAKE APPROXIMATELY 48 BISCUITS

150g unsalted butter, softened
115g icing sugar, sifted
½ vanilla pod, seeds only
2½ large, free-range egg yolks (40g)
250g soft pastry flour
5g Maldon sea salt, finely ground
caster sugar for sprinkling

1. Preheat the oven to 160°C.

2. Cream the butter with the sifted icing sugar and the vanilla seeds, then beat in the egg yolks. Sift the flour and salt onto the bench and make a well in the centre. Scrape the butter mix into the well and, using your fingertips, gradually bring the flour into the butter mix, working as little as possible. Once a homogenous dough has been formed, wrap in cling film, flatten then chill for a minimum of 1 hour.

3. Roll out the dough to a thickness of 4mm. Cut out 7cm discs and place on baking trays lined with baking parchment or a Silpat mat.

4. Bake for around 8 minutes until pale golden in colour. Remove from the oven and sprinkle with caster sugar. Allow to cool for 5 minutes and then transfer to a wire rack to cool completely.

SEASONAL EATING

VEG

		WINTER			SPRING			SUMMER			AUTUMN		
		DEC	JAN	FEB	MAR	APR	MAY	JUN	JUL	AUG	SEP	OCT	NOV
ARTICHOKE, Globe	🛒							□	●	●	●	●	□
Jerusalem	🛒	●	●	●								□	●
ASPARAGUS	🛒				●	●	●	●	●				
AUBERGINE	🛒					□	●	●	●	●	●	●	
BEETROOT	🛒	●	●	□				□	●	●	●	●	●
BORLOTTI BEAN	🔍								●	●	●		
BROAD BEANS	🛒					□	●	●	●	□			
BROCCOLI	🛒						●	●	●	●	●	●	□
BRUSSELS SPROUTS	🛒	●	●	□	□						□	□	●
CABBAGES, Cavolo Nero	🛒	●	●	●	●			●	●	●	●	●	●
Chinese Leaf	🛒						□	●	●	●	●	●	□
January King	🔍		●	●	□								
Kale	🛒	●	●	●							□	●	●
Red Cabbage	🛒							●	●	●	●	□	●
Savoy	🛒	●	●	●				●		●			
Spring Greens	🛒				●	●	●	□	□	□			
White	🛒	●	●	●							●	●	●
CARROTS	🛒	●	●	●				●	●	●	●	●	●
CAULIFLOWER	🛒	●	●	●	●	●							□
CELERIAC	🛒	●	●	●	□						●	●	●
CELERY	🛒	●	●	●	□						●	●	●
CHARD	🔍							●	●	●	●	●	●
CHICORY	🔍	●	●	●	□							●	●
CHILLI	🛒								●	●	●	●	
COURGETTES	🛒							●	●	●	●	□	
COURGETTE FLOWERS	🔍						●	●	●	●	□		
CUCUMBERS	🛒							□	□	●	●	□	
FENNEL	🛒							●	●	●	●	●	□
FRENCH BEANS	🛒							●	●	●	●	□	
GARLIC (Cultivated)	🛒							●	●	□	□	□	
HORSERADISH	🔍	●	●	□							●	●	●
KOHLRABI	🔍	□	□	□					●	●	●	●	●
LEEKS	🛒	●	●	●	□						□	●	●

KEY

 You should find this at your local supermarket

 Just as tasty, but not as widely available

Available but may not be at its seasonal best

 Wild

 Very wild

VEG (cont.)

Seasonal availability chart (■ = in season / available, □ = limited or stored)

	WINTER			SPRING			SUMMER			AUTUMN		
	DEC	JAN	FEB	MAR	APR	MAY	JUN	JUL	AUG	SEP	OCT	NOV
LETTUCES, LEAVES, Cos					■	■	■	■	■	■	□	
Crisp					■	■	■	■	■	■	□	
Gem					■	■	■	■	■	■	□	
Iceberg					■	■	■	■	■	■	□	
Rosso					■	■	■	■	■	■	□	
Rocket					■	■	■	■	■	■	□	
Round					■	■	■	■	■	■	□	
MANGETOUT						■	■	■				
MARROW										□	■	■
ONIONS	■	■	■	■	□	■		■	■	■	■	■
PAK CHOI							□	■	■	■	□	
PARSNIPS	■	■	■	□						□	■	■
PEAS						■	■	■	■	□		
PEPPERS								□	■	■	□	
POTATOES, EARLY	A selection of new early and second early potatoes											
Duke of York (roast)					■	■	■					
Jersey Royals (boil)					□	■	■					
Maris Bard (boil/chip)						■	■					
Maris Peer (boil)							■	■	■	■		
Osprey (salad)							■	■	■	■		
Pentland Javelin (salad)						■	■	■				
POTATOES, MAIN CROP	A selection of main crop potatoes											
Anya (salad)	■	■	■	□	□	□	■	■	■	■	■	■
King Edward (mash)	■	■	■	□	□	□	■	■	■	■	■	■
Marfona (jacket)	■	■	■	□	□	□	■	■	■	■	■	■
Maris Piper (roast)	■	■	■	□	□	□	■	■	■	■	■	■
Pink Fir Apple (boil)	■	■	■	□	□	□	■	■	■	■	■	■
Rooster (chip)	■	■	■	□	□	□	■	■	■	■	■	■
PURPLE SPR. BROCCOLI			□	■	■	■						
RADISH							■	■	■	■	□	□
RUNNER BEANS							□	■	■	■	□	
SALSIFY	■	■	■	□							□	■
SAMPHIRE, Marsh							□	■	■	□		
Rock				□	■	■	□					
SHALLOT	■	■	■	□							□	■
SPINACH	□	□	■	■	■	□	□	□	□	□	□	□

VEG (cont.)

		DECEMBER	JANUARY	FEBRUARY	MARCH	APRIL	MAY	JUNE	JULY	AUGUST	SEPTEMBER	OCTOBER	NOVEMBER
		WINTER			**SPRING**			**SUMMER**			**AUTUMN**		
SPRING ONIONS	🛒					○	○	●	●	●	●		○
SQUASHES* (pumpkins, etc)	🛒	○	○								●	●	○
SWEDE	🛒	●	●	○							○	●	●
SWEETCORN	🛒									○	●		○
SWISS CHARD	🔍								○	●	●	●	●
TOMATOES*	🛒							○	●	●	●		○
TURNIPS, Baby	🛒							●	●	○	○		
Mature	🛒	●	●							○	○	●	●
WATERCRESS	🛒				●	●	●	○	●	○			

* Strictly, these are a fruit!

FRUIT

		DECEMBER	JANUARY	FEBRUARY	MARCH	APRIL	MAY	JUNE	JULY	AUGUST	SEPTEMBER	OCTOBER	NOVEMBER
APPLES, Cox	🛒	●	○									●	●
Bramley	🛒								○	●	●		
Discovery	🔍									●	●		
Egremont Russet	🔍										●	●	●
APRICOTS	🛒					○	○	●	●		○		
BILBERRIES	🔍								●	●		○	
BLACKBERRIES	🛒								●	●	○	○	○
BLACKCURRANTS	🛒								●	●	○		
BLUEBERRIES	🛒								○	●	○		
CHERRIES	🛒							○	●	●			
ELDERBERRIES	🛒									○	●	●	
FIGS (BRITISH)	🛒								○	●	●	○	
GOOSEBERRIES	🛒							○	●	●			
LOGANBERRIES	🔍							○	●	●	○		
MEDLARS	🔍	○										○	●
MULBERRIES	🔍									●	●	○	
PEARS, Concorde	🛒	●	○								○	●	●
Conference	🛒										○	●	●
Onward	🔍										●	●	

FRUIT (cont.)

Legend: ■ = in season · □ = limited / coming in · 🔍 = seasonal · 🛒 = available to buy

Fruit		WINTER Dec	Jan	Feb	SPRING Mar	Apr	May	SUMMER Jun	Jul	Aug	AUTUMN Sep	Oct	Nov
Williams	🔍									□	■		
PLUMS & GAGES, Falstaff	🔍								□	■	□		
GREENGAGE	🔍								□	■	■		
VICTORIA (most common)	🛒								□	■			
QUINCE	🔍										□	■	
RASPBERRIES	🛒							□	■	■	■	□	
REDCURRANTS	🛒							□	■	■	□		
RHUBARB, Forced	🛒		■	■	■								
Field	🛒				■	■	■	□					
STRAWBERRIES	🛒					□	■	■	■	□			
WHITECURRANTS	🔍								■	■			

FISH

Fish		WINTER Dec	Jan	Feb	SPRING Mar	Apr	May	SUMMER Jun	Jul	Aug	AUTUMN Sep	Oct	Nov
BLACK BREAM	🔍	□					□	■	■	■	■	□	□
COCKLES	🔍	■	■	■	■	□					■	□	■
COD	🛒	■	■	■			□	□	□	□	■	□	■
COLEY	🛒	■				□	□	□			■	■	■
CRAB (brown male)	🛒	□	■	■	■	■	■	■	■	■	■	■	■
CRAB (brown female)	🛒	■	■	■	□	□	■	■	■	■	■	■	■
CRAB (spider male)	🔍					□	■	■	■	■	■	■	□
CRAB (spider female)	🔍							□	■	■	■	■	□
CRAYFISH (signal/freshwater)	🛒					□	■	■	■	■	■	■	□
CUTTLEFISH	🔍					□	■	■					
GURNARD (grey and red)	🔍	■	■	■							■	■	■
HERRING	🛒							■	■	■	■	■	■
LEMON SOLE	🛒	■	■	■	■	■					■	■	■
LOBSTER	🛒	■	□	□	□	□	□	□	■	■	■	■	■
MACKEREL	🛒	□	□	□	□	□	■	■	■	■	■	■	■
MEGRIM	🔍	□					■	■	■	■	■	■	■
MUSSELS	🛒	■	■	□	□	□	□				■	■	■
OYSTERS (native)	🛒	■	□	□	□	□					■	■	■
OYSTERS (rock)	🛒	■	■	■	■	□	□	□	□	□	■	■	■

FISH (cont.)

Legend: ■ = in season (filled) · □ = available (outline) · 🛒 = buy · 🔍 = forage

		WINTER			SPRING			SUMMER			AUTUMN	
		DEC	JAN	FEB	MAR	APR	MAY	JUN	JUL	AUG	SEP	OCT	NOV
PILCHARD (Cornish sardine)	🛒	□	□								■	■	□
PLAICE	🛒	■				■	■	■	■	■	■	■	■
POLLOCK	🛒	□	□	■	■	■	■				□	■	■
PRAWNS	🛒	■						□	□	□	■	■	■
RAZOR CLAMS	🔍	■	■	■	□	□	□			□			
SALMON (farmed)	🛒	■	■	■	■	■	■	■	■	■	■	■	■
SALMON (wild)	🔍				□	■	■	■	■	■	■	□	
SARDINE	🛒	□	□								■	■	□
SCALLOPS	🛒	■	□	□	□	□					■	■	■
SEA BASS	🛒	□	□	□	□					■	■	■	■
SHRIMP	🛒				■	■	■	■	■	■	■	■	■
SQUID	🛒	□								■	■	■	□
TROUT (farmed)	🛒	■	■	■	■	■	■	■	■	■	■	■	■
(freshwater, brown, rainbow)	🛒				□	■	■	■	■	■	■	□	
WHELKS	🔍				■	■	■	■	■	■	□	□	■
WHITING	🛒	■	■	□				□	■	■	■	■	■
WINKLES	🔍	■	□	□	□	□					■	■	■
WITCH (Torbay sole)	🔍	■	■	■	□						■	■	■

MEAT & GAME

		DEC	JAN	FEB	MAR	APR	MAY	JUN	JUL	AUG	SEP	OCT	NOV
DUCK (farmed)	🛒	■	■	■	□					■	■	■	■
DUCK (wild e.g. teal mallard)	🔍	■	□								■	■	■
GOOSE (farmed)	🛒	■	■									□	■
GOOSE (wild)	🔍	■	□									□	■
GROUSE	🛒	■								■	■	■	■
HARE	🔍	■	■	■	□							■	■
PHEASANT	🛒	■	■	□								□	■
PARTRIDGE	🛒	■	■	□								□	■
RABBIT	🔍	■	■	■	□	□	□	□	□	□	■	■	■
ROOK	🔍				□	□	■	■	□				
SNIPE	🔍	■	■									■	■
SQUIRREL (grey)	🔍	■	■	□	□	□	□	□	□	□	■	■	■

MEAT & GAME (cont.)

		WINTER			SPRING			SUMMER			AUTUMN		
		DEC	JAN	FEB	MAR	APR	MAY	JUN	JUL	AUG	SEP	OCT	NOV
VENISON													
(fallow deer, stag)	🛒	□	■	■		□					■	■	□
(fallow deer, hind)	🛒	■	■	■	■								■
(red deer, stag)	🛒	□	□	□	□						■	□	□
(red deer, hind)	🛒	■	□	□									
(roe deer, stag)	🛒					■	■	■	■				
(roe deer, hind)	🛒	■											■
WILD BOAR (farmed)	🛒	■	■	■	■	□	□	□	□	□	■	■	■
WILD BOAR (wild/feral)	🔍	■	■	■	□						■	■	■
WOODCOCK	🔍	■	■									□	□
WOOD PIGEON	🔍	□	□	□	□	□	■	■	■	■	■	■	□

HEDGEROW HARVEST

		DEC	JAN	FEB	MAR	APR	MAY	JUN	JUL	AUG	SEP	OCT	NOV
ALEXANDERS	🌲				■	■	■						
BLACKBERRIES	🍃								□	■	■	□	□
COBNUTS	🍃									□	■	■	
CRAB APPLES	🌲	□									■	■	■
DAMSONS	🍃									□	■		
DANDELIONS	🍃				□	■	■						
ELDERBERRIES	🍃										■	□	
ELDERFLOWERS	🍃					□	■	■					
HAZELNUTS	🍃	□									■	■	■
MARSH SAMPHIRE	🌲							□	■	■	□		
MORELS	🍃				■	■							
NETTLES	🍃	■	□	□	■	■	□	□	□	□	□		
PENNY BUN MUSHROOMS	🌲									■	■	■	■
ROCK SAMPHIRE	🍃					■	■	□					
ROSEHIPS	🌲	□									■	■	■
SLOES	🍃										□	■	■
ST. GEORGES MUSHROOMS	🌲					■	■	■					
SWEET CHESTNUT	🍃										□	■	■
WILD CHERVIL	🌲	□	□	■	■							□	□
WILD GARLIC	🌲				■	■	■						

HERBS

Herb		Dec	Jan	Feb	Mar	Apr	May	Jun	Jul	Aug	Sep	Oct	Nov
		Winter			**Spring**			**Summer**			**Autumn**		
BAY (use dried only)	🛒	■	■	■	■	■	■	■	■	■	■		■
BASIL	🛒					□	□	■	■	■	■	□	
BORAGE	🔍						■	■	■	■	■	□	□
CHERVIL	🔍					□	■	□	□	□			
CHAMOMILE	🔍						■	■	■	■	□		
CHIVES	🛒				□	■	■	■	■	■	■	□	□
CORIANDER	🛒							□	■	■	□		
LAVENDER	🔍							□	■	■	□		
LEMON THYME	🛒						■	■	■	■	□	□	
LOVAGE	🔍					□	■	■					
MACE	🛒							□	■	■	□		
MARJORAM	🛒							□	■	■			
MINT	🛒							□	■	■	■	■	□
OREGANO	🛒							□	■	■	□		
PARSLEY, Curly	🛒					□	■	■	■	■	■	□	
Flat	🛒	□	□	□	□	□	■	■	■	■	■	■	□
ROSEMARY	🛒	□				□	■	■	■	■	■	■	□
SAGE	🛒					□	■	■	■	■	□	□	□
SAVORY, Summer	🔍						□	■	■	■	□	□	□
Winter	🔍	■	■	■	■			□	□	□	□	□	■
SORREL	🔍					□	□	■	■	■	■	□	
TARRAGON	🛒							□	■	■	■	□	□
THYME, Common	🛒							■	■	■	□	□	
Lemon	🛒							■	■	■	■	□	

References, resources and suppliers

GROWING
Royal Horticultural Society
Planting and growing your own vegetables 020 3176 5800 • rhs.org.uk

GAME
British Association for Shooting & Conservation
Conservation and legal seasons for game species 01244 573 000 • basc.org.uk

The Game & Wildlife Conservation Trust
Game and wildlife management for nature conservation 01425 652381 • gwct.org.uk

FISH
Marine Conservation Society
Protection of our seas, beaches and wildlife 01989 566017 • mcsuk.org

Marine Stewardship Council
Sustainable fishing and certifying ethically sourced seafood 020 7246 8913 • msc.org

WILDLIFE
British Divers Marine Life Rescue
Injured marine and coastal wildlife 01825 765546 • bdmlr.org.uk

Royal Society for the Prevention of Cruelty to Animals (RSPCA)
Sick or injured wildlife 0300 1234 999 • rspca.org.uk

Royal Society for the Protection of Birds (RSPB)
Bird identification and protection 01767 693690 • rspb.org.uk

The Wildlife Trusts
Protection of species and habitats 01636 677711 • wildlifetrusts.org

OUTDOOR ACTIVITIES
Met Office
Weather and tide tables 0370 900 0100 • metoffice.gov.uk

The National Trust
Conservation of heritage buildings and landscapes 0344 800 1895 • nationaltrust.org.uk

Rogers Mushroom Guide
Mushroom identification rogersmushrooms.com

Sustrans
Information on the National Cycle Network 0117 926 8893 • sustrans.org.uk

Wild Swimming
Information on wild swimming wildswimming.co.uk

INGREDIENTS
Walter Rose and Sons
Traditional butchers, Wiltshire walterroseandson.co.uk

Shipton Mill flour
shipton-mill.com

Sous Chef
Specialist online supplier souschef.co.uk

The Cornish Fishmonger
Extensive online fish and shellfish supply thecornishfishmonger.co.uk

West Country Catch
Weymouth-based fishmonger's westcountrycatch.com

Sharp's Brewery
Cornish brewery producing a wide range of beers with a passion for beer and food pairings sharpsbrewery.co.uk

EQUIPMENT
Continental Chef Supplies
Everything for the chef, kitchen and dining room chefs.net

Steamer Trading Cook Shops
steamer.co.uk

PHOTOGRAPHY
The Flash Centre
theflashcentre.com

Nikon
europe-nikon.com

Index

Acknowledgements

I should begin with all the food writers, authors, journalists and chefs who have helped to feed my love of food writing over the years. Books, magazines, newspapers, web articles, they have all been a hugely important part of my career. A pivotal moment was reading Pierre Koffmann's book *La Tante Claire* about twenty-five years ago; it opened up a new world and started me on an amazing path. *The Caterer* magazine has also been an important part of my culinary career and I am extremely proud to contribute to it today. Many other authors and their work have been influential and have helped me to learn and grow; the continual learning is half the fun!

The chefs I have worked for and with also deserve a good deal of credit. Colin Gilbert was the head chef who took a chance and gave me my first full-time job in the industry, Peter Gorton inspired me and helped to take my cooking to another level, but equally important are the chefs who worked for me over the years and helped us to build a successful restaurant, so thanks all.

As far as *Well Seasoned* is concerned I must say thanks to James Whetlor who introduced Jon and I and also to Jon himself. It has been a real pleasure working with you, Jon. What a journey!

On a purely personal level I am indebted to David Williams for encouraging and being willing to criticize my photography, and to Toby Frere for his endless interest and enthusiasm for the book, a bunch of props and the best coffee in the area. To Brian Keene for the use of your greenhouse and some superb allotment produce. To Jack and all the team at Walter Rose for supplying the best meat, game and poultry; to West Country catch my local fish supplier; to Continental Chef Supplies for their help with beautiful crockery, boards and utensils and to Matt Inwood for all his help, encouragement and the brilliant design of *Well Seasoned*.

Lastly, to Eléna my wonderful wife, who has shared every bit of the journey and has been a vital part of any success I may have achieved – thank you will never be enough.

Russell Brown

I'm going to start with my family. To Mum and Dad – growing up on Cold Norton Farm was an idyllic childhood and one which I wish every child could experience. Thanks to my brothers Chris, Nick and Al for ensuring we were never bored and for continuing to compete in the life-long fishing and shooting biathlon. (Round 41 and I'm pretty sure I'm in the lead.)

In terms of influences, Hugh Fearnley-Whittingstall and Valentine Warner both deserve a mention for reawakening my interest in food ethics and the vital link between the landscape, the seasons and our food.

The original *Well Seasoned* team, Patrick Tolhurst, Joey O'Hare and Alex Melrose all deserve huge thanks. The name of this book is theirs as much as it is mine.

Tom, Ben, Doug, Jon and Gary – BICLAA – who have fished with me for some twenty years now and only occasionally gone home without me.

Russ has already mentioned James Whetlor and it's true that we owe him a great debt. I intend to pay it off by eating lots of goat.

Russ himself is a man with a rare combination of talents. There are plenty of good chefs out there, and plenty of good photographers, but they are rarely the same people and this book wouldn't have been half as good without him. Thanks for eating my mackerel recipe and being polite about it.

Finally, to my patient wife Helen and our two fantastic children, Grace and Thomas. Thanks for testing the recipes, traipsing round the farmers' markets and listening to the seasonal food facts many, many times.

Jonathan Haley

We are lucky to have a great agent in Georgina Capel and will be ever grateful to her and to Anima and Head of Zeus for taking a chance on us as new authors. Ellen Parnavelas has been a patient and gentle editor who, along with the whole team at Zeus, have made the production of our first book a pleasurable process.

Russell Brown & Jonathan Haley

The End?

So, you've reached the end of your first year of the seasonal life. The good news is that you can simply turn to the front of the book and start again. The even better news is that you're now well on your way to becoming a *Well Seasoned* expert. So, this definitely isn't the end. It's just a new seasonal beginning.